Python High Performance

Second Edition

Build robust application by implementing concurrent and distributed processing techniques

Gabriele Lanaro

BIRMINGHAM - MUMBAI

Python High Performance

Second Edition

Copyright © 2017 Packt Publishing

First published: December 2013

Second edition: May 2017

Production reference: 1180517

Published by Packt Publishing Ltd.
Livery Place
35 Livery Street
Birmingham
B3 2PB, UK.
ISBN 978-1-78728-289-6

www.packtpub.com

Credits

Author
Gabriele Lanaro

Reviewer
Will Brennan

Commissioning Editor
Kunal Parikh

Acquisition Editor
Chaitanya Nair

Content Development Editor
Vikas Tiwari

Technical Editor
Jijo Maliyekal

Copy Editor
Shaila Kusanale

Project Coordinator
Ulhas Kambali

Proofreader
Safis Editing

Indexer
Tejal Daruwale Soni

Graphics
Abhinash Sahu

Production Coordinator
Shantanu Zagade

About the Author

Dr. Gabriele Lanaro has been conducting research to study the formation and growth of crystals using medium and large-scale computer simulations. In 2017, he obtained his PhD in theoretical chemistry. His interests span machine learning, numerical computing visualization, and web technologies. He has a sheer passion for good software and is the author of the chemlab and chemview open source packages. In 2013, he authored the first edition of the book *"High Performance Python Programming"*.

I'd like to acknowledge the support from Packt editors, including Vikas Tiwari. I would also like to thank my girlfriend, Harani, who had to tolerate the way-too-long writing nights, and friends who provided company and support throughout. Also, as always, I'd love to thank my parents for giving me the opportunity to pursue my ambitions.

Lastly, I would like to thank Blenz coffee for powering the execution engine of this book through electricity and caffeine.

About the Reviewer

Will Brennan is a C++/Python developer based in London with previous experience in writing molecular dynamics simulations. He is currently working on high-performance image processing and machine learning applications. You can refer to his repositories at `https://github.com/WillBrennan`.

www.PacktPub.com

For support files and downloads related to your book, please visit www.PacktPub.com.

Did you know that Packt offers eBook versions of every book published, with PDF and ePub files available? You can upgrade to the eBook version at www.PacktPub.com and as a print book customer, you are entitled to a discount on the eBook copy. Get in touch with us at service@packtpub.com for more details.

At www.PacktPub.com, you can also read a collection of free technical articles, sign up for a range of free newsletters and receive exclusive discounts and offers on Packt books and eBooks.

https://www.packtpub.com/mapt

Get the most in-demand software skills with Mapt. Mapt gives you full access to all Packt books and video courses, as well as industry-leading tools to help you plan your personal development and advance your career.

Why subscribe?

- Fully searchable across every book published by Packt
- Copy and paste, print, and bookmark content
- On demand and accessible via a web browser

Customer Feedback

Thanks for purchasing this Packt book. At Packt, quality is at the heart of our editorial process. To help us improve, please leave us an honest review on this book's Amazon page at https://www.amazon.com/dp/1787282899.

If you'd like to join our team of regular reviewers, you can e-mail us at customerreviews@packtpub.com. We award our regular reviewers with free eBooks and videos in exchange for their valuable feedback. Help us be relentless in improving our products!

Table of Contents

Preface

The Python programming language has seen a huge surge in popularity in recent years, thanks to its intuitive, fun syntax, and its vast array of top-quality third-party libraries. Python has been the language of choice for many introductory and advanced university courses as well as for numerically intense fields, such as the sciences and engineering. Its primary applications also lies in machine learning, system scripting, and web applications.

The reference Python interpreter, CPython, is generally regarded as inefficient when compared to lower-level languages, such as C, C++, and Fortran. CPython's poor performance lies in the fact that the program instructions are processed by an interpreter rather than being compiled to efficient machine code. While using an interpreter has several advantages, such as portability and the additional compilation step, it does introduce an extra layer of indirection between the program and the machine, which causes a less efficient execution.

Over the years, many strategies have been developed to overcome CPython's performance shortcomings. This book aims to fill this gap and will teach how to consistently achieve strong performance out of your Python programs.

This book will appeal to a broad audience as it covers both the optimization of numerical and scientific codes as well as strategies to improve the response times of web services and applications.

The book can be read cover-to-cover ; however, chapters are designed to be self-contained so that you can skip to a section of interest if you are already familiar with the previous topics.

What this book covers

Chapter 1, *Benchmark and Profiling*, will teach you how to assess the performance of Python programs and practical strategies on how to identify and isolate the slow sections of your code.

Chapter 2, *Pure Python Optimizations*, discusses how to improve your running times by order of magnitudes using the efficient data structures and algorithms available in the Python standard library and pure-Python third-party modules.

Chapter 3, *Fast Array Operations with NumPy and Pandas*, is a guide to the NumPy and Pandas packages. Mastery of these packages will allow you to implement fast numerical algorithms with an expressive, concise interface.

Chapter 4, *C Performance with Cython*, is a tutorial on Cython, a language that uses a Python-compatible syntax to generate efficient C code.

Chapter 5, *Exploring Compilers*, covers tools that can be used to compile Python to efficient machine code. The chapter will teach you how to use Numba, an optimizing compiler for Python functions, and PyPy, an alternative interpreter that can execute and optimize Python programs on the fly.

Chapter 6, *Implementing Concurrency*, is a guide to asynchronous and reactive programming. We will learn about key terms and concepts, and demonstrate how to write clean, concurrent code using the asyncio and RxPy frameworks.

Chapter 7, *Parallel Processing*, is an introduction to parallel programming on multi-core processors and GPUs. In this chapter, you will learn to achieve parallelism using the multiprocessing module and by expressing your code using Theano and Tensorflow.

Chapter 8, *Distributed Processing*, extends the content of the preceding chapter by focusing on running parallel algorithms on distributed systems for large-scale problems and big data. This chapter will cover the Dask, PySpark, and mpi4py libraries.

Chapter 9, *Designing for High Performance*, discusses general optimization strategies and best practices to develop, test, and deploy your high-performance Python applications.

What you need for this book

The software in this book is tested on Python version 3.5 and on Ubuntu version 16.04. However, majority of the examples can also be run on the Windows and Mac OS X operating systems.

The recommended way to install Python and the associated libraries is through the Anaconda distribution, which can be downloaded from https://www.continuum.io/downloads, for Linux, Windows, and Mac OS X.

Who this book is for

The book is aimed at Python developers who want to improve the performance of their application; basic knowledge of Python is expected.

Conventions

In this book, you will find a number of text styles that distinguish between different kinds of information. Here are some examples of these styles and an explanation of their meaning.

Code words in text, database table names, folder names, filenames, file extensions, pathnames, dummy URLs, user input, and Twitter handles are shown as follows: "To summarize, we will implement a method called `ParticleSimulator.evolve_numpy` and benchmark it against the pure Python version, renamed as `ParticleSimulator.evolve_python`"

A block of code is set as follows:

```
def square(x):
    return x * x

inputs = [0, 1, 2, 3, 4]
outputs = pool.map(square, inputs)
```

When we wish to draw your attention to a particular part of a code block, the relevant lines or items are set in bold:

```
def square(x):
    return x * x

inputs = [0, 1, 2, 3, 4]
outputs = pool.map(square, inputs)
```

Any command-line input or output is written as follows:

```
$ time python -c 'import pi; pi.pi_serial()'
real 0m0.734s
user 0m0.731s
sys 0m0.004s
```

New terms and **important words** are shown in bold. Words that you see on the screen, for example, in menus or dialog boxes, appear in the text like this: "On the right, clicking on the tab **Callee Map** will display a diagram of the function costs."

Warnings or important notes appear in a box like this.

 Tips and tricks appear like this.

Reader feedback

Feedback from our readers is always welcome. Let us know what you think about this book-what you liked or disliked. Reader feedback is important for us as it helps us develop titles that you will really get the most out of.

To send us general feedback, simply e-mail feedback@packtpub.com, and mention the book's title in the subject of your message.

If there is a topic that you have expertise in and you are interested in either writing or contributing to a book, see our author guide at www.packtpub.com/authors.

Customer support

Now that you are the proud owner of a Packt book, we have a number of things to help you to get the most from your purchase.

Downloading the example code

You can download the example code files for this book from your account at http://www.packtpub.com. If you purchased this book elsewhere, you can visit http://www.packtpub.com/support and register to have the files e-mailed directly to you.

You can download the code files by following these steps:

1. Log in or register to our website using your e-mail address and password.
2. Hover the mouse pointer on the **SUPPORT** tab at the top.
3. Click on **Code Downloads & Errata**.
4. Enter the name of the book in the **Search** box.
5. Select the book for which you're looking to download the code files.
6. Choose from the drop-down menu where you purchased this book from.
7. Click on **Code Download**.

Once the file is downloaded, please make sure that you unzip or extract the folder using the latest version of:

- WinRAR / 7-Zip for Windows
- Zipeg / iZip / UnRarX for Mac
- 7-Zip / PeaZip for Linux

The code bundle for the book is also hosted on GitHub at `https://github.com/PacktPubl ishing/Python-High-Performance-Second-Edition`. We also have other code bundles from our rich catalog of books and videos available at `https://github.com/PacktPublish ing/`. Check them out!

Downloading the color images of this book

We also provide you with a PDF file that has color images of the screenshots/diagrams used in this book. The color images will help you better understand the changes in the output. You can download this file from `https://www.packtpub.com/sites/default/files/down loads/PythonHighPerformanceSecondEdition_ColorImages.pdf`.

Errata

Although we have taken every care to ensure the accuracy of our content, mistakes do happen. If you find a mistake in one of our books-maybe a mistake in the text or the code-we would be grateful if you could report this to us. By doing so, you can save other readers from frustration and help us improve subsequent versions of this book. If you find any errata, please report them by visiting `http://www.packtpub.com/submit-errata`, selecting your book, clicking on the **Errata Submission Form** link, and entering the details of your errata. Once your errata are verified, your submission will be accepted and the errata will be uploaded to our website or added to any list of existing errata under the Errata section of that title.

To view the previously submitted errata, go to `https://www.packtpub.com/books/content/support` and enter the name of the book in the search field. The required information will appear under the **Errata** section.

Piracy

Piracy of copyrighted material on the Internet is an ongoing problem across all media. At Packt, we take the protection of our copyright and licenses very seriously. If you come across any illegal copies of our works in any form on the Internet, please provide us with the location address or website name immediately so that we can pursue a remedy.

Please contact us at `copyright@packtpub.com` with a link to the suspected pirated material.

We appreciate your help in protecting our authors and our ability to bring you valuable content.

Questions

If you have a problem with any aspect of this book, you can contact us at `questions@packtpub.com`, and we will do our best to address the problem.

1
Benchmarking and Profiling

Recognizing the slow parts of your program is the single most important task when it comes to speeding up your code. Luckily, in most cases, the code that causes the application to slow down is a very small fraction of the program. By locating those critical sections, you can focus on the parts that need improvement without wasting time in micro-optimization.

Profiling is the technique that allows us to pinpoint the most resource-intensive spots in an application. A **profiler** is a program that runs an application and monitors how long each function takes to execute, thus detecting the functions in which your application spends most of its time.

Python provides several tools to help us find these bottlenecks and measure important performance metrics. In this chapter, we will learn how to use the standard `cProfile` module and the `line_profiler` third-party package. We will also learn how to profile an application's memory consumption through the `memory_profiler` tool. Another useful tool that we will cover is *KCachegrind*, which can be used to graphically display the data produced by various profilers.

Benchmarks are small scripts used to assess the total execution time of your application. We will learn how to write benchmarks and how to accurately time your programs.

The list of topics we will cover in this chapter is as follows:

- General principles of high performance programming
- Writing tests and benchmarks
- The Unix `time` command
- The Python `timeit` module
- Testing and benchmarking with `pytest`
- Profiling your application
- The `cProfile` standard tool

- Interpreting profiling results with KCachegrind
- `line_profiler` and `memory_profiler` tools
- Disassembling Python code through the `dis` module

Designing your application

When designing a performance-intensive program, the very first step is to write your code without bothering with small optimizations:

"Premature optimization is the root of all evil."

- Donald Knuth

In the early development stages, the design of the program can change quickly and may require large rewrites and reorganizations of the code base. By testing different prototypes without the burden of optimization, you are free to devote your time and energy to ensure that the program produces correct results and that the design is flexible. After all, who needs an application that runs fast but gives the wrong answer?

The mantras that you should remember when optimizing your code are as follows:

- **Make it run**: We have to get the software in a working state, and ensure that it produces the correct results. This exploratory phase serves to better understand the application and to spot major design issues in the early stages.
- **Make it right**: We want to ensure that the design of the program is solid. Refactoring should be done before attempting any performance optimization. This really helps separate the application into independent and cohesive units that are easier to maintain.
- **Make it fast**: Once our program is working and is well structured, we can focus on performance optimization. We may also want to optimize memory usage if that constitutes an issue.

In this section, we will write and profile a *particle simulator* test application. The **simulator** is a program that takes some particles and simulates their movement over time according to a set of laws that we impose. These particles can be abstract entities or correspond to physical objects, for example, billiard balls moving on a table, molecules in gas, stars moving through space, smoke particles, fluids in a chamber, and so on.

Computer simulations are useful in fields such as Physics, Chemistry, Astronomy, and many other disciplines. The applications used to simulate systems are particularly performance-intensive and scientists and engineers spend an inordinate amount of time optimizing these codes. In order to study realistic systems, it is often necessary to simulate a very high number of bodies and every small increase in performance counts.

In our first example, we will simulate a system containing particles that constantly rotate around a central point at various speeds, just like the hands of a clock.

The necessary information to run our simulation will be the starting positions of the particles, the speed, and the rotation direction. From these elements, we have to calculate the position of the particle in the next instant of time. An example system is shown in the following figure. The origin of the system is the (0, 0) point, the position is indicated by the **x**, **y** vector and the velocity is indicated by the **vx**, **vy** vector:

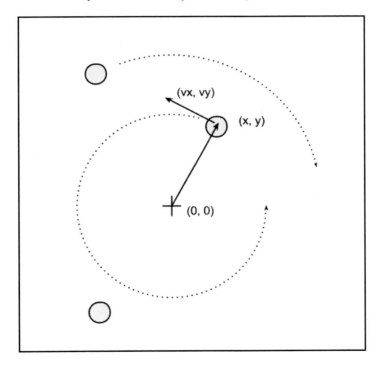

The basic feature of a circular motion is that the particles always move perpendicular to the direction connecting the particle and the center. To move the particle, we simply change the position by taking a series of very small steps (which correspond to advancing the system for a small interval of time) in the direction of motion, as shown in the following figure:

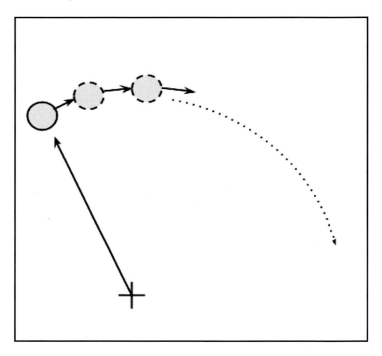

We will start by designing the application in an object-oriented way. According to our requirements, it is natural to have a generic Particle class that stores the particle positions, x and y, and their angular velocity, ang_vel:

```
class Particle:
    def __init__(self, x, y, ang_vel):
        self.x = x
        self.y = y
        self.ang_vel = ang_vel
```

Note that we accept positive and negative numbers for all the parameters (the sign of ang_vel will simply determine the direction of rotation).

Another class, called `ParticleSimulator`, will encapsulate the laws of motion and will be responsible for changing the positions of the particles over time. The __init__ method will store a list of `Particle` instances and the `evolve` method will change the particle positions according to our laws.

We want the particles to rotate around the position corresponding to the x=0 and y=0 coordinates, at a constant speed. The direction of the particles will always be perpendicular to the direction from the center (refer to the first figure of this chapter). To find the direction of the movement along the *x* and *y* axes (corresponding to the Python v_x and v_y variables), it is sufficient to use these formulae:

```
v_x = -y / (x**2 + y**2)**0.5
v_y = x / (x**2 + y**2)**0.5
```

If we let one of our particles move, after a certain time *t*, it will reach another position following a circular path. We can approximate a circular trajectory by dividing the time interval, *t*, into tiny time steps, *dt*, where the particle moves in a straight line tangentially to the circle. The final result is just an approximation of a circular motion. In order to avoid a strong divergence, such as the one illustrated in the following figure, it is necessary to take very small time steps:

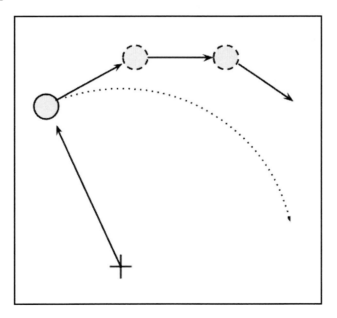

In a more schematic way, we have to carry out the following steps to calculate the particle position at time *t*:

1. Calculate the direction of motion (v_x and v_y).
2. Calculate the displacement (d_x and d_y), which is the product of time step, angular velocity, and direction of motion.
3. Repeat steps 1 and 2 for enough times to cover the total time *t*.

The following code shows the full ParticleSimulator implementation:

```
class ParticleSimulator:

    def __init__(self, particles):
        self.particles = particles

    def evolve(self, dt):
        timestep = 0.00001
        nsteps = int(dt/timestep)

        for i in range(nsteps):
            for p in self.particles:
                # 1. calculate the direction
                norm = (p.x**2 + p.y**2)**0.5
                v_x = -p.y/norm
                v_y = p.x/norm

                # 2. calculate the displacement
                d_x = timestep * p.ang_vel * v_x
                d_y = timestep * p.ang_vel * v_y

                p.x += d_x
                p.y += d_y
                # 3. repeat for all the time steps
```

We can use the matplotlib library to visualize our particles. This library is not included in the Python standard library, and it can be easily installed using the pip install matplotlib command.

Alternatively, you can use the Anaconda Python distribution (https://store.continuum.io/cshop/anaconda/) that includes matplotlib and most of the other third-party packages used in this book. Anaconda is free and is available for Linux, Windows, and Mac.

To make an interactive visualization, we will use the `matplotlib.pyplot.plot` function to display the particles as points and the `matplotlib.animation.FuncAnimation` class to animate the evolution of the particles over time.

The `visualize` function takes a particle `ParticleSimulator` instance as an argument and displays the trajectory in an animated plot. The steps necessary to display the particle trajectory using the `matplotlib` tools are as follows:

- Set up the axes and use the `plot` function to display the particles. `plot` takes a list of *x* and *y* coordinates.
- Write an initialization function, `init`, and a function, `animate`, that updates the *x* and *y* coordinates using the `line.set_data` method.
- Create a `FuncAnimation` instance by passing the `init` and `animate` functions plus the `interval` parameters, which specify the update interval, and `blit`, which improves the update rate of the image.
- Run the animation with `plt.show()`:

```python
from matplotlib import pyplot as plt
from matplotlib import animation

def visualize(simulator):

    X = [p.x for p in simulator.particles]
    Y = [p.y for p in simulator.particles]

    fig = plt.figure()
    ax = plt.subplot(111, aspect='equal')
    line, = ax.plot(X, Y, 'ro')

    # Axis limits
    plt.xlim(-1, 1)
    plt.ylim(-1, 1)

    # It will be run when the animation starts
    def init():
        line.set_data([], [])
        return line, # The comma is important!

    def animate(i):
        # We let the particle evolve for 0.01 time units
        simulator.evolve(0.01)
        X = [p.x for p in simulator.particles]
        Y = [p.y for p in simulator.particles]

        line.set_data(X, Y)
```

```
        return line,

    # Call the animate function each 10 ms
    anim = animation.FuncAnimation(fig,
                                   animate,
                                   init_func=init,
                                   blit=True,
                                   interval=10)
    plt.show()
```

To test things out, we define a small function, `test_visualize`, that animates a system of three particles rotating in different directions. Note that the third particle completes a round three times faster than the others:

```
def test_visualize():
    particles = [Particle(0.3, 0.5, 1),
                 Particle(0.0, -0.5, -1),
                 Particle(-0.1, -0.4, 3)]

    simulator = ParticleSimulator(particles)
    visualize(simulator)

if __name__ == '__main__':
    test_visualize()
```

The `test_visualize` function is helpful to graphically understand the system time evolution. In the following section, we will write more test functions to properly verify program correctness and measure performance.

Writing tests and benchmarks

Now that we have a working simulator, we can start measuring our performance and tune-up our code so that the simulator can handle as many particles as possible. As a first step, we will write a test and a benchmark.

We need a test that checks whether the results produced by the simulation are correct or not. Optimizing a program commonly requires employing multiple strategies; as we rewrite our code multiple times, bugs may easily be introduced. A solid test suite ensures that the implementation is correct at every iteration so that we are free to go wild and try different things with the confidence that, if the test suite passes, the code will still work as expected.

Our test will take three particles, simulate them for 0.1 time units, and compare the results with those from a reference implementation. A good way to organize your tests is using a separate function for each different aspect (or unit) of your application. Since our current functionality is included in the `evolve` method, our function will be named `test_evolve`. The following code shows the `test_evolve` implementation. Note that, in this case, we compare floating point numbers up to a certain precision through the `fequal` function:

```
def test_evolve():
    particles = [Particle( 0.3,  0.5, +1),
                 Particle( 0.0, -0.5, -1),
                 Particle(-0.1, -0.4, +3)]

    simulator = ParticleSimulator(particles)

    simulator.evolve(0.1)

    p0, p1, p2 = particles

    def fequal(a, b, eps=1e-5):
        return abs(a - b) < eps

    assert fequal(p0.x,  0.210269)
    assert fequal(p0.y,  0.543863)

    assert fequal(p1.x, -0.099334)
    assert fequal(p1.y, -0.490034)

    assert fequal(p2.x,  0.191358)
    assert fequal(p2.y, -0.365227)

if __name__ == '__main__':
    test_evolve()
```

A test ensures the correctness of our functionality but gives little information about its running time. A benchmark is a simple and representative use case that can be run to assess the running time of an application. Benchmarks are very useful to keep score of how fast our program is with each new version that we implement.

We can write a representative benchmark by instantiating a thousand `Particle` objects with random coordinates and angular velocity, and feed them to a `ParticleSimulator` class. We then let the system evolve for 0.1 time units:

```
from random import uniform

def benchmark():
    particles = [Particle(uniform(-1.0, 1.0),
```

```
                          uniform(-1.0, 1.0),
                          uniform(-1.0, 1.0))
                 for i in range(1000)]

    simulator = ParticleSimulator(particles)
    simulator.evolve(0.1)

if __name__ == '__main__':
    benchmark()
```

Timing your benchmark

A very simple way to time a benchmark is through the Unix time command. Using the time command, as follows, you can easily measure the execution time of an arbitrary process:

```
    $ time python simul.py
real    0m1.051s
user    0m1.022s
sys     0m0.028s
```

 The time command is not available for Windows. To install Unix tools, such as time, on Windows you can use the cygwin shell, downloadable from the official website (http://www.cygwin.com/). Alternatively, you can use similar PowerShell commands, such as Measure-Command (https://msdn.microsoft.com/en-us/powershell/reference/5.1/microsoft.powershell.utility/measure-command), to measure execution time.

By default, time displays three metrics:

- real: The actual time spent running the process from start to finish, as if it was measured by a human with a stopwatch
- user: The cumulative time spent by all the CPUs during the computation
- sys: The cumulative time spent by all the CPUs during system-related tasks, such as memory allocation

Note that sometimes user + sys might be greater than real, as multiple processors may work in parallel.

`time` also offers richer formatting options. For an overview, you can explore its manual (using the `man time` command). If you want a summary of all the metrics available, you can use the `-v` option.

The Unix `time` command is one of the simplest and more direct ways to benchmark a program. For an accurate measurement, the benchmark should be designed to have a long enough execution time (in the order of seconds) so that the setup and tear-down of the process is small compared to the execution time of the application. The `user` metric is suitable as a monitor for the CPU performance, while the `real` metric also includes the time spent in other processes while waiting for I/O operations.

Another convenient way to time Python scripts is the `timeit` module. This module runs a snippet of code in a loop for *n* times and measures the total execution times. Then, it repeats the same operation *r* times (by default, the value of *r* is 3) and records the time of the best run. Due to this timing scheme, `timeit` is an appropriate tool to accurately time small statements in isolation.

The `timeit` module can be used as a Python package, from the command line or from *IPython*.

IPython is a Python shell design that improves the interactivity of the Python interpreter. It boosts tab completion and many utilities to time, profile, and debug your code. We will use this shell to try out snippets throughout the book. The IPython shell accepts **magic commands**--statements that start with a % symbol--that enhance the shell with special behaviors. Commands that start with %% are called **cell magics**, which can be applied on multi-line snippets (termed as **cells**).

IPython is available on most Linux distributions through `pip` and is included in Anaconda.

You can use IPython as a regular Python shell (`ipython`), but it is also available in a Qt-based version (`ipython qtconsole`) and as a powerful browser-based interface (`jupyter notebook`).

In IPython and command-line interfaces, it is possible to specify the number of loops or repetitions with the −n and −r options. If not specified, they will be automatically inferred by timeit. When invoking timeit from the command line, you can also pass some setup code, through the −s option, which will execute before the benchmark. In the following snippet, the IPython command line and Python module version of timeit are demonstrated:

```
# IPython Interface
$ ipython
In [1]: from simul import benchmark
In [2]: %timeit benchmark()
1 loops, best of 3: 782 ms per loop

# Command Line Interface
$ python −m timeit −s 'from simul import benchmark' 'benchmark()'
10 loops, best of 3: 826 msec per loop

# Python Interface
# put this function into the simul.py script

import timeit
result = timeit.timeit('benchmark()',
 setup='from __main__ import benchmark',
 number=10)

# result is the time (in seconds) to run the whole loop
result = timeit.repeat('benchmark()',
 setup='from __main__ import benchmark',
 number=10,
 repeat=3)
# result is a list containing the time of each repetition (repeat=3 in this
case)
```

Note that while the command line and IPython interfaces automatically infer a reasonable number of loops n, the Python interface requires you to explicitly specify a value through the number argument.

Better tests and benchmarks with pytest-benchmark

The Unix `time` command is a versatile tool that can be used to assess the running time of small programs on a variety of platforms. For larger Python applications and libraries, a more comprehensive solution that deals with both testing and benchmarking is `pytest`, in combination with its `pytest-benchmark` plugin.

In this section, we will write a simple benchmark for our application using the `pytest` testing framework. For the interested reader, the `pytest` documentation, which can be found at `http://doc.pytest.org/en/latest/`, is the best resource to learn more about the framework and its uses.

 You can install `pytest` from the console using the `pip install pytest` command. The benchmarking plugin can be installed, similarly, by issuing the `pip install pytest-benchmark` command.

A testing framework is a set of tools that simplifies writing, executing, and debugging tests and provides rich reports and summaries of the test results. When using the `pytest` framework, it is recommended to place tests separately from the application code. In the following example, we create the `test_simul.py` file, which contains the `test_evolve` function:

```python
from simul import Particle, ParticleSimulator

def test_evolve():
    particles = [Particle( 0.3,  0.5, +1),
                 Particle( 0.0, -0.5, -1),
                 Particle(-0.1, -0.4, +3)]

    simulator = ParticleSimulator(particles)

    simulator.evolve(0.1)

    p0, p1, p2 = particles

    def fequal(a, b, eps=1e-5):
        return abs(a - b) < eps

    assert fequal(p0.x,  0.210269)
    assert fequal(p0.y,  0.543863)

    assert fequal(p1.x, -0.099334)
```

```
assert fequal(p1.y, -0.490034)

assert fequal(p2.x,  0.191358)
assert fequal(p2.y, -0.365227)
```

The `pytest` executable can be used from the command line to discover and run tests contained in Python modules. To execute a specific test, we can use the `pytest path/to/module.py::function_name` syntax. To execute `test_evolve`, we can type the following command in a console to obtain simple but informative output:

```
$ pytest test_simul.py::test_evolve

platform linux -- Python 3.5.2, pytest-3.0.5, py-1.4.32, pluggy-0.4.0
rootdir: /home/gabriele/workspace/hiperf/chapter1, inifile: plugins:
collected 2 items

test_simul.py .

=========================== 1 passed in 0.43 seconds
===========================
```

Once we have a test in place, it is possible for you to execute your test as a benchmark using the `pytest-benchmark` plugin. If we change our `test` function so that it accepts an argument named `benchmark`, the `pytest` framework will automatically pass the `benchmark` resource as an argument (in `pytest` terminology, these resources are called *fixtures*). The benchmark resource can be called by passing the function that we intend to benchmark as the first argument, followed by the additional arguments. In the following snippet, we illustrate the edits necessary to benchmark the `ParticleSimulator.evolve` function:

```
from simul import Particle, ParticleSimulator

def test_evolve(benchmark):
    # ... previous code
    benchmark(simulator.evolve, 0.1)
```

To run the benchmark, it is sufficient to rerun the `pytest`
`test_simul.py::test_evolve` command. The resulting output will contain detailed
timing information regarding the `test_evolve` function, as shown:

```
=================================== test session starts ====================================
platform linux -- Python 3.5.2, pytest-3.0.5, py-1.4.32, pluggy-0.4.0
benchmark: 3.0.0 (defaults: timer=time.perf_counter disable_gc=False min_rounds=5 min_time=5.00us max_time=1.00s cal
ibration_precision=10 warmup=False warmup_iterations=100000)
rootdir: /home/gabriele/workspace/hiperf/chapter1, inifile:
plugins: benchmark-3.0.0
collected 2 items

test_simul.py .


----------------------------------- benchmark: 1 tests -------------------------------------
Name (time in ms)         Min      Max     Mean   StdDev   Median     IQR  Outliers(*)  Rounds  Iterations
--------------------------------------------------------------------------------------------
test_evolve           29.4716  41.1791  30.4622   2.0234  29.9630  0.7376         2;2      34           1
--------------------------------------------------------------------------------------------

(*) Outliers: 1 Standard Deviation from Mean; 1.5 IQR (InterQuartile Range) from 1st Quartile and 3rd Quartile.
=============================== 1 passed in 2.52 seconds ====================================
```

For each test collected, `pytest-benchmark` will execute the benchmark function several
times and provide a statistic summary of its running time. The output shown earlier is very
interesting as it shows how running times vary between runs.

In this example, the benchmark in `test_evolve` was run 34 times (column `Rounds`), its
timings ranged between 29 and 41 ms (Min and Max), and the Average and Median times
were fairly similar at about 30 ms, which is actually very close to the best timing obtained.
This example demonstrates how there can be substantial performance variability between
runs, and that when taking timings with one-shot tools such as `time`, it is a good idea to run
the program multiple times and record a representative value, such as the minimum or the
median.

`pytest-benchmark` has many more features and options that can be used to take accurate
timings and analyze the results. For more information, consult the documentation at `http
://pytest-benchmark.readthedocs.io/en/stable/usage.html`.

Finding bottlenecks with cProfile

After assessing the correctness and timing the execution time of the program, we are ready to identify the parts of the code that need to be tuned for performance. Those parts are typically quite small compared to the size of the program.

Two profiling modules are available through the Python standard library:

- **The** `profile` **module**: This module is written in pure Python and adds a significant overhead to the program execution. Its presence in the standard library is because of its vast platform support and because it is easier to extend.
- **The** `cProfile` **module**: This is the main profiling module, with an interface equivalent to `profile`. It is written in C, has a small overhead, and is suitable as a general purpose profiler.

The `cProfile` module can be used in three different ways:

- From the command line
- As a Python module
- With IPython

`cProfile` does not require any change in the source code and can be executed directly on an existing Python script or function. You can use `cProfile` from the command line in this way:

```
$ python -m cProfile simul.py
```

This will print a long output containing several profiling metrics of all of the functions called in the application. You can use the `-s` option to sort the output by a specific metric. In the following snippet ,the output is sorted by the `tottime` metric, which will be described here:

```
$ python -m cProfile -s tottime simul.py
```

The data produced by `cProfile` can be saved in an output file by passing the `-o` option. The format that `cProfile` uses is readable by the `stats` module and other tools. The usage of the `-o` option is as follows:

```
$ python -m cProfile -o prof.out simul.py
```

The usage of cProfile as a Python module requires invoking the `cProfile.run` function in the following way:

```
from simul import benchmark
import cProfile

cProfile.run("benchmark()")
```

You can also wrap a section of code between method calls of a `cProfile.Profile` object, as shown:

```
from simul import benchmark
import cProfile

pr = cProfile.Profile()
pr.enable()
benchmark()
pr.disable()
pr.print_stats()
```

`cProfile` can also be used interactively with IPython. The `%prun` magic command lets you profile an individual function call, as illustrated:

```
IPython: chapter1/codes
(hperf) → codes ipython
Python 3.5.2 |Continuum Analytics, Inc.| (default, Jul  2 2016, 17:53:06)
Type "copyright", "credits" or "license" for more information.

IPython 5.1.0 -- An enhanced Interactive Python.
?         -> Introduction and overview of IPython's features.
%quickref -> Quick reference.
help      -> Python's own help system.
object?   -> Details about 'object', use 'object??' for extra details.

In [1]: from simul import benchmark

In [2]: %prun benchmark()
         707 function calls in 1.231 seconds

   Ordered by: internal time

   ncalls  tottime  percall  cumtime  percall filename:lineno(function)
        1    1.230    1.230    1.230    1.230 simul.py:21(evolve)
        1    0.000    0.000    0.001    0.001 simul.py:118(<listcomp>)
      300    0.000    0.000    0.000    0.000 random.py:342(uniform)
      100    0.000    0.000    0.000    0.000 simul.py:10(__init__)
      300    0.000    0.000    0.000    0.000 {method 'random' of '_random.Random' objects}
        1    0.000    0.000    1.231    1.231 {built-in method builtins.exec}
        1    0.000    0.000    1.231    1.231 <string>:1(<module>)
        1    0.000    0.000    1.231    1.231 simul.py:117(benchmark)
        1    0.000    0.000    0.000    0.000 simul.py:18(__init__)
        1    0.000    0.000    0.000    0.000 {method 'disable' of '_lsprof.Profiler' objects}

In [3]:
```

The `cProfile` output is divided into five columns:

- `ncalls`: The number of times the function was called.
- `tottime`: The total time spent in the function without taking into account the calls to other functions.
- `cumtime`: The time in the function including other function calls.
- `percall`: The time spent for a single call of the function--it can be obtained by dividing the total or cumulative time by the number of calls.
- `filename:lineno`: The filename and corresponding line numbers. This information is not available when calling C extensions modules.

The most important metric is `tottime`, the actual time spent in the function body excluding subcalls, which tell us exactly where the bottleneck is.

Unsurprisingly, the largest portion of time is spent in the `evolve` function. We can imagine that the loop is the section of the code that needs performance tuning. `cProfile` only provides information at the function level and does not tell us which specific statements are responsible for the bottleneck. Fortunately, as we will see in the next section, the `line_profiler` tool is capable of providing line-by-line information of the time spent in the function.

Analyzing the `cProfile` text output can be daunting for big programs with a lot of calls and subcalls. Some visual tools aid the task by improving navigation with an interactive, graphical interface.

KCachegrind is a **Graphical User Interface (GUI)** useful to analyze the profiling output emitted by `cProfile`.

 KCachegrind is available in the Ubuntu 16.04 official repositories. The Qt port, QCacheGrind, can be downloaded for Windows from `http://sourc eforge.net/projects/qcachegrindwin/`. Mac users can compile QCacheGrind using Mac Ports (`http://www.macports.org/`) by following the instructions present in the blog post at `http://blogs.perl.org/user s/rurban/2013/04/install-kachegrind-on-macosx-with-ports.html`.

KCachegrind can't directly read the output files produced by `cProfile`. Luckily, the `pyprof2calltree` third-party Python module is able to convert the `cProfile` output file into a format readable by KCachegrind.

You can install `pyprof2calltree` from the Python Package Index using the command `pip install pyprof2calltree`.

To best show the KCachegrind features, we will use another example with a more diversified structure. We define a `recursive` function, `factorial`, and two other functions that use `factorial`, named `taylor_exp` and `taylor_sin`. They represent the polynomial coefficients of the Taylor approximations of `exp(x)` and `sin(x)`:

```python
def factorial(n):
    if n == 0:
        return 1.0
    else:
        return n * factorial(n-1)

def taylor_exp(n):
    return [1.0/factorial(i) for i in range(n)]

def taylor_sin(n):
    res = []
    for i in range(n):
        if i % 2 == 1:
            res.append((-1)**((i-1)/2)/float(factorial(i)))
        else:
            res.append(0.0)
    return res

def benchmark():
    taylor_exp(500)
    taylor_sin(500)

if __name__ == '__main__':
    benchmark()
```

To access profile information, we first need to generate the `cProfile` output file:

```
$ python -m cProfile -o prof.out taylor.py
```

Then, we can convert the output file with `pyprof2calltree` and launch KCachegrind:

```
$ pyprof2calltree -i prof.out -o prof.calltree
$ kcachegrind prof.calltree # or qcachegrind prof.calltree
```

The output is shown in the following screenshot:

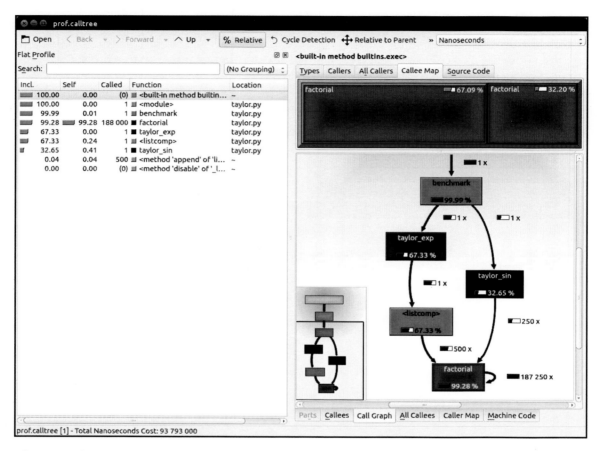

The preceding screenshot shows the KCachegrind user interface. On the left, we have an output fairly similar to cProfile. The actual column names are slightly different: **Incl.** translates to cProfile module's cumtime and **Self** translates to tottime. The values are given in percentages by clicking on the **Relative** button on the menu bar. By clicking on the column headers, you can sort them by the corresponding property.

On the top right, a click on the **Callee Map** tab will display a diagram of the function costs. In the diagram, the time percentage spent by the function is proportional to the area of the rectangle. Rectangles can contain sub-rectangles that represent subcalls to other functions. In this case, we can easily see that there are two rectangles for the factorial function. The one on the left corresponds to the calls made by taylor_exp and the one on the right to the calls made by taylor_sin.

On the bottom right, you can display another diagram, the *call graph*, by clicking on the **Call Graph** tab. A call graph is a graphical representation of the calling relationship between the functions; each square represents a function and the arrows imply a calling relationship. For example, taylor_exp calls factorial **500** times, and taylor_sin calls factorial **250** times. KCachegrind also detects recursive calls: factorial calls itself **187250** times.

You can navigate to the **Call Graph** or the **Caller Map** tab by double-clicking on the rectangles; the interface will update accordingly, showing that the timing properties are relative to the selected function. For example, double-clicking on taylor_exp will cause the graph to change, showing only the contribution of taylor_exp to the total cost.

 Gprof2Dot (https://github.com/jrfonseca/gprof2dot) is another popular tool used to produce call graphs. Starting from output files produced by one of the supported profilers, it will generate a .dot diagram representing the call graph.

Profile line by line with line_profiler

Now that we know which function we have to optimize, we can use the line_profiler module that provides information on how time is spent in a line-by-line fashion. This is very useful in situations where it's difficult to determine which statements are costly. The line_profiler module is a third-party module that is available on the Python Package Index and can be installed by following the instructions at https://github.com/rkern/line_profiler.

In order to use line_profiler, we need to apply a @profile decorator to the functions we intend to monitor. Note that you don't have to import the profile function from another module as it gets injected in the global namespace when running the kernprof.py profiling script. To produce profiling output for our program, we need to add the @profile decorator to the evolve function:

```
@profile
def evolve(self, dt):
    # code
```

The `kernprof.py` script will produce an output file and will print the result of the profiling on the standard output. We should run the script with two options:

- `-l` to use the `line_profiler` function
- `-v` to immediately print the results on screen

The usage of `kernprof.py` is illustrated in the following line of code:

```
$ kernprof.py -l -v simul.py
```

It is also possible to run the profiler in an IPython shell for interactive editing. You should first load the `line_profiler` extension that will provide the `lprun` magic command. Using that command, you can avoid adding the `@profile` decorator:

```
IPython: chapter1/codes

In [1]: %load_ext line_profiler

In [2]: from simul import benchmark, ParticleSimulator

In [3]: %lprun -f ParticleSimulator.evolve benchmark()
Timer unit: 1e-06 s

Total time: 8.66675 s
File: /home/gabriele/workspace/hiperf/chapter1/codes/simul.py
Function: evolve at line 21

Line #      Hits         Time  Per Hit   % Time  Line Contents
==============================================================
    21                                           def evolve(self, dt):
    22         1            2      2.0      0.0       timestep = 0.00001
    23         1            4      4.0      0.0       nsteps = int(dt/timestep)
    24
    25     10001        12561      1.3      0.1       for i in range(nsteps):
    26   1010000       867457      0.9     10.0           for p in self.particles:
    27
    28   1000000      1859312      1.9     21.5               norm = (p.x**2 + p.y**2)**0.5
    29   1000000       972028      1.0     11.2               v_x = (-p.y)/norm
    30   1000000       921008      0.9     10.6               v_y = p.x/norm
    31
    32   1000000       982441      1.0     11.3               d_x = timestep * p.ang_vel * v_x
    33   1000000       974838      1.0     11.2               d_y = timestep * p.ang_vel * v_y
    34
    35   1000000      1058183      1.1     12.2               p.x += d_x
    36   1000000      1018915      1.0     11.8               p.y += d_y

In [4]:
```

The output is quite intuitive and is divided into six columns:

- `Line #`: The number of the line that was run
- `Hits`: The number of times that line was run
- `Time`: The execution time of the line in microseconds (`Time`)
- `Per Hit`: Time/hits
- `% Time`: Fraction of the total time spent executing that line
- `Line Contents`: The content of the line

By looking at the percentage column, we can get a pretty good idea of where the time is spent. In this case, there are a few statements in the `for` loop body with a cost of around 10-20 percent each.

Optimizing our code

Now that we have identified where exactly our application is spending most of its time, we can make some changes and assess the change in performance.

There are different ways to tune up our pure Python code. The way that produces the most remarkable results is to improve the *algorithms* used. In this case, instead of calculating the velocity and adding small steps, it will be more efficient (and correct as it is not an approximation) to express the equations of motion in terms of radius, r, and angle, `alpha`, (instead of x and y), and then calculate the points on a circle using the following equation:

```
x = r * cos(alpha)
y = r * sin(alpha)
```

Another way lies in minimizing the number of instructions. For example, we can precalculate the `timestep * p.ang_vel` factor that doesn't change with time. We can exchange the loop order (first we iterate on particles, then we iterate on time steps) and put the calculation of the factor outside the loop on the particles.

The line-by-line profiling also showed that even simple assignment operations can take a considerable amount of time. For example, the following statement takes more than 10 percent of the total time:

```
v_x = (-p.y)/norm
```

We can improve the performance of the loop by reducing the number of assignment operations performed. To do that, we can avoid intermediate variables by rewriting the expression into a single, slightly more complex statement (note that the right-hand side gets evaluated completely before being assigned to the variables):

```
p.x, p.y = p.x - t_x_ang*p.y/norm, p.y + t_x_ang * p.x/norm
```

This leads to the following code:

```
def evolve_fast(self, dt):
    timestep = 0.00001
    nsteps = int(dt/timestep)

    # Loop order is changed
    for p in self.particles:
        t_x_ang = timestep * p.ang_vel
        for i in range(nsteps):
            norm = (p.x**2 + p.y**2)**0.5
            p.x, p.y = (p.x - t_x_ang * p.y/norm,
                        p.y + t_x_ang * p.x/norm)
```

After applying the changes, we should verify that the result is still the same by running our test. We can then compare the execution times using our benchmark:

```
$ time python simul.py # Performance Tuned
real    0m0.756s
user    0m0.714s
sys     0m0.036s

$ time python simul.py # Original
real    0m0.863s
user    0m0.831s
sys     0m0.028s
```

As you can see, we obtained only a modest increment in speed by making a pure Python micro-optimization.

The dis module

Sometimes it's not easy to estimate how many operations a Python statement will take. In this section, we will dig into the Python internals to estimate the performance of individual statements. In the CPython interpreter, Python code is first converted to an intermediate representation, the **bytecode**, and then executed by the Python interpreter.

To inspect how the code is converted to bytecode, we can use the dis Python module (dis stands for disassemble). Its usage is really simple; all that is needed is to call the dis.dis function on the ParticleSimulator.evolve method:

```
import dis
from simul import ParticleSimulator
dis.dis(ParticleSimulator.evolve)
```

This will print, for each line in the function, a list of bytecode instructions. For example, the v_x = (-p.y)/norm statement is expanded in the following set of instructions:

```
29              85 LOAD_FAST              5 (p)
                88 LOAD_ATTR              4 (y)
                91 UNARY_NEGATIVE
                92 LOAD_FAST              6 (norm)
                95 BINARY_TRUE_DIVIDE
                96 STORE_FAST             7 (v_x)
```

LOAD_FAST loads a reference of the p variable onto the stack and LOAD_ATTR loads the y attribute of the item present on top of the stack. The other instructions, UNARY_NEGATIVE and BINARY_TRUE_DIVIDE, simply do arithmetic operations on top-of-stack items. Finally, the result is stored in v_x (STORE_FAST).

By analyzing the dis output, we can see that the first version of the loop produces 51 bytecode instructions while the second gets converted into 35 instructions.

The dis module helps discover how the statements get converted and serves mainly as an exploration and learning tool of the Python bytecode representation.

To improve our performance even further, we can keep trying to figure out other approaches to reduce the amount of instructions. It's clear, however, that this approach is ultimately limited by the speed of the Python interpreter and it is probably not the right tool for the job. In the following chapters, we will see how to speed up interpreter-limited calculations by executing fast specialized versions written in a lower level language (such as C or Fortran).

Profiling memory usage with memory_profiler

In some cases, high memory usage constitutes an issue. For example, if we want to handle a huge number of particles, we will incur a memory overhead due to the creation of many Particle instances.

The memory_profiler module summarizes, in a way similar to line_profiler, the memory usage of the process.

 The memory_profiler package is also available on the Python Package Index. You should also install the psutil module (https://github.com /giampaolo/psutil) as an optional dependency that will make memory_profiler considerably faster.

Just like line_profiler, memory_profiler also requires the instrumentation of the source code by placing a @profile decorator on the function we intend to monitor. In our case, we want to analyze the benchmark function.

We can slightly change benchmark to instantiate a considerable amount (100000) of Particle instances and decrease the simulation time:

```
def benchmark_memory():
    particles = [Particle(uniform(-1.0, 1.0),
                          uniform(-1.0, 1.0),
                          uniform(-1.0, 1.0))
                 for i in range(100000)]

    simulator = ParticleSimulator(particles)
    simulator.evolve(0.001)
```

We can use memory_profiler from an IPython shell through the %mprun magic command as shown in the following screenshot:

```
⊗ ⊖ ⊡  IPython: chapter1/codes

IPython 5.1.0 -- An enhanced Interactive Python.
?          -> Introduction and overview of IPython's features.
%quickref -> Quick reference.
help       -> Python's own help system.
object?    -> Details about 'object', use 'object??' for extra details.

In [1]: %load_ext memory_profiler

In [2]: from simul import benchmark_memory

In [3]: %mprun -f benchmark_memory benchmark_memory()
Filename: /home/gabriele/workspace/hiperf/chapter1/codes/simul.py

Line #    Mem usage    Increment   Line Contents
================================================
   142     37.8 MiB     0.0 MiB    def benchmark_memory():
   143     61.5 MiB    23.7 MiB        particles = [Particle(uniform(-1.0, 1.0),
   144                                                        uniform(-1.0, 1.0),
   145                                                        uniform(-1.0, 1.0))
   146     61.5 MiB     0.0 MiB                    for i in range(100000)]
   147
   148     61.5 MiB     0.0 MiB        simulator = ParticleSimulator(particles)
   149     61.5 MiB     0.0 MiB        simulator.evolve(0.001)

In [4]: █
```

It is possible to run `memory_profiler` from the shell using the `mprof run` command after adding the `@profile` decorator.

From the `Increment` column, we can see that 100,000 `Particle` objects take `23.7 MiB` of memory.

1 MiB (mebibyte) is equivalent to 1,048,576 bytes. It is different from 1 MB (*megabyte*), which is equivalent to 1,000,000 bytes.

We can use __slots__ on the Particle class to reduce its memory footprint. This feature saves some memory by avoiding storing the variables of the instance in an internal dictionary. This strategy, however, has a drawback--it prevents the addition of attributes other than the ones specified in __slots__ :

```python
class Particle:
    __slots__ = ('x', 'y', 'ang_vel')

    def __init__(self, x, y, ang_vel):
        self.x = x
        self.y = y
        self.ang_vel = ang_vel
```

We can now rerun our benchmark to assess the change in memory consumption, the result is displayed in the following screenshot:

```
IPython: chapter1/codes

IPython 5.1.0 -- An enhanced Interactive Python.
?         -> Introduction and overview of IPython's features.
%quickref -> Quick reference.
help      -> Python's own help system.
object?   -> Details about 'object', use 'object??' for extra details.

In [1]: %load_ext memory_profiler

In [2]: from simul import benchmark_memory

In [3]: %mprun -f benchmark_memory benchmark_memory()
Filename: /home/gabriele/workspace/hiperf/chapter1/codes/simul.py

Line #    Mem usage    Increment   Line Contents
================================================
   142     38.0 MiB      0.0 MiB   def benchmark_memory():
   143     51.7 MiB     13.7 MiB       particles = [Particle(uniform(-1.0, 1.0),
   144                                                        uniform(-1.0, 1.0),
   145                                                        uniform(-1.0, 1.0))
   146     51.7 MiB      0.0 MiB                   for i in range(100000)]
   147
   148     51.7 MiB      0.0 MiB       simulator = ParticleSimulator(particles)
   149     51.7 MiB      0.0 MiB       simulator.evolve(0.001)

In [4]:
```

By rewriting the Particle class using __slots__, we can save about 10 MiB of memory.

Summary

In this chapter, we introduced the basic principles of optimization and applied those principles to a test application. When optimizing, the first thing to do is test and identify the bottlenecks in the application. We saw how to write and time a benchmark using the `time` Unix command, the Python `timeit` module, and the full-fledged `pytest-benchmark` package. We learned how to profile our application using `cProfile`, `line_profiler`, and `memory_profiler`, and how to analyze and navigate the profiling data graphically with KCachegrind.

In the next chapter, we will explore how to improve performance using algorithms and data structures available in the Python standard library. We will cover scaling, sample usage of several data structures, and learn techniques such as caching and memoization.

2
Pure Python Optimizations

As mentioned in the last chapter, one of the most effective ways of improving the performance of applications is through the use of better algorithms and data structures. The Python standard library provides a large variety of ready-to-use algorithms and data structures that can be directly incorporated in your applications. With the tools learned from this chapter, you will be able to use the right algorithm for the task and achieve massive speed gains.

Even though many algorithms have been around for quite a while, they are especially relevant in today's world as we continuously produce, consume, and analyze ever increasing amounts of data. Buying a larger server or microoptimizing can work for some time, but achieving better scaling through algorithmic improvement can solve the problem once and for all.

In this chapter, we will understand how to achieve better scaling using standard algorithms and data structures. More advanced use cases will also be covered by taking advantage of third-party libraries. We will also learn about tools to implement caching, a technique used to achieve faster response times by sacrificing some space on memory or on disk.

The list of topics to be covered in this chapter is as follows:

- Introduction to computational complexity
- Lists and deques
- Dictionaries
- How to build an inverted index using a dictionary
- Sets
- Heaps and priority queues
- Implementing autocompletion using tries
- Introduction to caching

- In-memory caching with the `functools.lru_cache` decorator
- On-disk cache with `joblib.Memory`
- Fast and memory-efficient loops with comprehensions and generators

Useful algorithms and data structures

Algorithmic improvements are especially effective in increasing performance because they typically allow the application to scale better with increasingly large inputs.

Algorithm running times can be classified according to their computational complexity, a characterization of the resources required to perform a task. Such classification is expressed through the Big-O notation, an upper bound on the operations required to execute the task, which usually depends on the input size.

For example, incrementing each element of a list can be implemented using a `for` loop, as follows:

```
input = list(range(10))
for i, _ in enumerate(input):
    input[i] += 1
```

If the operation does not depend on the size of the input (for example, accessing the first element of a list), the algorithm is said to take constant, or $O(1)$, time. This means that, no matter how much data we have, the time to run the algorithm will always be the same.

In this simple algorithm, the `input[i] += 1` operation will be repeated 10 times, which is the size of the input. If we double the size of the input array, the number of operations will increase proportionally. Since the number of operations is proportional to the input size, this algorithm is said to take $O(N)$ time, where N is the size of the input array.

In some instances, the running time may depend on the structure of the input (for example, if the collection is sorted or contains many duplicates). In these cases, an algorithm may have different best-case, average-case, and worst-case running times. Unless stated otherwise, the running times presented in this chapter are considered to be average running times.

In this section, we will examine the running times of the main algorithms and data structures that are implemented in the Python standard library, and understand how improving running times results in massive gains and allows us to solve large-scale problems with elegance.

You can find the code used to run the benchmarks in this chapter in the `Algorithms.ipynb` notebook, which can be opened using Jupyter.

Lists and deques

Python lists are ordered collections of elements and, in Python, are implemented as resizable arrays. An array is a basic data structure that consists of a series of contiguous memory locations, and each location contains a reference to a Python object.

Lists shine in accessing, modifying, and appending elements. Accessing or modifying an element involves fetching the object reference from the appropriate position of the underlying array and has complexity $O(1)$. Appending an element is also very fast. When an empty list is created, an array of fixed size is allocated and, as we insert elements, the slots in the array are gradually filled up. Once all the slots are occupied, the list needs to increase the size of its underlying array, thus triggering a memory reallocation that can take $O(N)$ time. Nevertheless, those memory allocations are infrequent, and the time complexity for the append operation is referred to as amortized $O(1)$ time.

The list operations that may have efficiency problems are those that add or remove elements at the beginning (or somewhere in the middle) of the list. When an item is inserted, or removed, from the beginning of a list, all the subsequent elements of the array need to be shifted by a position, thus taking $O(N)$ time.

In the following table, the timings for different operations on a list of size 10,000 are shown; you can see how insertion and removal performances vary quite dramatically if performed at the beginning or at the end of the list:

Code	N=10000 (µs)	N=20000 (µs)	N=30000 (µs)	Time
`list.pop()`	0.50	0.59	0.58	$O(1)$
`list.pop(0)`	4.20	8.36	12.09	$O(N)$
`list.append(1)`	0.43	0.45	0.46	$O(1)$
`list.insert(0, 1)`	6.20	11.97	17.41	$O(N)$

In some cases, it is necessary to efficiently perform insertion or removal of elements both at the beginning and at the end of the collection. Python provides a data structure with those properties in the `collections.deque` class. The word **deque** stands for double-ended queue because this data structure is designed to efficiently put and remove elements at the beginning and at the end of the collection, as it is in the case of queues. In Python, deques are implemented as doubly-linked lists.

Deques, in addition to `pop` and `append`, expose the `popleft` and `appendleft` methods that have $O(1)$ running time:

Code	N=10000 (µs)	N=20000 (µs)	N=30000 (µs)	Time
`deque.pop()`	0.41	0.47	0.51	$O(1)$
`deque.popleft()`	0.39	0.51	0.47	$O(1)$
`deque.append(1)`	0.42	0.48	0.50	$O(1)$
`deque.appendleft(1)`	0.38	0.47	0.51	$O(1)$

Despite these advantages, deques should not be used to replace regular lists in most cases. The efficiency gained by the `appendleft` and `popleft` operations comes at a cost: accessing an element in the middle of a deque is a $O(N)$ operation, as shown in the following table:

Code	N=10000 (µs)	N=20000 (µs)	N=30000 (µs)	Time
`deque[0]`	0.37	0.41	0.45	$O(1)$
`deque[N - 1]`	0.37	0.42	0.43	$O(1)$
`deque[int(N / 2)]`	1.14	1.71	2.48	$O(N)$

Searching for an item in a list is generally a $O(N)$ operation and is performed using the `list.index` method. A simple way to speed up searches in lists is to keep the array sorted and perform a binary search using the `bisect` module.

The `bisect` module allows fast searches on sorted arrays. The `bisect.bisect` function can be used on a sorted list to find the index to place an element while maintaining the array in sorted order. In the following example, we can see that if we want to insert the 3 element in the array while keeping `collection` in sorted order, we should put 3 in the third position (which corresponds to index 2):

```
insert bisect
collection = [1, 2, 4, 5, 6]
bisect.bisect(collection, 3)
# Result: 2
```

This function uses the binary search algorithm that has $O(log(N))$ running time. Such a running time is exceptionally fast, and basically means that your running time will increase by a constant amount every time you *double* your input size. This means that if, for example, your program takes 1 second to run on an input of size 1000, it will take 2 seconds to process an input of size 2000, 3 seconds to process an input of size 4000, and so on. If you had 100 seconds, you could theoretically process an input of size 10^{33}, which is larger than the number of atoms in your body!

If the value we are trying to insert is already present in the list, the `bisect.bisect` function will return the location *after* the already present value. Therefore, we can use the `bisect.bisect_left` variant, which returns the correct index in the following way (taken from the module documentation at `https://docs.python.org/3.5/library/bisect.html`):

```python
def index_bisect(a, x):
    'Locate the leftmost value exactly equal to x'
    i = bisect.bisect_left(a, x)
    if i != len(a) and a[i] == x:
    return i
    raise ValueError
```

In the following table, you can see how the running time of the `bisect` solution is barely affected at these input sizes, making it a suitable solution when searching through very large collections:

Code	N=10000 (μs)	N=20000 (μs)	N=30000 (μs)	Time
`list.index(a)`	87.55	171.06	263.17	$O(N)$
`index_bisect(list, a)`	3.16	3.20	4.71	$O(log(N))$

Dictionaries

Dictionaries are extremely versatile and extensively used in the Python language. Dictionaries are implemented as hash maps and are very good at element insertion, deletion, and access; all these operations have an average $O(1)$ time complexity.

In Python versions up to 3.5, dictionaries are unordered collections. Since Python 3.6, dictionaries are capable of maintaining their elements by order of insertion.

A hash map is a data structure that associates a set of key-value pairs. The principle behind hash maps is to assign a specific index to each key so that its associated value can be stored in an array. The index can be obtained through the use of a `hash` function; Python implements hash functions for several data types. As a demonstration, the generic function to obtain hash codes is `hash`. In the following example, we show you how to obtain the hash code given the `"hello"` string:

```
hash("hello")
# Result: -1182655621190490452

# To restrict the number to be a certain range you can use
# the modulo (%) operator
hash("hello") % 10
# Result: 8
```

Hash maps can be tricky to implement because they need to handle collisions that happen when two different objects have the same hash code. However, all the complexity is elegantly hidden behind the implementation and the default collision resolution works well in most real-world scenarios.

Access, insertion, and removal of an item in a dictionary scales as $O(1)$ with the size of the dictionary. However, note that the computation of the hash function still needs to happen and, for strings, the computation scales with the length of the string. As string keys are usually relatively small, this doesn't constitute a problem in practice.

A dictionary can be used to efficiently count unique elements in a list. In this example, we define the `counter_dict` function that takes a list and returns a dictionary containing the number of occurrences of each value in the list:

```
def counter_dict(items):
    counter = {}
    for item in items:
        if item not in counter:
            counter[item] = 0
        else:
            counter[item] += 1
    return counter
```

The code can be somewhat simplified using `collections.defaultdict`, which can be used to produce dictionaries where each new key is automatically assigned a default value. In the following code, the `defaultdict(int)` call produces a dictionary where every new element is automatically assigned a zero value, and can be used to streamline the counting:

```
from collections import defaultdict
def counter_defaultdict(items):
    counter = defaultdict(int)
    for item in items:
        counter[item] += 1
    return counter
```

The `collections` module also includes a `Counter` class that can be used for the same purpose with a single line of code:

```
from collections import Counter
counter = Counter(items)
```

Speed-wise, all these ways of counting have the same time complexity, but the `Counter` implementation is the most efficient, as shown in the following table:

Code	N=1000 (µs)	N=2000 (µs)	N=3000 (µs)	Time
Counter(items)	51.48	96.63	140.26	$O(N)$
counter_dict(items)	111.96	197.13	282.79	$O(N)$
counter_defaultdict(items)	120.90	238.27	359.60	$O(N)$

Building an in-memory search index using a hash map

Dictionaries can be used to quickly search for a word in a list of documents, similar to a search engine. In this subsection, we will learn how to build an inverted index based on a dictionary of lists. Let's say we have a collection of four documents:

```
docs = ["the cat is under the table",
        "the dog is under the table",
        "cats and dogs smell roses",
        "Carla eats an apple"]
```

A simple way to retrieve all the documents that match a query is to scan each document and test for the presence of a word. For example, if we want to look up the documents where the word `table` appears, we can employ the following filtering operation:

```
matches = [doc for doc in docs if "table" in doc]
```

This approach is simple and works well when we have one-off queries; however, if we need to query the collection very often, it can be beneficial to optimize querying time. Since the per-query cost of the linear scan is $O(N)$, you can imagine that a better scaling will allow us to handle much larger document collections.

A better strategy is to spend some time preprocessing the documents so that they are easier to find at query time. We can build a structure, called the **inverted index**, that associates each word in our collection with the list of documents where that word is present. In our earlier example, the word `"table"` will be associated to the `"the cat is under the table"` and `"the dog is under the table"` documents; they correspond to indices 0 and 1.

Such a mapping can be implemented by going over our collection of documents and storing in a dictionary the index of the documents where that term appears. The implementation is similar to the `counter_dict` function, except that, instead of accumulating a counter, we are growing the list of documents that match the current term:

```
# Building an index
index = {}
for i, doc in enumerate(docs):
    # We iterate over each term in the document
    for word in doc.split():
        # We build a list containing the indices
        # where the term appears
        if word not in index:
            index[word] = [i]
        else:
            index[word].append(i)
```

Once we have built our index, doing a query involves a simple dictionary lookup. For example, if we want to return all the documents containing the term table, we can simply query the index, and retrieve the corresponding documents:

```
results = index["table"]
result_documents = [docs[i] for i in results]
```

Since all it takes to query our collection is a dictionary access, the index can handle queries with time complexity $O(1)$! Thanks to the inverted index, we are now able to query any number of documents (as long as they fit in memory) in constant time. Needless to say, indexing is a technique widely used to quickly retrieve data not only in search engines, but also in databases and any system that requires fast searches.

Note that building an inverted index is an expensive operation and requires you to encode every possible query. This is a substantial drawback, but the benefits are great and it may be worthwhile to pay the price in terms of decreased flexibility.

Sets

Sets are unordered collections of elements, with the additional restriction that the elements must be unique. The main use-cases where sets are a good choice are membership tests (testing if an element is present in the collection) and, unsurprisingly, set operations such as union, difference, and intersection.

In Python, sets are implemented using a hash-based algorithm just like dictionaries; therefore, the time complexities for addition, deletion, and test for membership scale as $O(1)$ with the size of the collection.

Sets contain only unique elements. An immediate use case of sets is the removal of duplicates from a collection, which can be accomplished by simply passing the collection through the set constructor, as follows:

```
# create a list that contains duplicates
x = list(range(1000)) + list(range(500))
# the set *x_unique* will contain only
# the unique elements in x
x_unique = set(x)
```

The time complexity for removing duplicates is $O(N)$, as it requires to read the input and put each element in the set.

Sets expose a number of operations like union, intersection, and difference. The union of two sets is a new set containing all the elements of both the sets; the intersection is a new set that contains only the elements in common between the two sets, and the difference is a new set containing the element of the first set that are not contained in the second set. The time complexities for these operations are shown in the following table. Note that since we have two different input sizes, we will use the letter S to indicate the size of the first set (called `s`), and T to indicate the size of the second set (called `t`):

Code	Time
`s.union(t)`	$O(S + T)$
`s.intersection(t)`	$O(min(S, T))$
`s.difference(t)`	$O(S)$

An application of set operations are, for example, Boolean queries. Going back to the inverted index example of the previous subsection, we may want to support queries that include multiple terms. For example, we may want to search for all the documents that contain the words `cat` and `table`. This kind of a query can be efficiently computed by taking the intersection between the set of documents containing `cat` and the set of documents containing `table`.

In order to efficiently support those operations, we can change our indexing code so that each term is associated to a set of documents (rather than a list). After applying this change, calculating more advanced queries is a matter of applying the right set operation. In the following code, we show the inverted index based on sets and the query using set operations:

```
# Building an index using sets
index = {}
for i, doc in enumerate(docs):
    # We iterate over each term in the document
    for word in doc.split():
        # We build a set containing the indices
        # where the term appears
        if word not in index:
            index[word] = {i}
        else:
            index[word].add(i)

# Querying the documents containing both "cat" and "table"
index['cat'].intersection(index['table'])
```

Heaps

Heaps are data structures designed to quickly find and extract the maximum (or minimum) value in a collection. A typical use-case for heaps is to process a series of incoming tasks in order of maximum priority.

One can theoretically use a sorted list using the tools in the `bisect` module; however, while extracting the maximum value will take $O(1)$ time (using `list.pop`), insertion will still take $O(N)$ time (remember that, even if finding the insertion point takes $O(log(N))$ time, inserting an element in the middle of a list is still a $O(N)$ operation). A heap is a more efficient data structure that allows for insertion and extraction of maximum values with $O(log(N))$ time complexity.

In Python, heaps are built using the procedures contained in the `heapq` module on an underlying list. For example, if we have a list of 10 elements, we can reorganize it into a heap with the `heapq.heapify` function:

```
import heapq

collection = [10, 3, 3, 4, 5, 6]
heapq.heapify(collection)
```

To perform the insertion and extraction operations on the heap, we can use the `heapq.heappush` and `heapq.heappop` functions. The `heapq.heappop` function will extract the minimum value in the collection in $O(log(N))$ time and can be used in the following way:

```
heapq.heappop(collection)
# Returns: 3
```

Similarly, you can push the integer 1, with the `heapq.heappush` function, as follows:

```
heapq.heappush(collection, 1)
```

Another easy-to-use option is the `queue.PriorityQueue` class that, as a bonus, is thread and process-safe. The `PriorityQueue` class can be filled up with elements using the `PriorityQueue.put` method, while `PriorityQueue.get` can be used to extract the minimum value in the collection:

```
from queue import PriorityQueue

queue = PriorityQueue()
for element in collection:
    queue.put(element)

queue.get()
# Returns: 3
```

If the maximum element is required, a simple trick is to multiply each element of the list by -1. In this way, the order of the elements will be inverted. Also, if you want to associate an object (for example, a task to run) to each number (which can represent the priority), one can insert tuples of the `(number, object)` form; the comparison operator for the tuple will be ordered with respect to its first element, as shown in the following example:

```
queue = PriorityQueue()
queue.put((3, "priority 3"))
queue.put((2, "priority 2"))
queue.put((1, "priority 1"))
```

```
queue.get()
# Returns: (1, "priority 1")
```

Tries

A perhaps less popular data structure, very useful in practice, is the trie (sometimes called prefix tree). Tries are extremely fast at matching a list of strings against a prefix. This is especially useful when implementing features such as search-as-you type and autocompletion, where the list of available completions is very large and short response times are required.

Unfortunately, Python does not include a trie implementation in its standard library; however, many efficient implementations are readily available through PyPI. The one we will use in this subsection is `patricia-trie`, a single-file, pure Python implementation of trie. As an example, we will use `patricia-trie` to perform the task of finding the longest prefix in a set of strings (just like autocompletion).

As an example, we can demonstrate how fast a trie is able to search through a list of strings. In order to generate a large amount of unique random strings, we can define a function, `random_string`. The `random_string` function will return a string composed of random uppercase characters and, while there is a chance to get duplicates, we can greatly reduce the probability of duplicates to the point of being negligible if we make the string long enough. The implementation of the `random_string` function is shown as follows:

```
from random import choice
from string import ascii_uppercase

def random_string(length):
 """Produce a random string made of *length* uppercase ascii
 characters"""
 return ''.join(choice(ascii_uppercase) for i in range(length))
```

We can build a list of random strings and time how fast it searches for a prefix (in our case, the "AA" string) using the `str.startswith` function:

```
strings = [random_string(32) for i in range(10000)]
matches = [s for s in strings if s.startswith('AA')]
```

List comprehension and `str.startwith` are already very optimized operations and, on this small dataset, the search takes only a millisecond or so:

```
%timeit [s for s in strings if s.startswith('AA')]

1000 loops, best of 3: 1.76 ms per loop
```

Now, let's try using a trie for the same operation. In this example, we will use the `patricia-trie` library that is installable through `pip`. The `patricia.trie` class implements a variant of the trie data structure with an interface similar to a dictionary. We can initialize our trie by creating a dictionary from our list of strings, as follows:

```
from patricia import trie
strings_dict = {s:0 for s in strings}
# A dictionary where all values are 0
strings_trie = trie(**strings_dict)
```

To query `patricia-trie` for a matching prefix, we can use the `trie.iter` method, which returns an iterator over the matching strings:

```
matches = list(strings_trie.iter('AA'))
```

Now that we know how to initialize and query a trie, we can time the operation:

```
%timeit list(strings_trie.iter('AA'))
10000 loops, best of 3: 60.1 µs per loop
```

If you look closely, the timing for this input size is **60.1 µs**, which is about 30 times faster (1.76 ms = 1760 µs) than linear search! The speed up is so impressive because of the better computational complexity of the trie prefix search. Querying a trie has a time complexity $O(S)$, where S is the length of the longest string in the collection, while the time complexity of a simple linear scan is $O(N)$, where N is the size of the collection.

Note that if we want to return all the prefixes that match, the running time will be proportional to the number of results that match the prefix. Therefore, when designing timing benchmarks, care must be taken to ensure that we are always returning the same number of results.

The scaling properties of a trie versus a linear scan for datasets of different sizes that contains ten prefix matches are shown in the following table:

Algorithm	N=10000 (µs)	N=20000 (µs)	N=30000 (µs)	Time
Trie	17.12	17.27	17.47	$O(S)$
Linear scan	1978.44	4075.72	6398.06	$O(N)$

An interesting fact is that the implementation of `patricia-trie` is actually a single Python file; this clearly shows how simple and powerful a clever algorithm can be. For extra features and performance, other C-optimized trie libraries are also available, such as `datrie` and `marisa-trie`.

Caching and memoization

Caching is a great technique used to improve the performance of a wide range of applications. The idea behind caching is to store expensive results in a temporary location, called cache, that can be located in memory, on-disk, or in a remote location.

Web applications make extensive use of caching. In a web application, it often happens that users request a certain page at the same time. In this case, instead of recomputing the page for each user, the web application can compute it once and serve the user the already rendered page. Ideally, caching also needs a mechanism for invalidation so that if the page needs to be updated, we can recompute it before serving it again. Intelligent caching allows web applications to handle increasing number of users with less resources. Caching can also be done preemptively, such as the later sections of the video get buffered when watching a video online.

Caching is also used to improve the performance of certain algorithms. A great example is computing the Fibonacci sequence. Since computing the next number in the Fibonacci sequence requires the previous number in the sequence, one can store and reuse previous results, dramatically improving the running time. Storing and reusing the results of the previous function calls in an application is usually termed as **memoization**, and is one of the forms of caching. Several other algorithms can take advantage of memoization to gain impressive performance improvements, and this programming technique is commonly referred to as **dynamic programming**.

The benefits of caching, however, do not come for free. What we are actually doing is sacrificing some space to improve the speed of the application. Additionally, if the cache is stored in a location on the network, we may incur transfer costs and general time needed for communication. One should evaluate when it is convenient to use a cache and how much space we are willing to trade for an increase in speed.

Given the usefulness of this technique, the Python standard library includes a simple in-memory cache out of the box in the functools module. The functools.lru_cache decorator can be used to easily cache the results of a function. In the following example, we create a function, sum2, that prints a statement and returns the sum of two numbers. By running the function twice, you can see that the first time the sum2 function is executed the "Calculating ..." string is produced, while the second time the result is returned without running the function:

```
from functools import lru_cache

@lru_cache()
def sum2(a, b):
    print("Calculating {} + {}".format(a, b))
    return a + b

print(sum2(1, 2))
# Output:
# Calculating 1 + 2
# 3

print(sum2(1, 2))
# Output:
# 3
```

The lru_cache decorator also provides other basic features. To restrict the size of the cache, one can set the number of elements that we intend to maintain through the max_size argument. If we want our cache size to be unbounded, we can specify a value of None. An example usage of max_size is shown here:

```
@lru_cache(max_size=16)
def sum2(a, b):
    ...
```

In this way, as we execute sum2 with different arguments, the cache will reach a maximum size of 16 and, as we keep requesting more calculations, new values will replace older values in the cache. The lru prefix originates from this strategy, which means least recently used.

The `lru_cache` decorator also adds extra functionalities to the decorated function. For example, it is possible to examine the cache performance using the `cache_info` method, and it is possible to reset the cache using the `cache_clear` method, as follows:

```
sum2.cache_info()
# Output: CacheInfo(hits=0, misses=1, maxsize=128, currsize=1)
sum2.cache_clear()
```

As an example, we can see how a problem, such as computing the fibonacci series, may benefit from caching. We can define a `fibonacci` function and time its execution:

```
def fibonacci(n):
    if n < 1:
        return 1
    else:
        return fibonacci(n - 1) + fibonacci(n - 2)

# Non-memoized version
%timeit fibonacci(20)
100 loops, best of 3: 5.57 ms per loop
```

The execution takes 5.57 ms, which is very high. The scaling of the function written in this way has poor performance; the previously computed fibonacci sequences are not reused, causing this algorithm to have an exponential scaling of roughly $O(2^N)$.

Caching can improve this algorithm by storing and reusing the already-computed fibonacci numbers. To implement the cached version, it is sufficient to apply the `lru_cache` decorator to the original `fibonacci` function. Also, to design a proper benchmark, we need to ensure that a new cache is instantiated for every run; to do this, we can use the `timeit.repeat` function, as shown in the following example:

```
import timeit
setup_code = '''
from functools import lru_cache
from __main__ import fibonacci
fibonacci_memoized = lru_cache(maxsize=None)(fibonacci)
'''

results = timeit.repeat('fibonacci_memoized(20)',
                        setup=setup_code,
                        repeat=1000,
                        number=1)
print("Fibonacci took {:.2f} us".format(min(results)))
# Output: Fibonacci took 0.01 us
```

Even though we changed the algorithm by adding a simple decorator, the running time now is much less than a microsecond. The reason is that, thanks to caching, we now have a linear time algorithm instead of an exponential one.

The `lru_cache` decorator can be used to implement simple in-memory caching in your application. For more advanced use cases, third-party modules can be used for more powerful implementation and on-disk caching.

Joblib

A simple library that, among other things, provides a simple on-disk cache is `joblib`. The package can be used in a similar way as `lru_cache`, except that the results will be stored on disk and will persist between runs.

 The `joblib` module can be installed from PyPI using the `pip install joblib` command.

The `joblib` module provides the `Memory` class that can be used to memoize functions using the `Memory.cache` decorator:

```
from joblib import Memory
memory = Memory(cachedir='/path/to/cachedir')

@memory.cache
def sum2(a, b):
    return a + b
```

The function will behave similar to `lru_cache`, with the exception that the results will be stored on-disk in the directory specified by the `cachedir` argument during `Memory` initialization. Additionally, the cached results will persist over subsequent runs!

The `Memory.cache` method also allows to limit recomputation only when certain arguments change, and the resulting decorated function supports basic functionalities to clear and analyze the cache.

Perhaps the best `joblib` feature is that, thanks to intelligent hashing algorithms, it provides efficient memoization of functions that operate on `numpy` arrays, and is particularly useful in scientific and engineering applications.

Comprehensions and generators

In this section, we will explore a few simple strategies to speed up Python loops using comprehension and generators. In Python, comprehension and generator expressions are fairly optimized operations and should be preferred in place of explicit for-loops. Another reason to use this construct is readability; even if the speedup over a standard loop is modest, the comprehension and generator syntax is more compact and (most of the times) more intuitive.

In the following example, we can see that both the list comprehension and generator expressions are faster than an explicit loop when combined with the `sum` function:

```
def loop():
    res = []
    for i in range(100000):
        res.append(i * i)
    return sum(res)

def comprehension():
    return sum([i * i for i in range(100000)])

def generator():
    return sum(i * i for i in range(100000))

%timeit loop()
100 loops, best of 3: 16.1 ms per loop
%timeit comprehension()
100 loops, best of 3: 10.1 ms per loop
%timeit generator()
100 loops, best of 3: 12.4 ms per loop
```

Just like lists, it is possible to use `dict` comprehension to build dictionaries slightly more efficiently and compactly, as shown in the following code:

```
def loop():
    res = {}
    for i in range(100000):
        res[i] = i
    return res
```

```
def comprehension():
    return {i: i for i in range(100000)}
%timeit loop()
100 loops, best of 3: 13.2 ms per loop
%timeit comprehension()
100 loops, best of 3: 12.8 ms per loop
```

Efficient looping (especially in terms of memory) can be implemented using iterators and functions such as `filter` and `map`. As an example, consider the problem of applying a series of operations to a list using list comprehension and then taking the maximum value:

```
def map_comprehension(numbers):
    a = [n * 2 for n in numbers]
    b = [n ** 2 for n in a]
    c = [n ** 0.33 for n in b]
    return max(c)
```

The problem with this approach is that for every list comprehension, we are allocating a new list, increasing memory usage. Instead of using list comprehension, we can employ generators. Generators are objects that, when iterated upon, compute a value on the fly and return the result.

For example, the `map` function takes two arguments--a function and an iterator--and returns a generator that applies the function to every element of the collection. The important point is that the operation happens only *while we are iterating*, and not when `map` is invoked!

We can rewrite the previous function using `map` and by creating intermediate generators, rather than lists, thus saving memory by computing the values on the fly:

```
def map_normal(numbers):
    a = map(lambda n: n * 2, numbers)
    b = map(lambda n: n ** 2, a)
    c = map(lambda n: n ** 0.33, b)
    return max(c)
```

We can profile the memory of the two solutions using the `memory_profiler` extension from an IPython session. The extension provides a small utility, `%memit`, that will help us evaluate the memory usage of a Python statement in a way similar to `%timeit`, as illustrated in the following snippet:

```
%load_ext memory_profiler
numbers = range(1000000)
%memit map_comprehension(numbers)
peak memory: 166.33 MiB, increment: 102.54 MiB
%memit map_normal(numbers)
peak memory: 71.04 MiB, increment: 0.00 MiB
```

As you can see, the memory used by the first version is `102.54 MiB`, while the second version consumes `0.00 MiB`! For the interested reader, more functions that return generators can be found in the `itertools` module, which provides a set of utilities designed to handle common iteration patterns.

Summary

Algorithmic optimization can improve how your application scales as we process increasingly large data. In this chapter, we demonstrated use-cases and running times of the most common data structures available in Python, such as lists, deques, dictionaries, heaps, and tries. We also covered caching, a technique that can be used to trade some space, in memory or on-disk, in exchange for increased responsiveness of an application. We also demonstrated how to get modest speed gains by replacing for-loops with fast constructs, such as list comprehensions and generator expressions.

In the subsequent chapters, we will learn how to improve performance further using numerical libraries such as `numpy`, and how to write extension modules in a lower-level language with the help of *Cython*.

3
Fast Array Operations with NumPy and Pandas

NumPy is the *de facto* standard for scientific computing in Python. It extends Python with a flexible multidimensional array that allows fast and concise mathematical calculations.

NumPy provides common data structures and algorithms designed to express complex mathematical operations using a concise syntax. The multidimensional array, `numpy.ndarray`, is internally based on C arrays. Apart from the performance benefits, this choice allows NumPy code to easily interface with the existing C and FORTRAN routines; NumPy is helpful in bridging the gap between Python and the legacy code written using those languages.

In this chapter, we will learn how to create and manipulate NumPy arrays. We will also explore the NumPy broadcasting feature used to rewrite complex mathematical expressions in an efficient and succinct manner.

Pandas is a tool that relies heavily on NumPy and provides additional data structures and algorithms targeted toward data analysis. We will introduce the main Pandas features and its usage. We will also learn how to achieve high performance from Pandas data structures and vectorized operations.

The topics covered in this chapter are as follows:

- Creating and manipulating NumPy arrays
- Mastering NumPy's broadcasting feature for fast and succinct vectorized operations
- Improving our particle simulator with NumPy
- Reaching optimal performance with `numexpr`
- Pandas fundamentals
- Database-style operations with Pandas

Getting started with NumPy

The NumPy library revolves around its multidimensional array object, `numpy.ndarray`. NumPy arrays are collections of elements of the same data type; this fundamental restriction allows NumPy to pack the data in a way that allows for high-performance mathematical operations.

Creating arrays

You can create NumPy arrays using the `numpy.array` function. It takes a list-like object (or another array) as input and, optionally, a string expressing its data type. You can interactively test array creation using an IPython shell, as follows:

```
import numpy as np
a = np.array([0, 1, 2])
```

Every NumPy array has an associated data type that can be accessed using the `dtype` attribute. If we inspect the `a` array, we find that its `dtype` is `int64`, which stands for 64-bit integer:

```
a.dtype
# Result:
# dtype('int64')
```

We may decide to convert those integer numbers to `float` type. To do this, we can either pass the `dtype` argument at array initialization or cast the array to another data type using the `astype` method. The two ways to select a data type are shown in the following code:

```
a = np.array([1, 2, 3], dtype='float32')
a.astype('float32')
# Result:
# array([ 0.,   1.,   2.], dtype=float32)
```

To create an array with two dimensions (an array of arrays), we can perform the initialization using a nested sequence, as follows:

```
a = np.array([[0, 1, 2], [3, 4, 5]])
print(a)
# Output:
# [[0 1 2]
#  [3 4 5]]
```

The array created in this way has two dimensions, which are called **axes** in NumPy's jargon. An array formed in this way is like a table that contains two rows and three columns. We can access the axes using the `ndarray.shape` attribute:

```
a.shape
# Result:
# (2, 3)
```

Arrays can also be reshaped as long as the product of the shape dimensions is equal to the total number of elements in the array (that is, the total number of elements is conserved). For example, we can reshape an array containing 16 elements in the following ways: `(2, 8)`, `(4, 4)`, or `(2, 2, 4)`. To reshape an array, we can either use the `ndarray.reshape` method or assign a new value to the `ndarray.shape` tuple. The following code illustrates the use of the `ndarray.reshape` method:

```
a = np.array([0, 1, 2, 3, 4, 5, 6, 7, 8,
              9, 10, 11, 12, 13, 14, 15])
a.shape
# Output:
# (16,)

a.reshape(4, 4) # Equivalent: a.shape = (4, 4)
# Output:
# array([[ 0,  1,  2,  3],
#        [ 4,  5,  6,  7],
#        [ 8,  9, 10, 11],
#        [12, 13, 14, 15]])
```

Thanks to this property, you can freely add dimensions of size one. You can reshape an array with 16 elements to (16, 1), (1, 16), (16, 1, 1), and so on. In the next section, we will extensively use this feature to implement complex operations through *broadcasting*.

NumPy provides convenience functions, shown in the following code, to create arrays filled with zeros, ones, or with no initial value (in this case, their actual value is meaningless and depends on the memory state). Those functions take the array shape as a tuple and, optionally, its dtype:

```
np.zeros((3, 3))
np.empty((3, 3))
np.ones((3, 3), dtype='float32')
```

In our examples, we will use the numpy.random module to generate random floating point numbers in the (0, 1) interval. The numpy.random.rand will take a shape and return an array of random numbers with that shape:

```
np.random.rand(3, 3)
```

Sometimes it is convenient to initialize arrays that have the same shape as that of some other array. For that purpose, NumPy provides some handy functions, such as zeros_like, empty_like, and ones_like. These functions can be used as follows:

```
np.zeros_like(a)
np.empty_like(a)
np.ones_like(a)
```

Accessing arrays

The NumPy array interface is, on a shallow level, similar to that of Python lists. NumPy arrays can be indexed using integers and iterated using a for loop:

```
A = np.array([0, 1, 2, 3, 4, 5, 6, 7, 8])
A[0]
# Result:
# 0

[a for a in A]
# Result:
# [0, 1, 2, 3, 4, 5, 6, 7, 8]
```

In NumPy, array elements and sub-arrays can be conveniently accessed by using multiple values separated by commas inside the subscript operator, `[]`. If we take a `(3,3)` array (an array containing three triplets), and we access the element with index 0, we obtain the first row, as follows:

```
A = np.array([[0, 1, 2], [3, 4, 5], [6, 7, 8]])
A[0]
# Result:
# array([0, 1, 2])
```

We can index the row again by adding another index separated by a comma. To get the second element of the first row, we can use the `(0, 1)` index. An important observation is that the `A[0, 1]` notation is actually a shorthand for `A[(0, 1)]`, that is, we are actually indexing using a *tuple*! Both the versions are shown in the following snippet:

```
A[0, 1]
# Result:
# 1

# Equivalent version using tuple
A[(0, 1)]
```

NumPy allows you to slice arrays into multiple dimensions. If we slice on the first dimension, we can obtain a collection of triplets, shown as follows:

```
A[0:2]
# Result:
# array([[0, 1, 2],
#        [3, 4, 5]])
```

If we slice the array again on the second dimension with `0:2`, we are basically extracting the first two elements from the collection of triplets shown earlier. This results in an array of shape `(2, 2)`, shown in the following code:

```
A[0:2, 0:2]
# Result:
# array([[0, 1],
#        [3, 4]])
```

Intuitively, you can update the values in the array using both numerical indexes and slices. An example is illustrated in the following code snippet:

```
A[0, 1] = 8
A[0:2, 0:2] = [[1, 1], [1, 1]]
```

Indexing with the slicing syntax is very fast because, unlike lists, it doesn't produce a copy of the array. In NumPy's terminology, it returns a *view* of the same memory area. If we take a slice of the original array, and then we change one of its values, the original array will be updated as well. The following code illustrates an example of this feature:

```
a= np.array([1, 1, 1, 1])
a_view = a[0:2]
a_view[0] = 2
print(a)
# Output:
# [2 1 1 1]
```

It is important to be extra careful when mutating NumPy arrays. Since views share data, changing the values of a view can result in hard-to-find bugs. To prevent side effects, you can set the a.flags.writeable = False flag, which will prevent accidental mutation of the array or any of its views.

We can take a look at another example that shows how the slicing syntax can be used in a real-world setting. We define an r_i array, shown in the following line of code, which contains a set of 10 coordinates (*x*, *y*). Its shape will be (10, 2):

```
r_i = np.random.rand(10, 2)
```

If you have a hard time distinguishing arrays that differ in the axes order, for example between an a array of shape (10, 2) and (2, 10), it is useful to think that every time you say the word *of*, you should introduce a new dimension. An array with ten elements *of* size two will be (10, 2). Conversely, an array with two elements *of* size ten will be (2, 10).

A typical operation we may be interested in is the extraction of the *x* component from each coordinate. In other words, you want to extract the (0, 0), (1, 0), (2, 0), and so on items, resulting in an array with shape (10,). It is helpful to think that the first index is *moving* while the second one is *fixed* (at 0). With this in mind, we will slice every index on the first axis (the moving one) and take the first element (the fixed one) on the second axis, as shown in the following line of code:

```
x_i = r_i[:, 0]
```

On the other hand, the following expression will keep the first index fixed and the second index moving, returning the first (*x*, *y*) coordinate:

```
r_0 = r_i[0, :]
```

Slicing all the indexes over the last axis is optional; using `r_i[0]` has the same effect as `r_i[0, :]`.

NumPy allows you to index an array using another NumPy array made of either integer or Boolean values--a feature called *fancy indexing*.

If you index an array (say, `a`) with another array of integers (say, `idx`), NumPy will interpret the integers as indexes and will return an array containing their corresponding values. If we index an array containing 10 elements with `np.array([0, 2, 3])`, we obtain an array of shape `(3,)` containing the elements at positions 0, 2, and 3. The following code gives us an illustration of this concept:

```
a = np.array([9, 8, 7, 6, 5, 4, 3, 2, 1, 0])
idx = np.array([0, 2, 3])
a[idx]
# Result:
# array([9, 7, 6])
```

You can use fancy indexing on multiple dimensions by passing an array for each dimension. If we want to extract the `(0, 2)` and `(1, 3)` elements, we have to pack all the indexes acting on the first axis in one array, and the ones acting on the second axis in another. This can be seen in the following code:

```
a = np.array([[0, 1, 2], [3, 4, 5],
              [6, 7, 8], [9, 10, 11]])
idx1 = np.array([0, 1])
idx2 = np.array([2, 3])
a[idx1, idx2]
```

You can also use normal lists as index arrays, but not tuples. For example, the following two statements are equivalent:

```
a[np.array([0, 1])] # is equivalent to
a[[0, 1]]
```

However, if you use a tuple, NumPy will interpret the following statement as an index on multiple dimensions:

```
a[(0, 1)] # is equivalent to
a[0, 1]
```

The index arrays are not required to be one-dimensional; we can extract elements from the original array in any shape. For example, we can select elements from the original array to form a (2,2) array, as shown:

```
idx1 = [[0, 1], [3, 2]]
idx2 = [[0, 2], [1, 1]]
a[idx1, idx2]
# Output:
# array([[ 0,   5],
#        [10,   7]])
```

The array slicing and fancy-indexing features can be combined. This is useful, for instance, when we want to swap the *x* and *y* columns in a coordinate array. In the following code, the first index will be running over all the elements (a slice) and, for each of those, we extract the element in position 1 (the *y*) first and then the one in position 0 (the *x*):

```
r_i = np.random(10, 2)
r_i[:, [0, 1]] = r_i[:, [1, 0]]
```

When the index array is of the `bool` type, the rules are slightly different. The `bool` array will act like a *mask*; every element corresponding to `True` will be extracted and put in the output array. This procedure is shown in the following code:

```
a = np.array([0, 1, 2, 3, 4, 5])
mask = np.array([True, False, True, False, False, False])
a[mask]
# Output:
# array([0, 2])
```

The same rules apply when dealing with multiple dimensions. Furthermore, if the index array has the same shape as the original array, the elements corresponding to `True` will be selected and put in the resulting array.

Indexing in NumPy is a reasonably fast operation. Anyway, when speed is critical, you can use the slightly faster `numpy.take` and `numpy.compress` functions to squeeze out a little more performance. The first argument of `numpy.take` is the array we want to operate on, and the second is the list of indexes we want to extract. The last argument is `axis`; if not provided, the indexes will act on the flattened array; otherwise, they will act along the specified axis:

```
r_i = np.random(100, 2)
idx = np.arange(50) # integers 0 to 50

%timeit np.take(r_i, idx, axis=0)
1000000 loops, best of 3: 962 ns per loop
```

```
%timeit r_i[idx]
100000 loops, best of 3: 3.09 us per loop
```

The similar, but faster version for Boolean arrays is `numpy.compress`, which works in the same way. The use of `numpy.compress` is shown as follows:

```
In [51]: idx = np.ones(100, dtype='bool') # all True values
In [52]: %timeit np.compress(idx, r_i, axis=0)
1000000 loops, best of 3: 1.65 us per loop
In [53]: %timeit r_i[idx]
100000 loops, best of 3: 5.47 us per loop
```

Broadcasting

The true power of NumPy lies in its fast mathematical operations. The approach used by NumPy is to avoid stepping into the Python interpreter by performing element-wise calculation using optimized C code. **Broadcasting** is a clever set of rules that enables fast array calculations for arrays of similar (but not equal!) shape.

Whenever you do an arithmetic operation on two arrays (like a product), if the two operands have the same shape, the operation will be applied in an element-wise fashion. For example, upon multiplying two shape `(2,2)` arrays, the operation will be done between pairs of corresponding elements, producing another `(2, 2)` array, as shown in the following code:

```
A = np.array([[1, 2], [3, 4]])
B = np.array([[5, 6], [7, 8]])
A * B
# Output:
# array([[ 5, 12],
#        [21, 32]])
```

If the shapes of the operands don't match, NumPy will attempt to match them using broadcasting rules. If one of the operands is a *scalar* (for example, a number), it will be applied to every element of the array, as the following code illustrates:

```
A * 2
# Output:
# array([[2, 4],
#        [6, 8]])
```

If the operand is another array, NumPy will try to match the shapes starting from the last axis. For example, if we want to combine an array of shape (3, 2) with one of shape (2,), the second array will be repeated three times to generate a (3, 2) array. In other words, the array is *broadcasted* along a dimension to match the shape of the other operand, as shown in the following figure:

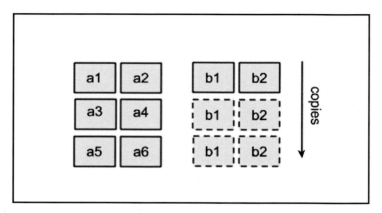

If the shapes mismatch, for example, when combining a (3, 2) array with a (2, 2) array, NumPy will throw an exception.

If one of the axis's size is 1, the array will be repeated over this axis until the shapes match. To illustrate that point, consider that we have an array of the following shape:

```
5, 10, 2
```

Now, consider that we want to broadcast it with an array of shape (5, 1, 2); the array will be repeated on the second axis 10 times, which is shown as follows:

```
5, 10, 2
5,  1, 2 → repeated
_ _ _ _
5, 10, 2
```

Earlier, we saw that it is possible to freely reshape arrays to add axes of size 1. Using the numpy.newaxis constant while indexing will introduce an extra dimension. For instance, if we have a (5, 2) array and we want to combine it with one of shape (5, 10, 2), we can add an extra axis in the middle, as shown in the following code, to obtain a compatible (5, 1, 2) array:

```
A = np.random.rand(5, 10, 2)
B = np.random.rand(5, 2)
A * B[:, np.newaxis, :]
```

This feature can be used, for example, to operate on all possible combinations of the two arrays. One of these applications is the *outer product*. Consider that we have the following two arrays:

```
a = [a1, a2, a3]
b = [b1, b2, b3]
```

The outer product is a matrix containing the product of all the possible combinations (i, j) of the two array elements, as shown in the following snippet:

```
a x b = a1*b1, a1*b2, a1*b3
        a2*b1, a2*b2, a2*b3
        a3*b1, a3*b2, a3*b3
```

To calculate this using NumPy, we will repeat the [a1, a2, a3] elements in one dimension, the [b1, b2, b3] elements in another dimension, and then take their element-wise product, as shown in the following figure:

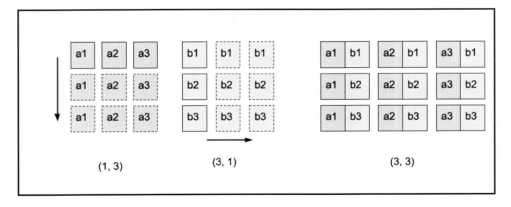

Using code, our strategy will be to transform the a array from shape (3,) to shape (3, 1), and the b array from shape (3,) to shape (1, 3). The two arrays are broadcasted in the two dimensions and get multiplied together using the following code:

```
AB = a[:, np.newaxis] * b[np.newaxis, :]
```

This operation is very fast and extremely effective as it avoids Python loops and is able to process a high number of elements at speeds comparable with pure C or FORTRAN code.

Mathematical operations

NumPy includes the most common mathematical operations available for broadcasting, by default, ranging from simple algebra to trigonometry, rounding, and logic. For instance, to take the square root of every element in the array, we can use `numpy.sqrt`, as shown in the following code:

```
np.sqrt(np.array([4, 9, 16]))
# Result:
# array([2., 3., 4.])
```

The comparison operators are useful when trying to filter certain elements based on a condition. Imagine that we have an array of random numbers from 0 to 1, and we want to extract all the numbers greater than 0.5. We can use the > operator on the array to obtain a `bool` array, as follows:

```
a = np.random.rand(5, 3)
a > 0.3
# Result:
# array([[ True, False,  True],
#        [ True,  True,  True],
#        [False,  True,  True],
#        [ True,  True, False],
#        [ True,  True, False]], dtype=bool)
```

The resulting `bool` array can then be reused as an index to retrieve the elements greater than 0.5:

```
a[a > 0.5]
print(a[a>0.5])
# Output:
# [ 0.9755  0.5977  0.8287  0.6214  0.5669  0.9553  0.5894
0.7196  0.9200  0.5781  0.8281 ]
```

NumPy also implements methods such as `ndarray.sum`, which takes the sum of all the elements on an axis. If we have an array of shape (5, 3), we can use the `ndarray.sum` method to sum the elements on the first axis, the second axis, or over all the elements of the array, as illustrated in the following snippet:

```
a = np.random.rand(5, 3)
a.sum(axis=0)
# Result:
# array([ 2.7454,  2.5517,  2.0303])

a.sum(axis=1)
# Result:
```

```
# array([ 1.7498,  1.2491,  1.8151,  1.9320,  0.5814])

a.sum() # With no argument operates on flattened array
# Result:
# 7.3275
```

Note that by summing the elements over an axis, we eliminate that axis. From the preceding example, the sum on the axis 0 produces an array of shape (3,), while the sum on the axis 1 produces an array of shape (5,).

Calculating the norm

We can review the basic concepts illustrated in this section by calculating the *norm* of a set of coordinates. For a two-dimensional vector, the norm is defined as follows:

```
norm = sqrt(x**2 + y**2)
```

Given an array of 10 coordinates (x, y), we want to find the norm of each coordinate. We can calculate the norm by taking these steps:

1. Square the coordinates, obtaining an array that contains $(x**2, y**2)$ elements.
2. Sum those with numpy.sum over the last axis.
3. Take the square root, element-wise, with numpy.sqrt.

The final expression can be compressed in a single line:

```
r_i = np.random.rand(10, 2)
norm = np.sqrt((r_i ** 2).sum(axis=1))
print(norm)
# Output:
# [ 0.7314  0.9050  0.5063  0.2553  0.0778  0.9143  1.3245
0.9486  1.010   1.0212]
```

Rewriting the particle simulator in NumPy

In this section, we will optimize our particle simulator by rewriting some parts of it in NumPy. We found, from the profiling we did in Chapter 1, *Benchmarking and Profiling*, that the slowest part of our program is the following loop contained in the ParticleSimulator.evolve method:

```
for i in range(nsteps):
```

```
for p in self.particles:

    norm = (p.x**2 + p.y**2)**0.5
    v_x = (-p.y)/norm
    v_y = p.x/norm

    d_x = timestep * p.ang_vel * v_x
    d_y = timestep * p.ang_vel * v_y

    p.x += d_x
    p.y += d_y
```

You may have noticed that the body of the loop acts solely on the current particle. If we had an array containing the particle positions and angular speed, we could rewrite the loop using a broadcasted operation. In contrast, the loop's steps depend on the previous step and cannot be parallelized in this way.

It is natural then, to store all the array coordinates in an array of shape (nparticles, 2) and the angular speed in an array of shape (nparticles,), where nparticles is the number of particles. We'll call those arrays r_i and ang_vel_i:

```
r_i = np.array([[p.x, p.y] for p in self.particles])
ang_vel_i = np.array([p.ang_vel for p in self.particles])
```

The velocity direction, perpendicular to the vector (*x*, *y*), was defined as follows:

```
v_x = -y / norm
v_y = x / norm
```

The norm can be calculated using the strategy illustrated in the *Calculating the norm* section under the *Getting started with NumPy* heading:

```
norm_i = ((r_i ** 2).sum(axis=1))**0.5
```

For the (*-y*, *x*) components, we first need to swap the x and y columns in r_i and then multiply the first column by -1, as shown in the following code:

```
v_i = r_i[:, [1, 0]] / norm_i
v_i[:, 0] *= -1
```

To calculate the displacement, we need to compute the product of v_i, ang_vel_i, and timestep. Since ang_vel_i is of shape (nparticles,), it needs a new axis in order to operate with v_i of shape (nparticles, 2). We will do that using numpy.newaxis, as follows:

```
d_i = timestep * ang_vel_i[:, np.newaxis] * v_i
r_i += d_i
```

Outside the loop, we have to update the particle instances with the new coordinates, *x* and *y*, as follows:

```
for i, p in enumerate(self.particles):
  p.x, p.y = r_i[i]
```

To summarize, we will implement a method called `ParticleSimulator.evolve_numpy` and benchmark it against the pure Python version, renamed as `ParticleSimulator.evolve_python`:

```
def evolve_numpy(self, dt):
  timestep = 0.00001
  nsteps = int(dt/timestep)

  r_i = np.array([[p.x, p.y] for p in self.particles])
  ang_vel_i = np.array([p.ang_vel for p in self.particles])

  for i in range(nsteps):

    norm_i = np.sqrt((r_i ** 2).sum(axis=1))
    v_i = r_i[:, [1, 0]]
    v_i[:, 0] *= -1
    v_i /= norm_i[:, np.newaxis]
    d_i = timestep * ang_vel_i[:, np.newaxis] * v_i
    r_i += d_i

    for i, p in enumerate(self.particles):
      p.x, p.y = r_i[i]
```

We also update the benchmark to conveniently change the number of particles and the simulation method, as follows:

```
def benchmark(npart=100, method='python'):
  particles = [Particle(uniform(-1.0, 1.0),
                        uniform(-1.0, 1.0),
                        uniform(-1.0, 1.0))
               for i in range(npart)]

  simulator = ParticleSimulator(particles)

  if method=='python':
    simulator.evolve_python(0.1)

  elif method == 'numpy':
    simulator.evolve_numpy(0.1)
```

Let's run the benchmark in an IPython session:

```
from simul import benchmark
%timeit benchmark(100, 'python')
1 loops, best of 3: 614 ms per loop
%timeit benchmark(100, 'numpy')
1 loops, best of 3: 415 ms per loop
```

We have some improvement, but it doesn't look like a huge speed boost. The power of NumPy is revealed when handling big arrays. If we increase the number of particles, we will note a more significant performance boost:

```
%timeit benchmark(1000, 'python')
1 loops, best of 3: 6.13 s per loop
%timeit benchmark(1000, 'numpy')
1 loops, best of 3: 852 ms per loop
```

The plot in the following figure was produced by running the benchmark with different particle numbers:

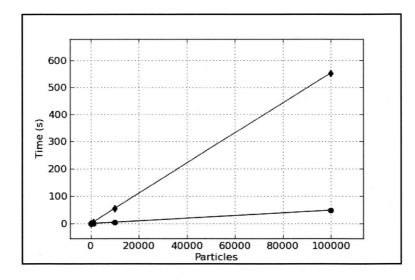

The plot shows that both the implementations scale linearly with particle size, but the runtime in the pure Python version grows much faster than the NumPy version; at greater sizes, we have a greater NumPy advantage. In general, when using NumPy, you should try to pack things into large arrays and group the calculations using the broadcasting feature.

Reaching optimal performance with numexpr

When handling complex expressions, NumPy stores intermediate results in memory. David M. Cooke wrote a package called `numexpr`, which optimizes and compiles array expressions on the fly. It works by optimizing the usage of the CPU cache and by taking advantage of multiple processors.

Its usage is generally straightforward and is based on a single function-- `numexpr.evaluate`. The function takes a string containing an array expression as its first argument. The syntax is basically identical to that of NumPy. For example, we can calculate a simple `a + b * c` expression in the following way:

```
a = np.random.rand(10000)
b = np.random.rand(10000)
c = np.random.rand(10000)
d = ne.evaluate('a + b * c')
```

The `numexpr` package increases the performances in almost all cases, but to get a substantial advantage, you should use it with large arrays. An application that involves a large array is the calculation of a *distance matrix*. In a particle system, a distance matrix contains all the possible distances between the particles. To calculate it, we should first calculate all the vectors connecting any two particles `(i,j)`, as follows:

```
x_ij = x_j - x_i
y_ij = y_j - y_i.
```

Then, we calculate the length of this vector by taking its norm, as in the following code:

```
d_ij = sqrt(x_ij**2 + y_ij**2)
```

We can write this in NumPy by employing the usual broadcasting rules (the operation is similar to the outer product):

```
r = np.random.rand(10000, 2)
r_i = r[:, np.newaxis]
r_j = r[np.newaxis, :]
d_ij = r_j - r_i
```

Finally, we calculate the norm over the last axis using the following line of code:

```
d_ij = np.sqrt((d_ij ** 2).sum(axis=2))
```

Rewriting the same expression using the `numexpr` syntax is extremely easy. The `numexpr` package doesn't support slicing in its array expression; therefore, we first need to prepare the operands for broadcasting by adding an extra dimension, as follows:

```
r = np.random(10000, 2)
r_i = r[:, np.newaxis]
r_j = r[np.newaxis, :]
```

At that point, we should try to pack as many operations as possible in a single expression to allow a significant optimization.

Most of the NumPy mathematical functions are also available in `numexpr`. However, there is a limitation--the reduction operations (the ones that reduce an axis, such as sum) have to happen last. Therefore, we have to first calculate the sum, then step out of `numexpr`, and finally calculate the square root in another expression:

```
d_ij = ne.evaluate('sum((r_j - r_i)**2, 2)')
d_ij = ne.evaluate('sqrt(d_ij)')
```

The `numexpr` compiler will avoid redundant memory allocation by not storing intermediate results. When possible, it will also distribute the operations over multiple processors. In the `distance_matrix.py` file, you will find two functions that implement the two versions: `distance_matrix_numpy` and `distance_matrix_numexpr`:

```
from distance_matrix import (distance_matrix_numpy,
                             distance_matrix_numexpr)
%timeit distance_matrix_numpy(10000)
1 loops, best of 3: 3.56 s per loop
%timeit distance_matrix_numexpr(10000)
1 loops, best of 3: 858 ms per loop
```

By simply converting the expressions to use `numexpr`, we were able to obtain a 4.5x increase in performance over standard NumPy. The `numexpr` package can be used every time you need to optimize a NumPy expression that involves large arrays and complex operations, and you can do so with minimal changes in the code.

Pandas

Pandas is a library originally developed by Wes McKinney, which was designed to analyze datasets in a seamless and performant way. In recent years, this powerful library has seen an incredible growth and huge adoption by the Python community. In this section, we will introduce the main concepts and tools provided in this library, and we will use it to increase performance of various usecases that can't otherwise be addressed with NumPy's vectorized operations and broadcasting.

Pandas fundamentals

While NumPy deals mostly with arrays, Pandas main data structures are `pandas.Series`, `pandas.DataFrame`, and `pandas.Panel`. In the rest of this chapter, we will abbreviate `pandas` with `pd`.

The main difference between a `pd.Series` object and an `np.array` is that a `pd.Series` object associates a specific *key* to each element of an array. Let's see how this works in practice with an example.

Let's assume that we are trying to test a new blood pressure drug, and we want to store, for each patient, whether the patient's blood pressure improved after administering the drug. We can encode this information by associating to each subject ID (represented by an integer), `True` if the drug was effective, and `False` otherwise.

We can create a `pd.Series` object by associating an array of keys, the patients, to the array of values that represent the drug effectiveness. The array of keys can be passed to the `Series` constructor using the `index` argument, as shown in the following snippet:

```
import pandas as pd
patients = [0, 1, 2, 3]
effective = [True, True, False, False]

effective_series = pd.Series(effective, index=patients)
```

Associating a set of integers from 0 to *N* to a set of values can technically be implemented with np.array, since, in this case, the key will simply be the position of the element in the array. In Pandas, keys are not limited to integers but can also be strings, floating point numbers, and also generic (hashable) Python objects. For example, we can easily turn our IDs into strings with little effort, as shown in the following code:

```
patients = ["a", "b", "c", "d"]
effective = [True, True, False, False]

effective_series = pd.Series(effective, index=patients)
```

An interesting observation is that, while NumPy arrays can be thought of as a contiguous collection of values similar to Python lists, the Pandas pd.Series object can be thought of as a structure that maps keys to values, similar to Python dictionaries.

What if you want to store the initial and final blood pressure for each patient? In Pandas, one can use a pd.DataFrame object to associate multiple data to each key.

pd.DataFrame can be initialized, similarly to a pd.Series object, by passing a dictionary of columns and an index. In the following example, we will see how to create a pd.DataFrame containing four columns that represent the initial and final measurements of systolic and dyastolic blood pressure for our patients:

```
patients = ["a", "b", "c", "d"]

columns = {
  "sys_initial": [120, 126, 130, 115],
  "dia_initial": [75, 85, 90, 87],
  "sys_final": [115, 123, 130, 118],
  "dia_final": [70, 82, 92, 87]
}

df = pd.DataFrame(columns, index=patients)
```

Equivalently, you can think of a pd.DataFrame as a collection of pd.Series. In fact, it is possible to directly initialize a pd.DataFrame, using a dictionary of pd.Series instances:

```
columns = {
  "sys_initial": pd.Series([120, 126, 130, 115], index=patients),
  "dia_initial": pd.Series([75, 85, 90, 87], index=patients),
  "sys_final": pd.Series([115, 123, 130, 118], index=patients),
  "dia_final": pd.Series([70, 82, 92, 87], index=patients)
}
df = pd.DataFrame(columns)
```

To inspect the content of a `pd.DataFrame` or `pd.Series` object, you can use the `pd.Series.head` and `pd.DataFrame.head` methods, which print the first few rows of the dataset:

```
effective_series.head()
# Output:
# a  True
# b  True
# c  False
# d  False
# dtype: bool

df.head()
# Output:
#    dia_final   dia_initial   sys_final   sys_initial
# a         70            75         115           120
# b         82            85         123           126
# c         92            90         130           130
# d         87            87         118           115
```

Just like a `pd.DataFrame` can be used to store a collection of `pd.Series`, you can use a `pd.Panel` to store a collection of `pd.DataFrames`. We will not cover the usage of `pd.Panel` as it is not used as often as `pd.Series` and `pd.DataFrame`. To learn more about `pd.Panel`, ensure that you refer to the excellent documentation at `http://pandas.pydata.org/pandas-docs/stable/dsintro.html#panel`.

Indexing Series and DataFrame objects

Retrieving data from a `pd.Series`, given its *key*, can be done intuitively by indexing the `pd.Series.loc` attribute:

```
effective_series.loc["a"]
# Result:
# True
```

It is also possible to access the elements, given its *position* in the underlying array, using the `pd.Series.iloc` attribute:

```
effective_series.iloc[0]
# Result:
# True
```

You can also use the `pd.Series.ix` attribute for mixed access. If the key is not an integer, it will try to match by key, otherwise it will extract the element at the position indicated by the integer. A similar behavior will take place when you access the `pd.Series` directly. The following example demonstrates these concepts:

```
effective_series.ix["a"] # By key
effective_series.ix[0]   # By position

# Equivalent
effective_series["a"] # By key
effective_series[0]   # By position
```

Note that if the index is made of integers, this method will fall back to the key-only method (like `loc`). To index by position in this scenario, the `iloc` method is your only option.

Indexing `pd.DataFrame` works in a similar way. For example, you can use `pd.DataFrame.loc` to extract a row by key, and you can use `pd.DataFrame.iloc` to extract a row by position:

```
df.loc["a"]
df.iloc[0]
# Result:
# dia_final 70
# dia_initial 75
# sys_final 115
# sys_initial 120
# Name: a, dtype: int64
```

An important aspect is that the return type in this case is a `pd.Series`, where each column is a new key. In order to retrieve a specific row and column, you can use the following code. The `loc` attribute will index both row and column by key, while the `iloc` version will index row and column by an integer:

```
df.loc["a", "sys_initial"] # is equivalent to
df.loc["a"].loc["sys_initial"]

df.iloc[0, 1] # is equivalent to
df.iloc[0].iloc[1]
```

Indexing a `pd.DataFrame` using the `ix` attribute is convenient to mix and match index and location-based indexing. For example, retrieving the `"sys_initial"` column for the row at position 0 can be accomplished as follows:

```
df.ix[0, "sys_initial"]
```

Retrieving a column from a `pd.DataFrame` by name can be achieved by regular indexing or attribute access. To retrieve a column by position, you can either use `iloc` or use the `pd.DataFrame.column` attribute to retrieve the name of the column:

```
# Retrieve column by name
df["sys_initial"] # Equivalent to
df.sys_initial

# Retrieve column by position
df[df.columns[2]] # Equivalent to
df.iloc[:, 2]
```

The mentioned methods also support more advanced indexing similar to those of NumPy, such as `bool`, lists, and `int` arrays.

Now it's time for some performance considerations. There are some differences between an index in Pandas and a dictionary. For example, while the keys of a dictionary cannot contain duplicates, Pandas indexes can contain repeated elements. This flexibility, however, comes at a cost--if we try to access an element in a non-unique index, we may incur substantial performance loss--the access will be $O(N)$, like a linear search, rather than $O(1)$, like a dictionary.

A way to mitigate this effect is to sort the index; this will allow Pandas to use a binary search algorithm with a computational complexity of $O(log(N))$, which is much better. This can be accomplished using the `pd.Series.sort_index` function, as in the following code (the same applies for `pd.DataFrame`):

```
# Create a series with duplicate index
index = list(range(1000)) + list(range(1000))

# Accessing a normal series is a O(N) operation
series = pd.Series(range(2000), index=index)

# Sorting the will improve look-up scaling to O(log(N))
series.sort_index(inplace=True)
```

The timings for the different versions are summarized in the following table:

Index type	N=10000	N=20000	N=30000	Time
Unique	12.30	12.58	13.30	$O(1)$
Non unique	494.95	814.10	1129.95	$O(N)$
Non unique (sorted)	145.93	145.81	145.66	$O(log(N))$

Database-style operations with Pandas

You may have noted that the "tabular" data is similar to what is usually stored in a database. A database is usually indexed using a primary key, and the various columns can have different data types, just like in a `pd.DataFrame`.

The efficiency of the index operations in Pandas makes it suitable for database style manipulations, such as counting, joining, grouping, and aggregations.

Mapping

Pandas supports element-wise operations just like NumPy (after all, `pd.Series` stores their data using `np.array`). For example, it is possible to apply transformation very easily on both `pd.Series` and `pd.DataFrame`:

```
np.log(df.sys_initial)   # Logarithm of a series
df.sys_initial ** 2      # Square a series
np.log(df)               # Logarithm of a dataframe
df ** 2                  # Square of a dataframe
```

You can also perform element-wise operations between two `pd.Series` in a way similar to NumPy. An important difference is that the operands will be matched by key, rather than by position; if there is a mismatch in the index, the resulting value will be set to NaN. Both the scenarios are exemplified in the following example:

```
# Matching index
a = pd.Series([1, 2, 3], index=["a", "b", "c"])
b = pd.Series([4, 5, 6], index=["a", "b", "c"])
a + b
# Result:
# a 5
# b 7
# c 9
# dtype: int64

# Mismatching index
b = pd.Series([4, 5, 6], index=["a", "b", "d"])
# Result:
# a 5.0
# b 7.0
# c NaN
# d NaN
# dtype: float64
```

For added flexibility, Pandas exposes the `map`, `apply`, and `applymap` methods that can be used to apply specific transformations.

The `pd.Series.map` method can be used to execute a function to each value and return a `pd.Series` containing each result. In the following example, we show how to apply the `superstar` function to each element of a `pd.Series`:

```
a = pd.Series([1, 2, 3], index=["a", "b", "c"])
def superstar(x):
    return '*' + str(x) + '*'
a.map(superstar)

# Result:
# a *1*
# b *2*
# c *3*
# dtype: object
```

The `pd.DataFrame.applymap` function is the equivalent of `pd.Series.map`, but for DataFrames:

```
df.applymap(superstar)
# Result:
#    dia_final  dia_initial  sys_final  sys_initial
# a      *70*         *75*       *115*        *120*
# b      *82*         *85*       *123*        *126*
# c      *92*         *90*       *130*        *130*
# d      *87*         *87*       *118*        *115*
```

Finally, the `pd.DataFrame.apply` function can apply the passed function to each column or each row, rather than element-wise. The selection can be performed with the argument axis, where a value of 0 (the default) corresponds to columns, and 1 corresponds to rows. Also, note that the return value of `apply` is a `pd.Series`:

```
df.apply(superstar, axis=0)
# Result:
# dia_final *a 70nb 82nc 92nd 87nName: dia...
# dia_initial *a 75nb 85nc 90nd 87nName: dia...
# sys_final *a 115nb 123nc 130nd 118nName:...
# sys_initial *a 120nb 126nc 130nd 115nName:...
# dtype: object

df.apply(superstar, axis=1)
# Result:
# a *dia_final 70ndia_initial 75nsys_f...
# b *dia_final 82ndia_initial 85nsys_f...
# c *dia_final 92ndia_initial 90nsys_f...
```

```
# d *dia_final 87ndia_initial 87nsys_f...
# dtype: object
```

Pandas also supports efficient `numexpr`-style expressions with the convenient `eval` method. For example, if we want to calculate the difference in the final and initial blood pressure, we can write the expression as a string, as shown in the following code:

```
df.eval("sys_final - sys_initial")
# Result:
# a -5
# b -3
# c 0
# d 3
# dtype: int64
```

It is also possible to create new columns using the assignment operator in the `pd.DataFrame.eval` expression. Note that, if the `inplace=True` argument is used, the operation will be applied directly on the original `pd.DataFrame`; otherwise, the function will return a new dataframe. In the next example, we compute the difference between `sys_final` and `sys_initial`, and we store it in the `sys_delta` column:

```
df.eval("sys_delta = sys_final - sys_initial", inplace=False)
# Result:
#      dia_final   dia_initial   sys_final   sys_initial   sys_delta
# a           70            75         115           120          -5
# b           82            85         123           126          -3
# c           92            90         130           130           0
# d           87            87         118           115           3
```

Grouping, aggregations, and transforms

One of the most appreciated features of Pandas is the simple and concise expression of data analysis pipelines that requires grouping, transforming, and aggregating the data. To demonstrate this concept, let's extend our dataset by adding two new patients to whom we didn't administer the treatment (this is usually called a *control group*). We also include a column, `drug_admst`, which records whether the patient was administered the treatment:

```
patients = ["a", "b", "c", "d", "e", "f"]

columns = {
    "sys_initial": [120, 126, 130, 115, 150, 117],
    "dia_initial": [75, 85, 90, 87, 90, 74],
    "sys_final": [115, 123, 130, 118, 130, 121],
    "dia_final": [70, 82, 92, 87, 85, 74],
```

```
    "drug_admst": [True, True, True, True, False, False]
}

df = pd.DataFrame(columns, index=patients)
```

At this point, we may be interested to know how the blood pressure changed between the two groups. You can group the patients according to drug_amst using the pd.DataFrame.groupby function. The return value will be the DataFrameGroupBy object, which can be iterated to obtain a new pd.DataFrame for each value of the drug_admst column:

```
df.groupby('drug_admst')
for value, group in df.groupby('drug_admst'):
    print("Value: {}".format(value))
    print("Group DataFrame:")
    print(group)
# Output:
# Value: False
# Group DataFrame:
#    dia_final  dia_initial  drug_admst  sys_final  sys_initial
# e         85           90       False        130          150
# f         74           74       False        121          117
# Value: True
# Group DataFrame:
#    dia_final  dia_initial  drug_admst  sys_final  sys_initial
# a         70           75        True        115          120
# b         82           85        True        123          126
# c         92           90        True        130          130
# d         87           87        True        118          115
```

Iterating on the DataFrameGroupBy object is almost never necessary, because, thanks to method chaining, it is possible to calculate group-related properties directly. For example, we may want to calculate mean, max, or standard deviation for each group. All those operations that summarize the data in some way are called aggregations and can be performed using the agg method. The result of agg is another pd.DataFrame that relates the grouping variables and the result of the aggregation, as illustrated in the following code:

```
df.groupby('drug_admst').agg(np.mean)
#             dia_final  dia_initial  sys_final  sys_initial
# drug_admst
# False           79.50        82.00      125.5       133.50
# True            82.75        84.25      121.5       122.75
```

It is also possible to perform processing on the DataFrame groups that do not represent a summarization. One common example of such an operation is filling in missing values. Those intermediate steps are called *transforms*.

We can illustrate this concept with an example. Let's assume that we have a few missing values in our dataset, and we want to replace those values with the average of the other values in the same group. This can be accomplished using a transform, as follows:

```
df.loc['a','sys_initial'] = None
df.groupby('drug_admst').transform(lambda df: df.fillna(df.mean()))
#      dia_final    dia_initial    sys_final    sys_initial
# a           70             75          115     123.666667
# b           82             85          123     126.000000
# c           92             90          130     130.000000
# d           87             87          118     115.000000
# e           85             90          130     150.000000
# f           74             74          121     117.000000
```

Joining

Joins are useful to aggregate data that is scattered among different tables. Let's say that we want to include the location of the hospital in which patient measurements were taken in our dataset. We can reference the location for each patient using the H1, H2, and H3 labels, and we can store the address and identifier of the hospital in a hospital table:

```
hospitals = pd.DataFrame(
  { "name" : ["City 1", "City 2", "City 3"],
    "address" : ["Address 1", "Address 2", "Address 3"],
    "city": ["City 1", "City 2", "City 3"] },
  index=["H1", "H2", "H3"])

hospital_id = ["H1", "H2", "H2", "H3", "H3", "H3"]
df['hospital_id'] = hospital_id
```

Now, we want to find the city where the measure was taken for each patient. We need to *map* the keys from the hospital_id column to the city stored in the hospitals table.

This can surely be implemented in Python using dictionaries:

```
hospital_dict = {
  "H1": ("City 1", "Name 1", "Address 1"),
  "H2": ("City 2", "Name 2", "Address 2"),
  "H3": ("City 3", "Name 3", "Address 3")
}
cities = [hospital_dict[key][0]
          for key in hospital_id]
```

This algorithm runs efficiently with an $O(N)$ time complexity, where N is the size of `hospital_id`. Pandas allows you to encode the same operation using simple indexing; the advantage is that the join will be performed in heavily optimized Cython and with efficient hashing algorithms. The preceding simple Python expression can be easily converted to Pandas in this way:

```
cities = hospitals.loc[hospital_id, "city"]
```

More advanced joins can also be performed with the `pd.DataFrame.join` method, which will produce a new `pd.DataFrame` that will attach the hospital information for each patient:

```
result = df.join(hospitals, on='hospital_id')
result.columns
# Result:
# Index(['dia_final', 'dia_initial', 'drug_admst',
# 'sys_final', 'sys_initial',
# 'hospital_id', 'address', 'city', 'name'],
# dtype='object')
```

Summary

In this chapter, we learned how to manipulate NumPy arrays and how to write fast mathematical expressions using array broadcasting. This knowledge will help you write more concise, expressive code and, at the same time, to obtain substantial performance gains. We also introduced the `numexpr` library to further speed up NumPy calculations with minimal effort.

Pandas implements efficient data structures that are useful when analyzing large datasets. In particular, Pandas shines when the data is indexed by non-integer keys and provides very fast hashing algorithms.

NumPy and Pandas work well when handling large, homogenous inputs, but they are not suitable when the expressions grow complex and the operations cannot be expressed using the tools provided by these libraries. In such cases, we can leverage Python capabilities as a glue language by interfacing it with C using the Cython package.

4

C Performance with Cython

Cython is a language that extends Python by supporting the declaration of types for functions, variables, and classes. These typed declarations enable Cython to compile Python scripts to efficient C code. Cython can also act as a bridge between Python and C as it provides easy-to-use constructs to write interfaces to external C and C++ routines.

In this chapter, we will learn the following things:

- Cython syntax basics
- How to compile Cython programs
- How to use **static typing** to generate fast code
- How to efficiently manipulate arrays using typed **memoryviews**
- Optimizing a sample particle simulator
- Tips on using Cython in the Jupyter notebook
- The profiling tools available for Cython

While a minimum knowledge of C is helpful, this chapter focuses only on Cython in the context of Python optimization. Therefore, it doesn't require any C background.

Compiling Cython extensions

The Cython syntax is, by design, a superset of Python. Cython can compile, with a few exceptions, most Python modules without requiring any change. Cython source files have the `.pyx` extension and can be compiled to produce a C file using the `cython` command.

Our first Cython script will contain a simple function that prints `Hello, World!` as the output.

Create a new `hello.pyx` file containing the following code:

```
def hello():
    print('Hello, World!')
```

The `cython` command will read `hello.pyx` and generate the `hello.c` file:

$ cython hello.pyx

To compile `hello.c` to a Python extension module, we will use the GCC compiler. We need to add some Python-specific compilation options that depend on the operating system. It's important to specify the directory that contains the header files; in the following example, the directory is `/usr/include/python3.5/`:

$ gcc -shared -pthread -fPIC -fwrapv -O2 -Wall -fno-strict-aliasing -lm -I/usr/include/python3.5/ -o hello.so hello.c

> To find your Python include directory, you can use the `distutils` utility: `sysconfig.get_python_inc`. To execute it, you can simply issue the following `python -c "from distutils import sysconfig; print(sysconfig.get_python_inc())"` command.

This will produce a file called `hello.so`, a C extension module that is directly importable into a Python session:

```
>>> import hello
>>> hello.hello()
Hello, World!
```

Cython accepts both Python 2 and Python 3 as input and output languages. In other words, you can compile a Python 3 script `hello.pyx` file using the `-3` option:

$ cython -3 hello.pyx

The generated `hello.c` can be compiled without any changes to Python 2 and Python 3 by including the corresponding headers with the `-I` option, as follows:

$ gcc -I/usr/include/python3.5 # ... other options
$ gcc -I/usr/include/python2.7 # ... other options

A Cython program can be compiled in a more straightforward way using `distutils`, the standard Python packaging tool. By writing a `setup.py` script, we can compile the `.pyx` file directly to an extension module. To compile our `hello.pyx` example, we can write a minimal `setup.py` containing the following code:

```
from distutils.core import setup
```

```
from Cython.Build import cythonize

setup(
  name='Hello',
  ext_modules = cythonize('hello.pyx')
)
```

In the first two lines of the preceding code, we import the `setup` function and the `cythonize` helper. The `setup` function contains a few key-value pairs that specify the name of the application and the extensions that need to be built.

The `cythonize` helper takes either a string or a list of strings containing the Cython modules we want to compile. You can also use glob patterns using the following code:

```
cythonize(['hello.pyx', 'world.pyx', '*.pyx'])
```

To compile our extension module using `distutils`, you can execute the `setup.py` script using the following code:

```
$ python setup.py build_ext --inplace
```

The `build_ext` option tells the script to build the extension modules indicated in `ext_modules`, while the `--inplace` option tells the script to place the `hello.so` output file in the same location as the source file (instead of a build directory).

Cython modules can also be automatically compiled using `pyximport`. All that's needed is a call to `pyximport.install()` at the beginning of your script (or you need to issue the command in your interpreter). After doing that, you can import `.pyx` files directly and `pyximport` will transparently compile the corresponding Cython modules:

```
>>> import pyximport
>>> pyximport.install()
>>> import hello # This will compile hello.pyx
```

Unfortunately, `pyximport` will not work for all kinds of configurations (for example, when they involve a combination of C and Cython files), but it comes handy for testing simple scripts.

Since version 0.13, IPython includes the `cythonmagic` extension to interactively write and test a series of Cython statements. You can load the extensions in an IPython shell using `load_ext`:

```
%load_ext cythonmagic
```

Once the extension is loaded, you can use the `%%cython` *cell magic* to write a multiline Cython snippet. In the following example, we define a `hello_snippet` function that will be compiled and added to the IPython session namespace:

```
%%cython
def hello_snippet():
    print("Hello, Cython!")

hello_snippet()
Hello,  Cython!
```

Adding static types

In Python, a variable can be associated to objects of different types during the execution of the program. While this feature is desirable as it makes the language flexible and dynamic, it also adds a significant overhead to the interpreter as it needs to look up type and methods of the variables at runtime, making it difficult to perform various optimizations. Cython extends the Python language with explicit type declarations so that it can generate efficient C extensions through compilation.

The main way to declare data types in Cython is through `cdef` statements. The `cdef` keyword can be used in multiple contexts, such as variables, functions, and extension types (statically-typed classes).

Variables

In Cython, you can declare the type of a variable by prepending the variable with `cdef` and its respective type. For example, we can declare the `i` variable as a 16 bit integer in the following way:

```
cdef int i
```

The `cdef` statement supports multiple variable names on the same line along with optional initialization, as seen in the following line:

```
cdef double a, b = 2.0, c = 3.0
```

Typed variables are treated differently in comparison to regular variables. In Python, variables are often described as *labels* that refer to objects in memory. For example, we could assign the value `'hello'` to the `a` variable at any point in the program without restriction:

```
a = 'hello'
```

The a variable holds a reference to the `'hello'` string. We can also freely assign another value (for example, the integer 1) to the same variable later in the code:

```
a = 1
```

Python will assign the integer 1 to the a variable without any problem.

Typed variables behave quite differently and are usually described as *data containers:* we can only store values that fit into the container that is determined by its data type. For example, if we declare the a variable as `int`, and then we try to assign it to a `double`, Cython will trigger an error, as shown in the following code:

```
%%cython
cdef int i
i = 3.0

# Output has been cut
...cf4b.pyx:2:4 Cannot assign type 'double' to 'int'
```

Static typing makes it easy for the compiler to perform useful optimizations. For example, if we declare a loop index as `int`, Cython will rewrite the loop in pure C without needing to step into the Python interpreter. The typing declaration guarantees that the type of the index will always be `int` and cannot be overwritten at runtime so that the compiler is free to perform the optimizations without compromising the program correctness.

We can assess the speed gain in this case with a small test case. In the following example, we implement a simple loop that increments a variable 100 times. With Cython, the `example` function can be coded as follows:

```
%%cython
def example():
    cdef int i, j=0
    for i in range(100):
        j += 1
    return j

example()
# Result:
# 100
```

We can compare the speed of an analogous, untyped, pure Python loop:

```
def example_python():
    j=0
    for i in range(100):
        j += 1
```

```
        return j

%timeit example()
10000000 loops, best of 3: 25 ns per loop
%timeit example_python()
100000 loops, best of 3: 2.74 us per loop
```

The speedup obtained by implementing this simple type declaration is a whopping 100x! This works because the Cython loop has first been converted to pure C and then to efficient machine code, while the Python loop still relies on the slow interpreter.

In Cython, it is possible to declare a variable to be of any standard C type, and it is also possible to define custom types using classic C constructs, such as struct, enum, and typedef.

An interesting example is that if we declare a variable to be of the object type, the variable will accept any kind of Python object:

```
cdef object a_py
# both 'hello' and 1 are Python objects
a_py = 'hello'
a_py = 1
```

Note that declaring a variable as object has no performance benefits as accessing and operating on the object will still require the interpreter to look up the underlying type of the variable and its attributes and methods.

Sometimes, certain data types (such as float and int numbers) are compatible in the sense that they can be converted into each other. In Cython, it is possible to convert (*cast*) between types by surrounding the destination type between pointy brackets, as shown in the following snippet:

```
cdef int a = 0
cdef double b
b = <double> a
```

Functions

You can add type information to the arguments of a Python function by specifying the type in front of each of the argument names. Functions specified in this way will work and perform like regular Python functions, but their arguments will be type-checked. We can write a max_python function, which returns the greater value between two integers:

```
def max_python(int a, int b):
    return a if a > b else b
```

A function specified in this way will perform type-checking and treat the arguments as typed variables, just like in `cdef` definitions. However, the function will still be a Python function, and calling it multiple times will still need to switch back to the interpreter. To allow Cython for function call optimizations, we should declare the type of the return type using a `cdef` statement:

```
cdef int max_cython(int a, int b):
    return a if a > b else b
```

Functions declared in this way are translated to native C functions and have much less overhead compared to Python functions. A substantial drawback is that they can't be used from Python, but only from Cython, and their scope is restricted to the same Cython file unless they're exposed in a definition file (refer to the *Sharing declarations* section).

Fortunately, Cython allows you to define functions that are both callable from Python and translatable to performant C functions. If you declare a function with a `cpdef` statement, Cython will generate two versions of the function: a Python version available to the interpreter, and a fast C function usable from Cython. The `cpdef` syntax is equivalent to `cdef`, shown as follows:

```
cpdef int max_hybrid(int a, int b):
    return a if a > b else b
```

Sometimes, the call overhead can be a performance issue even with C functions, especially when the same function is called many times in a critical loop. When the function body is small, it is convenient to add the `inline` keyword in front of the function definition; the function call will be replaced by the function body itself. Our `max` function is a good candidate for *inlining*:

```
cdef inline int max_inline(int a, int b):
    return a if a > b else b
```

Classes

We can define an extension type using the `cdef class` statement and declaring its attributes in the class body. For example, we can create an extension type--Point--as shown in the following code, which stores two coordinates (*x*, *y*) of the `double` type:

```
cdef class Point
    cdef double x
    cdef double y
```

```
def __init__(self, double x, double y):
    self.x = x
    self.y = y
```

Accessing the declared attributes in the class methods allows Cython to bypass expensive Python attribute look-ups by direct access to the given fields in the underlying C `struct`. For this reason, attribute access in typed classes is an extremely fast operation.

To use the `cdef class` in your code, you need to explicitly declare the type of the variables you intend to use at compile time. You can use the extension type name (such as `Point`) in any context where you will use a standard type (such as `double`, `float`, and `int`). For example, if we want a Cython function that calculates the distance from the origin (in the example, the function is called `norm`) of a `Point`, we have to declare the input variable as `Point`, as shown in the following code:

```
cdef double norm(Point p):
    return (p.x**2 + p.y**2)**0.5
```

Just like typed functions, typed classes have some limitations. If you try to access an extension type attribute from Python, you will get an `AttributeError`, as follows:

```
>>> a = Point(0.0, 0.0)
>>> a.x
AttributeError: 'Point' object has no attribute 'x'
```

In order to access attributes from Python code, you have to use the `public` (for read/write access) or `readonly` specifiers in the attribute declaration, as shown in the following code:

```
cdef class Point:
    cdef public double x
```

Additionally, methods can be declared with the `cpdef` statement, just like regular functions.

Extension types do not support the addition of extra attributes at runtime. In order to do that, a solution is defining a Python class that is a subclass of the typed class and extends its attributes and methods in pure Python.

Sharing declarations

When writing your Cython modules, you may want to reorganize your most used functions and classes declaration in a separate file so that they can be reused in different modules. Cython allows you to put these components in a *definition file* and access them with `cimport` statements.

Let's say that we have a module with the `max` and `min` functions, and we want to reuse those functions in multiple Cython programs. If we simply write a bunch of functions in a `.pyx` file, the declarations will be confined to the same file.

 Definition files are also used to interface Cython with external C code. The idea is to copy (or, more accurately, translate) the types and function prototypes in the definition file and leave the implementation in the external C code that will be compiled and linked in a separate step.

To share the `max` and `min` functions, we need to write a definition file with a `.pxd` extension. Such a file only contains the types and function prototypes that we want to share with other modules--a *public* interface. We can declare the prototypes of our `max` and `min` functions in a file named `mathlib.pxd`, as follows:

```
cdef int max(int a, int b)
cdef int min(int a, int b)
```

As you can see, we only write the function name and arguments without implementing the function body.

The function implementation goes into the implementation file with the same base name but the `.pyx` extension--`mathlib.pyx`:

```
cdef int max(int a, int b):
    return a if a > b else b

cdef int min(int a, int b):
    return a if a < b else b
```

The `mathlib` module is now importable from another Cython module.

To test our new Cython module, we will create a file named `distance.pyx` containing a function named `chebyshev`. The function will calculate the Chebyshev distance between two points, as shown in the following code. The Chebyshev distance between two coordinates-- (x1, y1) and (x2, y2)--is defined as the maximum value of the difference between each coordinate:

```
max(abs(x1 - x2), abs(y1 - y2))
```

To implement the `chebyshev` function, we will use the `max` function declared in `mathlib.pxd` by importing it with the `cimport` statement, as shown in the following code snippet:

```
from mathlib cimport max

def chebyshev(int x1, int y1, int x2, int y2):
    return max(abs(x1 - x2), abs(y1 - y2))
```

The `cimport` statement will read `hello.pxd` and the `max` definition will be used to generate the `distance.c` file.

Working with arrays

Numerical and high performance calculations often make use of arrays. Cython provides an easy way to interact with them, using directly low-level C arrays, or the more general *typed memoryviews*.

C arrays and pointers

C arrays are a collection of items of the same type, stored contiguously in memory. Before digging into the details, it is helpful to understand (or review) how memory is managed in C.

Variables in C are like containers. When creating a variable, a space in memory is reserved to store its value. For example, if we create a variable containing a 64 bit floating point number (`double`), the program will allocate 64 bit (16 bytes) of memory. This portion of memory can be accessed through an address to that memory location.

To obtain the address of a variable, we can use the *address operator* denoted by the & symbol. We can also use the printf function, as follows, available in the libc.stdio Cython module to print the address of this variable:

```
%%cython
cdef double a
from libc.stdio cimport printf
printf("%p", &a)
# Output:
# 0x7fc8bb611210
```

Memory addresses can be stored in special variables, *pointers*, that can be declared by putting a * prefix in front of the variable name, as follows:

```
from libc.stdio cimport printf
cdef double a
cdef double *a_pointer
a_pointer = &a # a_pointer and &a are of the same type
```

If we have a pointer, and we want to grab the value contained in the address it's pointing at, we can use the *dereference operator* denoted by the * symbol. Be careful, the * used in this context has a different meaning from the * used in the variable declaration:

```
cdef double a
cdef double *a_pointer
a_pointer = &a

a = 3.0
print(*a_pointer) # prints 3.0
```

When declaring a C array, the program allocates enough space to accommodate all the elements requested. For instance, to create an array that has 10 double values (16 bytes each), the program will reserve *16 * 10 = 160* bytes of contiguous space in memory. In Cython, we can declare such arrays using the following syntax:

```
cdef double arr[10]
```

We can also declare a multidimensional array, such as an array with 5 rows and 2 columns, using the following syntax:

```
cdef double arr[5][2]
```

The memory will be allocated in a single block of memory, row after row. This order is commonly referred to as *row-major* and is depicted in the following figure. Arrays can also be ordered *column-major*, as is the case for the FORTRAN programming language:

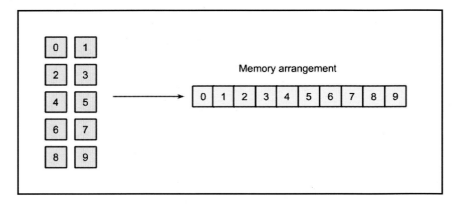

 Array ordering has important consequences. When iterating a C array over the last dimension, we access contiguous memory blocks (in our example, 0, 1, 2, 3 ...) while when we iterate on the first dimension, we skip a few positions (0, 2, 4, 6, 8, 1 ...). You should always try to access memory sequentially as this optimizes cache and memory usage.

We can store and retrieve elements from the array using standard indexing; C arrays don't support fancy indexing or slices:

```
arr[0] = 1.0
```

C arrays have many of the same behaviors as pointers. The `arr` variable, in fact, points to the memory location of the first element of the array. We can verify that the address of the first element of the array is the same as the address contained in the `arr` variable using the dereference operator, as follows:

```
%%cython
from libc.stdio cimport printf
cdef double arr[10]
printf("%pn", arr)
printf("%pn", &arr[0])

# Output
# 0x7ff6de204220
# 0x7ff6de204220
```

You should use C arrays and pointers when interfacing with the existing C libraries or when you need a fine control over the memory (also, they are very performant). This level of fine control is also prone to mistakes as it doesn't prevent you from accessing the wrong memory locations. For more common use cases and improved safety, you can use NumPy arrays or typed memoryviews.

NumPy arrays

NumPy arrays can be used as normal Python objects in Cython using their already optimized broadcasted operations. However, Cython provides a `numpy` module with better support for direct iteration.

When we normally access an element of a NumPy array, a few other operations take place at the interpreter level causing a major overhead. Cython can bypass those operations and checks by acting directly on the underlying memory area used by NumPy arrays, and thus obtaining impressive performance gains.

NumPy arrays can be declared as the `ndarray` data type. To use the data type in our code, we first need to `cimport` the `numpy` Cython module (which is not the same as the Python NumPy module). We will bind the module to the `c_np` variable to make the difference with the Python `numpy` module more explicit:

```
cimport numpy as c_np
import numpy as np
```

We can now declare a NumPy array by specifying its type and the number of dimensions between square brackets (this is called *buffer syntax*). To declare a two-dimensional array of type `double`, we can use the following code:

```
cdef c_np.ndarray[double, ndim=2] arr
```

Access to this array will be performed by directly operating on the underlying memory area; the operation will avoid stepping into the interpreter, giving us a tremendous speed boost.

In the next example, we will show the usage of typed numpy arrays and compare them with the normal Python version.

We first write the `numpy_bench_py` function that increments each element of `py_arr`. We declare the `i` index as an integer so that we avoid the for-loop overhead:

```
%%cython
import numpy as np
def numpy_bench_py():
    py_arr = np.random.rand(1000)
    cdef int i
    for i in range(1000):
        py_arr[i] += 1
```

Then, we write the same function using the `ndarray` type. Note that after we define the `c_arr` variable using `c_np.ndarray`, we can assign to it an array from the `numpy` Python module:

```
%%cython
import numpy as np
cimport numpy as c_np

def numpy_bench_c():
    cdef c_np.ndarray[double, ndim=1] c_arr
    c_arr = np.random.rand(1000)
    cdef int i

    for i in range(1000):
        c_arr[i] += 1
```

We can time the results using `timeit`, and we can see how the typed version is 50x faster:

```
%timeit numpy_bench_c()
100000 loops, best of 3: 11.5 us per loop
%timeit numpy_bench_py()
1000 loops, best of 3: 603 us per loop
```

Typed memoryviews

C and NumPy arrays as well as the built-in `bytes`, `bytearray`, and `array.array` objects are similar in the sense that they all operate on a contiguous memory area (also called memory *buffer*). Cython provides a universal interface--the *typed memoryview*--that unifies and simplifies the access to all these data types.

A **memoryview** is an object that maintains a reference on a specific memory area. It doesn't actually own the memory, but it can read and change its contents; in other words, it is a *view* on the underlying data. Memoryviews can be defined using a special syntax. For example, we can define a memoryview of int and a two-dimensional memoryview of double in the following way:

```
cdef int[:] a
cdef double[:, :] b
```

The same syntax applies to the declaration of any type in variables, function definitions, class attributes, and so on. Any object that exposes a buffer interface (for example, NumPy arrays, bytes, and array.array objects) will be bound to the memoryview automatically. For example, we can bind the memoryview to a NumPy array using a simple variable assignment:

```
import numpy as np

cdef int[:] arr
arr_np = np.zeros(10, dtype='int32')
arr = arr_np # We bind the array to the memoryview
```

It is important to note that the memoryview does not *own* the data, but it only provides a way to *access* and *change* the data it is bound to; the ownership, in this case, is left to the NumPy array. As you can see in the following example, changes made through the memoryview will act on the underlying memory area and will be reflected in the original NumPy structure (and vice versa):

```
arr[2] = 1 # Changing memoryview
print(arr_np)
# [0 0 1 0 0 0 0 0 0 0]
```

In a certain sense, the mechanism behind memoryviews is similar to what NumPy produces when we slice an array. As we have seen in Chapter 3, *Fast Array Operations with NumPy and Pandas*, slicing a NumPy array does not copy the data but returns a view on the same memory area, and changes to the view will reflect on the original array.

Memoryviews also support array slicing with the standard NumPy syntax:

```
cdef int[:, :, :] a
arr[0, :, :] # Is a 2-dimensional memoryview
arr[0, 0, :] # Is a 1-dimensional memoryview
arr[0, 0, 0] # Is an int
```

To copy data between one memoryview and another, you can use syntax similar to slice assignment, as shown in the following code:

```python
import numpy as np

cdef double[:, :] b
cdef double[:] r
b = np.random.rand(10, 3)
r = np.zeros(3, dtype='float64')

b[0, :] = r # Copy the value of r in the first row of b
```

In the next section, we will use the typed memoryviews to declare types for the arrays in our particle simulator.

Particle simulator in Cython

Now that we have a basic understanding of how Cython works, we can rewrite the ParticleSimulator.evolve method. Thanks to Cython, we can convert our loops in C, thus removing the overhead introduced by the Python interpreter.

In Chapter 3, *Fast Array Operations with NumPy and Pandas*, we wrote a fairly efficient version of the evolve method using NumPy. We can rename the old version as evolve_numpy to differentiate it from the new version:

```python
def evolve_numpy(self, dt):
    timestep = 0.00001
    nsteps = int(dt/timestep)

    r_i = np.array([[p.x, p.y] for p in self.particles])
    ang_speed_i = np.array([p.ang_speed for p in self.particles])
    v_i = np.empty_like(r_i)

    for i in range(nsteps):
        norm_i = np.sqrt((r_i ** 2).sum(axis=1))

        v_i = r_i[:, [1, 0]]
        v_i[:, 0] *= -1
        v_i /= norm_i[:, np.newaxis]

        d_i = timestep * ang_speed_i[:, np.newaxis] * v_i

        r_i += d_i
```

```
        for i, p in enumerate(self.particles):
            p.x, p.y = r_i[i]
```

We want to convert this code to Cython. Our strategy will be to take advantage of the fast indexing operations by removing the NumPy array broadcasting, thus reverting to an indexing-based algorithm. Since Cython generates efficient C code, we are free to use as many loops as we like without any performance penalty.

As a design choice, we can decide to encapsulate the loop in a function that we will rewrite in a Cython module called `cevolve.pyx`. The module will contain a single Python function, `c_evolve`, that will take the particle positions, angular velocities, timestep, and number of steps as input.

At first, we are not adding typing information; we just want to isolate the function and ensure that we can compile our module without errors:

```
# file: simul.py
def evolve_cython(self, dt):
    timestep = 0.00001
    nsteps = int(dt/timestep)

    r_i = np.array([[p.x, p.y] for p in self.particles])
    ang_speed_i = np.array([p.ang_speed for p in self.particles])

    c_evolve(r_i, ang_speed_i, timestep, nsteps)

    for i, p in enumerate(self.particles):
        p.x, p.y = r_i[i]

# file: cevolve.pyx
import numpy as np

def c_evolve(r_i, ang_speed_i, timestep, nsteps):
    v_i = np.empty_like(r_i)

    for i in range(nsteps):
        norm_i = np.sqrt((r_i ** 2).sum(axis=1))

        v_i = r_i[:, [1, 0]]
        v_i[:, 0] *= -1
        v_i /= norm_i[:, np.newaxis]

        d_i = timestep * ang_speed_i[:, np.newaxis] * v_i

        r_i += d_i
```

Note that we don't need a return value for `c_evolve` as values are updated in the `r_i` array in-place. We can benchmark the untyped Cython version against the old NumPy version by slightly changing our benchmark function, as follows:

```
def benchmark(npart=100, method='python'):
    particles = [Particle(uniform(-1.0, 1.0),
                          uniform(-1.0, 1.0),
                          uniform(-1.0, 1.0))
                          for i in range(npart)]
    simulator = ParticleSimulator(particles)
    if method=='python':
        simulator.evolve_python(0.1)
    elif method == 'cython':
        simulator.evolve_cython(0.1)
    elif method == 'numpy':
        simulator.evolve_numpy(0.1)
```

We can time the different versions in an IPython shell:

```
%timeit benchmark(100, 'cython')
1 loops, best of 3: 401 ms per loop
%timeit benchmark(100, 'numpy')
1 loops, best of 3: 413 ms per loop
```

The two versions have the same speed. Compiling the Cython module without static typing doesn't have any advantage over pure Python. The next step is to declare the type of all the important variables so that Cython can perform its optimizations.

We can start adding types to the function arguments and see how the performance changes. We can declare the arrays as typed memoryviews containing `double` values. It's worth mentioning that if we pass an array of the `int` or `float32` type, the casting won't happen automatically and we will get an error:

```
def c_evolve(double[:, :] r_i,
             double[:] ang_speed_i,
             double timestep,
             int nsteps):
```

At this point, we can rewrite the loops over the particles and timesteps. We can declare the i and j iteration indices and the nparticles particle number as int:

```
cdef int i, j
cdef int nparticles = r_i.shape[0]
```

The algorithm is very similar to the pure Python version; we iterate over the particles and timesteps, and we compute the velocity and displacement vectors for each particle coordinate using the following code:

```
for i in range(nsteps):
    for j in range(nparticles):
        x = r_i[j, 0]
        y = r_i[j, 1]
        ang_speed = ang_speed_i[j]

        norm = sqrt(x ** 2 + y ** 2)

        vx = (-y)/norm
        vy = x/norm

        dx = timestep * ang_speed * vx
        dy = timestep * ang_speed * vy

        r_i[j, 0] += dx
        r_i[j, 1] += dy
```

In the preceding code, we added the x, y, ang_speed, norm, vx, vy, dx, and dy variables. To avoid the Python interpreter overhead, we have to declare them with their corresponding types at the beginning of the function, as follows:

```
cdef double norm, x, y, vx, vy, dx, dy, ang_speed
```

We also used a function called sqrt to calculate the norm. If we use the sqrt present in the math module or the one in numpy, we will again include a slow Python function in our critical loop, thus killing our performance. A fast sqrt is available in the standard C library, already wrapped in the libc.math Cython module:

```
from libc.math cimport sqrt
```

We can rerun our benchmark to assess our improvements, as follows:

```
In [4]: %timeit benchmark(100, 'cython')
100 loops, best of 3: 13.4 ms per loop
In [5]: %timeit benchmark(100, 'numpy')
1 loops, best of 3: 429 ms per loop
```

For small particle numbers, the speed-up is massive as we obtained a 40x performance over the previous version. However, we should also try to test the performance scaling with a larger number of particles:

```
In [2]: %timeit benchmark(1000, 'cython')
10 loops, best of 3: 134 ms per loop
In [3]: %timeit benchmark(1000, 'numpy')
1 loops, best of 3: 877 ms per loop
```

As we increase the number of particles, the two versions get closer in speed. By increasing the particle size to 1000, we already decreased our speed-up to a more modest 6x. This is likely due to the fact that, as we increase the number of particles, the Python for-loop overhead becomes less and less significant compared to the speed of other operations.

Profiling Cython

Cython provides a feature, called *annotated view*, that helps find which lines are executed in the Python interpreter and which are good candidates for ulterior optimizations. We can turn this feature on by compiling a Cython file with the -a option. In this way, Cython will generate an HTML file containing our code annotated with some useful information. The usage of the -a option is as follows:

```
$ cython -a cevolve.pyx
$ firefox cevolve.html
```

The HTML file displayed in the following screenshot shows our Cython file line by line:

```
generated for it.

Raw output: cevolve.c

+01: import numpy as np
 02: cimport cython
 03: from libc.math cimport sqrt
 04:
+05: def c_evolve(double[:, :] r_i,double[:] ang_speed_i,
 06:              double timestep,int nsteps):
 07:     cdef int i
 08:     cdef int j
+09:     cdef int nparticles = r_i.shape[0]
 10:     cdef double norm, x, y, vx, vy, dx, dy, ang_speed
 11:
 12:
+13:     for i in range(nsteps):
+14:         for j in range(nparticles):
+15:             x = r_i[j, 0]
+16:             y = r_i[j, 1]
+17:             ang_speed = ang_speed_i[j]
 18:
+19:             norm = sqrt(x ** 2 + y ** 2)
 20:
+21:             vx = (-y)/norm
+22:             vy = x/norm
        if (unlikely(__pyx_v_norm == 0)) {
          #ifdef WITH_THREAD
          PyGILState_STATE __pyx_gilstate_save = PyGILState_Ensure();
          #endif
          PyErr_SetString(PyExc_ZeroDivisionError, "float division");
          #ifdef WITH_THREAD
          PyGILState_Release(__pyx_gilstate_save);
          #endif
          {__pyx_filename = __pyx_f[0]; __pyx_lineno = 22; __pyx_clineno = __LINE__; goto __pyx_L1_error;}
        }
        __pyx_v_vy = (__pyx_v_x / __pyx_v_norm);
 23:
+24:             dx = timestep * ang_speed * vx
+25:             dy = timestep * ang_speed * vy
 26:
+27:             r_i[j, 0] += dx
+28:             r_i[j, 1] += dy
 29:
```

Each line in the source code can appear in different shades of yellow. A more intense color corresponds to more interpreter-related calls, while white lines are translated to regular C code. Since interpreter calls substantially slow down execution, the objective is to make the function body as white as possible. By clicking on any of the lines, we can inspect the code generated by the Cython compiler. For example, the v_y = x/norm line checks that the norm is not 0 and raises a ZeroDivisionError if the condition is not verified. The x = r_i[j, 0] line shows that Cython checks whether the indexes are within the bounds of the array. You may note that the last line is of a very intense color; by inspecting the code, we can see that this is actually a glitch; the code refers to a boilerplate related to the end of the function.

Cython can shut down checks, such as division by zero, so that it can remove those extra interpreter related calls; this is usually accomplished through compiler directives. There are a few different ways to add compiler directives:

- Using a decorator or a context manager
- Using a comment at the beginning of the file
- Using the Cython command-line options

 For a complete list of the Cython compiler directives, you can refer to the official documentation at http://docs.cython.org/src/reference/comp ilation.html#compiler-directives.

For example, to disable bounds checking for arrays, it is sufficient to decorate a function with `cython.boundscheck`, in the following way:

```
cimport cython

@cython.boundscheck(False)
def myfunction():
    # Code here
```

Alternatively, we can use `cython.boundscheck` to wrap a block of code into a context manager, as follows:

```
with cython.boundscheck(False):
    # Code here
```

If we want to disable bounds checking for a whole module, we can add the following line of code at the beginning of the file:

```
# cython: boundscheck=False
```

To alter the directives with the command-line options, you can use the `-X` option as follows:

```
$ cython -X boundscheck=True
```

To disable the extra checks in our `c_evolve` function, we can disable the `boundscheck` directive and enable `cdivision` (this prevents checks for `ZeroDivisionError`), as in the following code:

```
cimport cython

@cython.boundscheck(False)
@cython.cdivision(True)
def c_evolve(double[:, :] r_i,
```

```
        double[:] ang_speed_i,
        double timestep,
        int nsteps):
```

If we look at the annotated view again, the loop body has become completely white--we removed all traces of the interpreter from the inner loop. In order to recompile, just type `python setup.py build_ext --inplace` again. By running the benchmark, however, we note that we didn't obtain a performance improvement, suggesting that those checks are not part of the bottleneck:

```
In [3]: %timeit benchmark(100, 'cython')
100 loops, best of 3: 13.4 ms per loop
```

Another way to profile Cython code is through the use of the `cProfile` module. As an example, we can write a simple function that calculates the Chebyshev distance between coordinate arrays. Create a `cheb.py` file:

```python
import numpy as np
from distance import chebyshev

def benchmark():
    a = np.random.rand(100, 2)
    b = np.random.rand(100, 2)
    for x1, y1 in a:
        for x2, y2 in b:
            chebyshev(x1, x2, y1, y2)
```

If we try profiling this script as-is, we won't get any statistics regarding the functions that we implemented in Cython. If we want to collect profiling information for the `max` and `min` functions, we need to add the `profile=True` option to the `mathlib.pyx` file, as shown in the following code:

```
# cython: profile=True

cdef int max(int a, int b):
    # Code here
```

We can now profile our script with `%prun` using IPython, as follows:

```
import cheb
%prun cheb.benchmark()

# Output:
2000005 function calls in 2.066 seconds

Ordered by: internal time
```

```
 ncalls tottime percall cumtime percall filename:lineno(function)
      1   1.664   1.664   2.066   2.066 cheb.py:4(benchmark)
1000000   0.351   0.000   0.401   0.000 {distance.chebyshev}
1000000   0.050   0.000   0.050   0.000 mathlib.pyx:2(max)
      2   0.000   0.000   0.000   0.000 {method 'rand' of
'mtrand.RandomState' objects}
      1   0.000   0.000   2.066   2.066 <string>:1(<module>)
      1   0.000   0.000   0.000   0.000 {method 'disable' of
'_lsprof.Profiler' objects}
```

From the output, we can see that the max function is present and is not a bottleneck. Most of the time seems to be spent in the benchmark function, meaning that the bottleneck is likely the pure Python for-loop. In this case, the best strategy will be rewriting the loop in NumPy or porting the code to Cython.

Using Cython with Jupyter

Optimizing Cython code requires substantial trial and error. Fortunately, Cython tools can be conveniently accessed through the Jupyter notebook for a more streamlined and integrated experience.

You can launch a notebook session by typing jupyter notebook in the command line and you can load the Cython magic by typing %load_ext cython in a cell.

As already mentioned earlier, the %%cython magic can be used to compile and load the Cython code inside the current session. As an example, we may copy the contents of cheb.py into a notebook cell:

```
%%cython
import numpy as np

cdef int max(int a, int b):
    return a if a > b else b

cdef int chebyshev(int x1, int y1, int x2, int y2):
    return max(abs(x1 - x2), abs(y1 - y2))

def c_benchmark():
    a = np.random.rand(1000, 2)
    b = np.random.rand(1000, 2)

    for x1, y1 in a:
        for x2, y2 in b:
            chebyshev(x1, x2, y1, y2)
```

A useful feature of the `%%cython` magic is the `-a` option that will compile the code and produce an annotated view (just like the command line `-a` option) of the source directly in the notebook, as shown in the following screenshot:

```
In [15]: %%cython -a
         import numpy as np

         cdef int max(int a, int b):
             return a if a > b else b

         cdef int chebyshev(int x1, int y1, int x2, int y2):
             return max(abs(x1 - x2), abs(y1 - y2))

         def c_benchmark():
             a = np.random.rand(1000, 2)
             b = np.random.rand(1000, 2)

             for x1, y1 in a:
                 for x2, y2 in b:
                     chebyshev(x1, x2, y1, y2)
```

Out[15]:

Generated by Cython 0.25.2

Yellow lines hint at Python interaction.
Click on a line that starts with a "+" to see the C code that Cython generated for it.

```
 01: # cython: profile=True
+02: import numpy as np
 03:
+04: cdef int max(int a, int b):
+05:     return a if a > b else b
 06:
+07: cdef int chebyshev(int x1, int y1, int x2, int y2):
+08:     return max(abs(x1 - x2), abs(y1 - y2))
 09:
+10: def c_benchmark():
+11:     a = np.random.rand(1000, 2)
+12:     b = np.random.rand(1000, 2)
 13:
+14:     for x1, y1 in a:
+15:         for x2, y2 in b:
+16:             chebyshev(x1, x2, y1, y2)
```

This allows you to quickly test different versions of your code and also use the other integrated tools available in Jupyter. For example, we can time and profile the code (provided that we activate the profile directive in the cell) in the same session using tools such as `%prun` and `%timeit`. For example, we can inspect the profiling results by taking advantage of the `%prun` magic, as shown in the following screenshot:

```
In [22]: %prun c_benchmark()


         2000005 function calls in 1.370 seconds

   Ordered by: internal time

   ncalls  tottime  percall  cumtime  percall filename:lineno(function)
        1    1.127    1.127    1.370    1.370 _cython_magic_c7d6eab16ab5658137c9af8534d5cafb.pyx:10(c_benchma
rk)
  1000000    0.191    0.000    0.243    0.000 _cython_magic_c7d6eab16ab5658137c9af8534d5cafb.pyx:7(chebyshev)
  1000000    0.052    0.000    0.052    0.000 _cython_magic_c7d6eab16ab5658137c9af8534d5cafb.pyx:4(max)
        1    0.000    0.000    1.370    1.370 <string>:1(<module>)
        1    0.000    0.000    1.370    1.370 {built-in method builtins.exec}
        1    0.000    0.000    1.370    1.370 {_cython_magic_c7d6eab16ab5658137c9af8534d5cafb.c_benchmark}
        1    0.000    0.000    0.000    0.000 {method 'disable' of '_lsprof.Profiler' objects}
```

It is also possible to use the `line_profiler` tool we discussed in Chapter 1, *Benchmarking and Profiling*, directly in the notebook. In order to support line annotations, it is necessary to do the following things:

- Enable the `linetrace=True` and `binding=True` compiler directives
- Enable the `CYTHON_TRACE=1` flag at compile time

This can be easily accomplished by adding the respective arguments to the `%%cython` magic, and by setting the compiler directives, as shown in the following code:

```
%%cython -a -f -c=-DCYTHON_TRACE=1
# cython: linetrace=True
# cython: binding=True

import numpy as np

cdef int max(int a, int b):
    return a if a > b else b

def chebyshev(int x1, int y1, int x2, int y2):
    return max(abs(x1 - x2), abs(y1 - y2))

def c_benchmark():
    a = np.random.rand(1000, 2)
    b = np.random.rand(1000, 2)
```

```
        for x1, y1 in a:
            for x2, y2 in b:
                chebyshev(x1, x2, y1, y2)
```

Once the code is instrumented, we can profile using the `%lprun` magic:

```
%lprun -f c_benchmark c_benchmark()
# Output:
Timer unit: 1e-06 s

Total time: 2.322 s
File:
/home/gabriele/.cache/ipython/cython/_cython_magic_18ad8204e9d29650f3b09feb
48ab0f44.pyx
Function: c_benchmark at line 11

Line #      Hits         Time  Per Hit   % Time  Line Contents
==============================================================
    11                                           def c_benchmark():
    12         1          226    226.0      0.0       a = np.random.rand...
    13         1           67     67.0      0.0       b = np.random.rand...
    14
    15      1001         1715      1.7      0.1       for x1, y1 in a:
    16   1001000      1299792      1.3     56.0           for x2, y2 in b:
    17   1000000      1020203      1.0     43.9               chebyshev...
```

As you can see, a good chunk of time is actually spent in line 16, which is a pure Python loop and a good candidate for further optimization.

The tools available in Jupyter notebook allow for a fast edit-compile-test cycle so that you can quickly prototype and save time when testing different solutions.

Summary

Cython is a tool that bridges the convenience of Python with the speed of C. Compared to C bindings, Cython programs are much easier to maintain and debug, thanks to the tight integration and compatibility with Python and the availability of excellent tools.

In this chapter, we introduced the basics of the Cython language and how to make our programs faster by adding static types to our variables and functions. We also learned how to work with C arrays, NumPy arrays, and memoryviews.

We optimized our particle simulator by rewriting the critical `evolve` function, obtaining a tremendous speed gain. Finally, we learned how to use the annotated view to spot hard-to-find interpreter related calls and how to enable `cProfile` support in Cython. Also, we learned how to take advantage of the Jupyter notebook for integrated profiling and analysis of Cython codes.

In the next chapter, we will explore other tools that can generate fast machine code on the fly, without requiring compilation of our code to C ahead of time.

5
Exploring Compilers

Python is a mature and widely used language and there is a large interest in improving its performance by compiling functions and methods directly to machine code rather than executing instructions in the interpreter. We have already seen a compiler example in Chapter 4, *C Performance with Cython*, where Python code is enhanced with types, compiled to efficient C code, and the interpreter calls are side-stepped.

In this chapter, we will explore two projects--Numba and PyPy--that approach compilation in a slightly different way. **Numba** is a library designed to compile small functions on the fly. Instead of transforming Python code to C, Numba analyzes and compiles Python functions directly to machine code. **PyPy** is a replacement interpreter that works by analyzing the code at runtime and optimizing the slow loops automatically.

These tools are called **Just-In-Time (JIT)** compilers because the compilation is performed at runtime rather than before running the code (in other cases, the compiler is called ahead-of-time or AOT).

The list of topics to be covered in this chapter is as follows:

- Getting started with Numba
- Implementing fast functions with native mode compilation
- Understanding and implementing universal functions
- JIT classes
- Setting up PyPy
- Running the particle simulator with PyPy
- Other interesting compilers

Numba

Numba was started in 2012 by Travis Oliphant, the original author of NumPy, as a library for compiling individual Python functions at runtime using the **Low-Level Virtual Machine (LLVM)** toolchain.

LLVM is a set of tools designed to write compilers. LLVM is language agnostic and is used to write compilers for a wide range of languages (an important example is the clang compiler). One of the core aspects of LLVM is the intermediate representation (the LLVM IR), a very low-level platform-agnostic language similar to assembly, that can be compiled to machine code for the specific target platform.

Numba works by inspecting Python functions and by compiling them, using LLVM, to the IR. As we have already seen in the last chapter, the speed gains can be obtained when we introduce types for variables and functions. Numba implements clever algorithms to guess the types (this is called type inference) and compiles type-aware versions of the functions for fast execution.

Note that Numba was developed to improve the performance of numerical code. The development efforts often prioritize the optimization of applications that intensively use NumPy arrays.

Numba is evolving really fast and can have substantial improvements between releases and, sometimes, backward incompatible changes. To keep up, ensure that you refer to the release notes for each version. In the rest of this chapter, we will use Numba version 0.30.1; ensure that you install the correct version to avoid any error.

The complete code examples in this chapter can be found in the `Numba.ipynb` notebook.

First steps with Numba

Getting started with Numba is fairly straightforward. As a first example, we will implement a function that calculates the sum of squares of an array. The function definition is as follows:

```
def sum_sq(a):
    result = 0
    N = len(a)
```

```
    for i in range(N):
        result += a[i]
    return result
```

To set up this function with Numba, it is sufficient to apply the nb.jit decorator:

```
from numba import nb

@nb.jit
def sum_sq(a):
    ...
```

The nb.jit decorator won't do much when applied. However, when the function will be invoked for the first time, Numba will detect the type of the input argument, a , and compile a specialized, performant version of the original function.

To measure the performance gain obtained by the Numba compiler, we can compare the timings of the original and the specialized functions. The original, undecorated function can be easily accessed through the py_func attribute. The timings for the two functions are as follows:

```
import numpy as np

x = np.random.rand(10000)

# Original
%timeit sum_sq.py_func(x)
100 loops, best of 3: 6.11 ms per loop

# Numba
%timeit sum_sq(x)
100000 loops, best of 3: 11.7 µs per loop
```

From the previous code, you can see how the Numba version (11.7 µs) is one order of magnitude faster than the Python version (6.11 ms). We can also compare how this implementation stacks up against NumPy standard operators:

```
%timeit (x**2).sum()
10000 loops, best of 3: 14.8 µs per loop
```

In this case, the Numba compiled function is marginally faster than NumPy vectorized operations. The reason for the extra speed of the Numba version is likely that the NumPy version allocates an extra array before performing the sum in comparison with the in-place operations performed by our sum_sq function.

As we didn't use array-specific methods in sum_sq, we can also try to apply the same function on a regular Python list of floating point numbers. Interestingly, Numba is able to obtain a substantial speed up even in this case, as compared to a list comprehension:

```
x_list = x.tolist()
%timeit sum_sq(x_list)
1000 loops, best of 3: 199 µs per loop

%timeit sum([x**2 for x in x_list])
1000 loops, best of 3: 1.28 ms per loop
```

Considering that all we needed to do was apply a simple decorator to obtain an incredible speed up over different data types, it's no wonder that what Numba does looks like magic. In the following sections, we will dig deeper and understand how Numba works and evaluate the benefits and limitations of the Numba compiler.

Type specializations

As shown earlier, the nb.jit decorator works by compiling a specialized version of the function once it encounters a new argument type. To better understand how this works, we can inspect the decorated function in the sum_sq example.

Numba exposes the specialized types using the signatures attribute. Right after the sum_sq definition, we can inspect the available specialization by accessing the sum_sq.signatures, as follows:

```
sum_sq.signatures
# Output:
# []
```

If we call this function with a specific argument, for instance, an array of float64 numbers, we can see how Numba compiles a specialized version on the fly. If we also apply the function on an array of float32, we can see how a new entry is added to the sum_sq.signatures list:

```
x = np.random.rand(1000).astype('float64')
sum_sq(x)
sum_sq.signatures
# Result:
# [(array(float64, 1d, C),)]

x = np.random.rand(1000).astype('float32')
sum_sq(x)
sum_sq.signatures
```

```
# Result:
# [(array(float64, 1d, C),), (array(float32, 1d, C),)]
```

It is possible to explicitly compile the function for certain types by passing a signature to the `nb.jit` function.

An individual signature can be passed as a tuple that contains the type we would like to accept. Numba provides a great variety of types that can be found in the `nb.types` module, and they are also available in the top-level `nb` namespace. If we want to specify an array of a specific type, we can use the slicing operator, `[:]`, on the type itself. In the following example, we demonstrate how to declare a function that takes an array of `float64` as its only argument:

```
@nb.jit((nb.float64[:],))
def sum_sq(a):
```

Note that when we explicitly declare a signature, we are prevented from using other types, as demonstrated in the following example. If we try to pass an array, x, as `float32`, Numba will raise a `TypeError`:

```
sum_sq(x.astype('float32'))
# TypeError: No matching definition for argument type(s)
array(float32, 1d, C)
```

Another way to declare signatures is through type strings. For example, a function that takes a `float64` as input and returns a `float64` as output can be declared with the `float64(float64)` string. Array types can be declared using a `[:]` suffix. To put this together, we can declare a signature for our `sum_sq` function, as follows:

```
@nb.jit("float64(float64[:])")
def sum_sq(a):
```

You can also pass multiple signatures by passing a list:

```
@nb.jit(["float64(float64[:])",
         "float64(float32[:])"])
def sum_sq(a):
```

Object mode versus native mode

So far, we have shown how Numba behaves when handling a fairly simple function. In this case, Numba worked exceptionally well, and we obtained great performance on arrays and lists.

The degree of optimization obtainable from Numba depends on how well Numba is able to infer the variable types and how well it can translate those standard Python operations to fast type-specific versions. If this happens, the interpreter is side-stepped and we can get performance gains similar to those of Cython.

When Numba cannot infer variable types, it will still try and compile the code, reverting to the interpreter when the types can't be determined or when certain operations are unsupported. In Numba, this is called **object mode** and is in contrast to the interpreter-free scenario, called **native mode**.

Numba provides a function, called `inspect_types`, that helps understand how effective the type inference was and which operations were optimized. As an example, we can take a look at the types inferred for our `sum_sq` function:

```
sum_sq.inspect_types()
```

When this function is called, Numba will print the type inferred for each specialized version of the function. The output consists of blocks that contain information about variables and types associated with them. For example, we can examine the `N = len(a)` line:

```
# --- LINE 4 ---
#    a = arg(0, name=a)  :: array(float64, 1d, A)
#    $0.1 = global(len: <built-in function len>)  ::
Function(<built-in function len>)
#    $0.3 = call $0.1(a)  :: (array(float64, 1d, A),) -> int64
#    N = $0.3  :: int64

N = len(a)
```

For each line, Numba prints a thorough description of variables, functions, and intermediate results. In the preceding example, you can see (second line) that the argument a is correctly identified as an array of `float64` numbers. At LINE 4, the input and return type of the `len` function is also correctly identified (and likely optimized) as taking an array of `float64` numbers and returning an `int64`.

If you scroll through the output, you can see how all the variables have a well-defined type. Therefore, we can be certain that Numba is able to compile the code quite efficiently. This form of compilation is called **native mode**.

As a counter example, we can see what happens if we write a function with unsupported operations. For example, as of version 0.30.1, Numba has limited support for string operations.

We can implement a function that concatenates a series of strings, and compiles it as follows:

```
@nb.jit
def concatenate(strings):
    result = ''
    for s in strings:
        result += s
    return result
```

Now, we can invoke this function with a list of strings and inspect the types:

```
concatenate(['hello', 'world'])
concatenate.signatures
# Output: [(reflected list(str),)]
concatenate.inspect_types()
```

Numba will return the output of the function for the `reflected list (str)` type. We can, for instance, examine how line 3 gets inferred. The output of `concatenate.inspect_types()` is reproduced here:

```
# --- LINE 3 ---
#    strings = arg(0, name=strings)   :: pyobject
#    $const0.1 = const(str, )   :: pyobject
#    result = $const0.1   :: pyobject
#    jump 6
# label 6

result = ''
```

You can see how this time, each variable or function is of the generic `pyobject` type rather than a specific one. This means that, in this case, Numba is unable to compile this operation without the help of the Python interpreter. Most importantly, if we time the original and compiled function, we note that the compiled function is about three times *slower* than the pure Python counterpart:

```
x = ['hello'] * 1000
%timeit concatenate.py_func(x)
10000 loops, best of 3: 111 µs per loop

%timeit concatenate(x)
1000 loops, best of 3: 317 µs per loop
```

This is because the Numba compiler is not able to optimize the code and adds some extra overhead to the function call.

As you may have noted, Numba compiled the code without complaints even if it is inefficient. The main reason for this is that Numba can still compile other sections of the code in an efficient manner while falling back to the Python interpreter for other parts of the code. This compilation strategy is called **object mode**.

It is possible to force the use of native mode by passing the `nopython=True` option to the `nb.jit` decorator. If, for example, we apply this decorator to our concatenate function, we observe that Numba throws an error on first invocation:

```
@nb.jit(nopython=True)
def concatenate(strings):
    result = ''
    for s in strings:
        result += s
    return result

concatenate(x)
# Exception:
# TypingError: Failed at nopython (nopython frontend)
```

This feature is quite useful for debugging and ensuring that all the code is fast and correctly typed.

Numba and NumPy

Numba was originally developed to easily increase performance of code that uses NumPy arrays. Currently, many NumPy features are implemented efficiently by the compiler.

Universal functions with Numba

Universal functions are special functions defined in NumPy that are able to operate on arrays of different sizes and shapes according to the broadcasting rules. One of the best features of Numba is the implementation of fast `ufuncs`.

We have already seen some `ufunc` examples in Chapter 3, *Fast Array Operations with NumPy and Pandas*. For instance, the `np.log` function is a `ufunc` because it can accept scalars and arrays of different sizes and shapes. Also, universal functions that take multiple arguments still work according to the broadcasting rules. Examples of universal functions that take multiple arguments are `np.sum` or `np.difference`.

Universal functions can be defined in standard NumPy by implementing the scalar version and using the `np.vectorize` function to enhance the function with the broadcasting feature. As an example, we will see how to write the *Cantor pairing function*.

A pairing function is a function that encodes two natural numbers into a single natural number so that you can easily interconvert between the two representations. The Cantor pairing function can be written as follows:

```
import numpy as np

def cantor(a, b):
    return  int(0.5 * (a + b)*(a + b + 1) + b)
```

As already mentioned, it is possible to create a ufunc in pure Python using the `np.vectorized` decorator:

```
@np.vectorize
def cantor(a, b):
    return  int(0.5 * (a + b)*(a + b + 1) + b)

cantor(np.array([1, 2]), 2)
# Result:
# array([ 8, 12])
```

Except for the convenience, defining universal functions in pure Python is not very useful as it requires a lot of function calls affected by interpreter overhead. For this reason, ufunc implementation is usually done in C or Cython, but Numba beats all these methods by its convenience.

All that is needed to do in order to perform the conversion is using the equivalent decorator, `nb.vectorize`. We can compare the speed of the standard `np.vectorized` version which, in the following code, is called `cantor_py`, and the same function is implemented using standard NumPy operations:

```
# Pure Python
%timeit cantor_py(x1, x2)
100 loops, best of 3: 6.06 ms per loop
# Numba
%timeit cantor(x1, x2)
100000 loops, best of 3: 15 µs per loop
# NumPy
%timeit (0.5 * (x1 + x2)*(x1 + x2 + 1) + x2).astype(int)
10000 loops, best of 3: 57.1 µs per loop
```

You can see how the Numba version beats all the other options by a large margin! Numba works extremely well because the function is simple and type inference is possible.

 An additional advantage of universal functions is that, since they depend on individual values, their evaluation can also be executed in parallel. Numba provides an easy way to parallelize such functions by passing the `target="cpu"` or `target="gpu"` keyword argument to the `nb.vectorize` decorator.

Generalized universal functions

One of the main limitations of universal functions is that they must be defined on scalar values. A generalized universal function, abbreviated `gufunc`, is an extension of universal functions to procedures that take arrays.

A classic example is the matrix multiplication. In NumPy, matrix multiplication can be applied using the `np.matmul` function, which takes two 2D arrays and returns another 2D array. An example usage of `np.matmul` is as follows:

```
a = np.random.rand(3, 3)
b = np.random.rand(3, 3)

c = np.matmul(a, b)
c.shape
# Result:
# (3, 3)
```

As we saw in the previous subsection, a `ufunc` broadcasts the operation over arrays of *scalars*, its natural generalization will be to broadcast over an array of *arrays*. If, for instance, we take two arrays of 3 by 3 matrices, we will expect `np.matmul` to take to match the matrices and take their product. In the following example, we take two arrays containing 10 matrices of shape (3, 3). If we apply `np.matmul`, the product will be applied *matrix-wise* to obtain a new array containing the 10 results (which are, again, (3, 3) matrices):

```
a = np.random.rand(10, 3, 3)
b = np.random.rand(10, 3, 3)

c = np.matmul(a, b)
c.shape
# Output
# (10, 3, 3)
```

The usual rules for broadcasting will work in a similar way. For example, if we have an array of (3, 3) matrices, which will have a shape of (10, 3, 3), we can use np.matmul to calculate the matrix multiplication of each element with a single (3, 3) matrix. According to the broadcasting rules, we obtain that the single matrix will be repeated to obtain a size of (10, 3, 3):

```
a = np.random.rand(10, 3, 3)
b = np.random.rand(3, 3) # Broadcasted to shape (10, 3, 3)
c = np.matmul(a, b)
c.shape
# Result:
# (10, 3, 3)
```

Numba supports the implementation of efficient generalized universal functions through the nb.guvectorize decorator. As an example, we will implement a function that computes the euclidean distance between two arrays as a gufunc. To create a gufunc, we have to define a function that takes the input arrays, plus an output array where we will store the result of our calculation.

The nb.guvectorize decorator requires two arguments:

- The types of the input and output: two 1D arrays as input and a scalar as output
- The so called layout string, which is a representation of the input and output sizes; in our case, we take two arrays of the same size (denoted arbitrarily by n), and we output a scalar

In the following example, we show the implementation of the euclidean function using the nb.guvectorize decorator:

```
@nb.guvectorize(['float64[:], float64[:], float64[:]'], '(n), (n) -
> ()')
def euclidean(a, b, out):
    N = a.shape[0]
    out[0] = 0.0
    for i in range(N):
        out[0] += (a[i] - b[i])**2
```

There are a few very important points to be made. Predictably, we declared the types of the inputs a and b as float64[:], because they are 1D arrays. However, what about the output argument? Wasn't it supposed to be a scalar? Yes, however, **Numba treats scalar argument as arrays of size 1**. That's why it was declared as float64[:].

Similarly, the layout string indicates that we have two arrays of size (n) and the output is a scalar, denoted by empty brackets-- (). However, the array out will be passed as an array of size 1.

Also, note that we don't return anything from the function; all the output has to be written in the out array.

 The letter n in the layout string is completely arbitrary; you may choose to use k or other letters of your liking. Also, if you want to combine arrays of uneven sizes, you can use layouts strings, such as (n, m).

Our brand new euclidean function can be conveniently used on arrays of different shapes, as shown in the following example:

```
a = np.random.rand(2)
b = np.random.rand(2)
c = euclidean(a, b) # Shape: (1,)

a = np.random.rand(10, 2)
b = np.random.rand(10, 2)
c = euclidean(a, b) # Shape: (10,)

a = np.random.rand(10, 2)
b = np.random.rand(2)
c = euclidean(a, b) # Shape: (10,)
```

How does the speed of euclidean compare to standard NumPy? In the following code, we benchmark a NumPy vectorized version with our previously defined euclidean function:

```
a = np.random.rand(10000, 2)
b = np.random.rand(10000, 2)

%timeit ((a - b)**2).sum(axis=1)
1000 loops, best of 3: 288 µs per loop

%timeit euclidean(a, b)
10000 loops, best of 3: 35.6 µs per loop
```

The Numba version, again, beats the NumPy version by a large margin!

JIT classes

As of today, Numba doesn't support optimization of generic Python objects. This limitation, however, doesn't have a huge impact on numerical codes as they usually involve arrays and math operations exclusively.

Nevertheless, certain data structures are much more naturally implemented using objects; therefore, Numba provides support for defining classes that can be used and compiled to fast, native code.

Bear in mind that this is one of the newest (almost experimental) features, and it is extremely useful as it allows us to extend Numba to support fast data structures that are not easily implemented with arrays.

As an example, we will show how to implement a simple linked list using JIT classes. A linked list can be implemented by defining a `Node` class that contains two fields: a value and the next item in the list. As you can see in the following figure, each **Node** connects to the next and holds a value, and the last node contains a broken link, to which we assign a value of **None**:

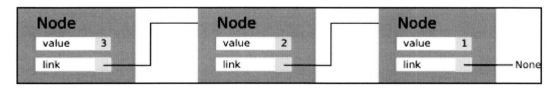

In Python, we can define the `Node` class as follows:

```
class Node:
    def __init__(self, value):
        self.next = None
        self.value = value
```

We can manage the collection of `Node` instances by creating another class, called `LinkedList`. This class will keep track of the head of the list (in the preceding figure, this corresponds to the **Node** with **value 3**). To insert an element in the front of the list, we can simply create a new **Node** and link it to the current head.

In the following code, we develop the initialization function for `LinkedList` and the `LinkedList.push_back` method that inserts an element in the front of the list using the strategy outlined earlier:

```
class LinkedList:
```

```
def __init__(self):
    self.head = None

def push_front(self, value):
    if self.head == None:
        self.head = Node(value)
    else:
        # We replace the head
        new_head = Node(value)
        new_head.next = self.head
        self.head = new_head
```

For debugging purposes, we can also implement the `LinkedList.show` method that traverses and prints each element in the list. The method is shown in the following snippet:

```
def show(self):
    node = self.head
    while node is not None:
        print(node.value)
        node = node.next
```

At this point, we can test our `LinkedList` and see whether it behaves correctly. We can create an empty list, add a few elements, and print its content. Note that since we are pushing elements at the front of the list, the last elements inserted will be the first to be printed:

```
lst = LinkedList()
lst.push_front(1)
lst.push_front(2)
lst.push_front(3)
lst.show()
# Output:
# 3
# 2
# 1
```

Finally, we can implement a function, `sum_list`, that returns the sum of the elements in the linked list. We will use this method to time differences between the Numba and pure Python version:

```
@nb.jit
def sum_list(lst):
    result = 0
    node = lst.head
    while node is not None:
```

```
        result += node.value
        node = node.next
    return result
```

If we measure the execution time of the original `sum_list` version and the `nb.jit` version, we see that there is not much difference. The reason is that Numba cannot infer the type of classes:

```
lst = LinkedList()
[lst.push_front(i) for i in range(10000)]

%timeit sum_list.py_func(lst)
1000 loops, best of 3: 2.36 ms per loop

%timeit sum_list(lst)
100 loops, best of 3: 1.75 ms per loop
```

We can improve the performance of `sum_list` by compiling the `Node` and `LinkedList` classes using the `nb.jitclass` decorator.

The `nb.jitclass` decorator takes a single argument that contains the attribute types. In the `Node` class, the attribute types are `int64` for `value` and `Node` for `next`. The `nb.jitclass` decorator will also compile all the methods defined for the class. Before delving into the code, there are two observations that need to be made.

First, the attribute declaration has to be done before the class is defined, but how do we declare a type we haven't defined yet? Numba provides the `nb.deferred_type()` function, which can be used for this purpose.

Second, the `next` attribute can be either `None` or a `Node` instance. This is what is called an optional type, and Numba provides a utility, called `nb.optional`, that lets you declare variables that can be (optionally) `None`.

This `Node` class is illustrated in the following code sample. As you can see, `node_type` is predeclared using `nb.deferred_type()`. The attributes are declared as a list of pairs containing the attribute name and the type (also note the use of `nb.optional`). After the class declaration, we are required to declare the deferred type:

```
node_type = nb.deferred_type()

node_spec = [
    ('next', nb.optional(node_type)),
    ('value', nb.int64)
]
```

```
@nb.jitclass(node_spec)
class Node:
    # Body of Node is unchanged

node_type.define(Node.class_type.instance_type)
```

The `LinkedList` class can be easily compiled, as follows. All that's needed is to define the `head` attribute and to apply the `nb.jitclass` decorator:

```
ll_spec = [
    ('head', nb.optional(Node.class_type.instance_type))
]

@nb.jitclass(ll_spec)
class LinkedList:
    # Body of LinkedList is unchanged
```

We can now measure the execution time of the `sum_list` function when we pass a JIT `LinkedList`:

```
lst = LinkedList()
[lst.push_front(i) for i in range(10000)]

%timeit sum_list(lst)
1000 loops, best of 3: 345 µs per loop

%timeit sum_list.py_func(lst)
100 loops, best of 3: 3.36 ms per loop
```

Interestingly, when using a JIT class from a compiled function, we obtain a substantial performance improvement against the pure Python version. However, using the JIT class from the original `sum_list.py_func` actually results in worse performance. Ensure that you use JIT classes only inside compiled functions!

Limitations in Numba

There are some instances where Numba cannot properly infer the variable types and will refuse to compile. In the following example, we define a function that takes a nested list of integers and returns the sum of the element in every sublist. In this case, Numba will raise `ValueError` and refuse to compile:

```
a = [[0, 1, 2],
     [3, 4],
     [5, 6, 7, 8]]
```

```
@nb.jit
def sum_sublists(a):
    result = []
    for sublist in a:
        result.append(sum(sublist))
    return result

sum_sublists(a)
# ValueError: cannot compute fingerprint of empty list
```

The problem with this code is that Numba is not able to determine the type of the list and fails. A way to fix this problem is to help the compiler determine the right type by initializing the list with a sample element and removing it at the end:

```
@nb.jit
def sum_sublists(a):
    result = [0]
    for sublist in a:
        result.append(sum(sublist))
    return result[1:]
```

Among other features that are not yet implemented in the Numba compiler are function and class definitions, list, set and dict comprehension, generators, the with statement, and try except blocks. Note, however, that many of these features may become supported in the future.

The PyPy project

PyPy is a very ambitious project at improving the performance of the Python interpreter. The way PyPy improves performance is by automatically compiling slow sections of the code at runtime.

PyPy is written in a special language called RPython (rather than C) that allows developers to quickly and reliably implement advanced features and improvements. RPython means *Restricted Python* because it implements a restricted subset of the Python language targeted to the compiler development.

As of today, PyPy version 5.6 supports a lot of Python features and is a possible choice for a large variety of applications.

PyPy compiles code using a very clever strategy, called *tracing JIT compilation*. At first, the code is executed normally using interpreter calls. PyPy then starts to profile the code and identifies the most intensive loops. After the identification takes place, the compiler then observes (*traces*) the operations and is able to compile its optimized, interpreter-free version.

Once an optimized version of the code is present, PyPy is able to run the slow loop much faster than the interpreted version.

This strategy can be contrasted with what Numba does. In Numba, the units of compilation are methods and functions, while the PyPy focus is just slow loops. Overall, the focus of the projects is also very different as Numba has a limited scope for numerical code and requires a lot of instrumentation while PyPy aims at replacing the CPython interpreter.

In this section, we will demonstrate and benchmark PyPy on our particle simulator application.

Setting up PyPy

PyPy is distributed as a precompiled binary that can be downloaded from `http://pypy.or g/download.html`, and it currently supports Python versions 2.7 (beta support in PyPy 5.6) and 3.3 (alpha support in PyPy 5.5). In this chapter, we will demonstrate the usage of the 2.7 version.

Once PyPy is downloaded and unpacked, you can locate the interpreter in the `bin/pypy` directory relative to the unpacked archive. You can initialize a new virtual environment where we can install additional packages using the following command:

```
$ /path/to/bin/pypy -m ensurepip
$ /path/to/bin/pypy -m pip install virtualenv
$ /path/to/bin/virtualenv my-pypy-env
```

To activate the environment, we will use the following command:

```
$ source my-pypy-env/bin/activate
```

At this point, you can verify that the binary Python is linked to the PyPy executable by typing `python -V`. At this point, we can go ahead and install some packages we may need. As of version 5.6, PyPy has limited support for software that uses the Python C API (most notably, packages such as `numpy` and `matplotlib`). We can go ahead and install them in the usual way:

```
(my-pypy-env) $ pip install numpy matplotlib
```

On certain platforms, installation of `numpy` and `matplotlib` can be tricky. You can skip the installation step and remove any imports on these two packages from the scripts we will run.

Running a particle simulator in PyPy

Now that we have successfully set up the PyPy installation, we can go ahead and run our particle simulator. As a first step, we will time the particle simulator from `Chapter 1`, *Benchmarking and Profiling*, on the standard Python interpreter. If the virtual environment is still active, you can issue the command deactivate to exit the environment. We can confirm that the Python interpreter is the standard one by using the `python -V` command:

```
(my-pypy-env) $ deactivate
$ python -V
Python 3.5.2 :: Continuum Analytics, Inc.
```

At this point, we can time our code using the `timeit` command-line interface:

```
$ python -m timeit --setup "from simul import benchmark" "benchmark()"
10 loops, best of 3: 886 msec per loop
```

We can reactivate the environment and run the exact same code from PyPy. On Ubuntu, you may have problems importing the `matplotlib.pyplot` module. You can try issuing the following `export` command to fix the issue or removing the `matplotlib` imports from `simul.py`:

```
$ export MPLBACKEND='agg'
```

Now, we can go ahead and time the code using PyPy:

```
$ source my-pypy-env/bin/activate
Python 2.7.12 (aff251e54385, Nov 09 2016, 18:02:49)
[PyPy 5.6.0 with GCC 4.8.2]

(my-pypy-env) $ python -m timeit --setup "from simul import benchmark"
"benchmark()"
WARNING: timeit is a very unreliable tool. use perf or something else for
real measurements
10 loops, average of 7: 106 +- 0.383 msec per loop (using standard
deviation)
```

Note that we obtained a large, more than eight times, speedup! PyPy, however, warns us that the `timeit` module can be unreliable. We can confirm our timings using the `perf` module, as suggested by PyPy:

```
(my-pypy-env) $ pip install perf
(my-pypy-env) $ python -m perf timeit --setup 'from simul import benchmark'
'benchmark()'
.......
Median +- std dev: 97.8 ms +- 2.3 ms
```

Other interesting projects

Over the years, many projects attempted to improve Python performance through several strategies and, sadly, many of them failed. As of today, there are a few projects that survive and hold the promise for a faster Python.

Numba and PyPy are mature projects that are steadily improving over the years. Features are continuously being added and they hold great promise for the future of Python.

Nuitka is a program developed by Kay Hayen that compiles Python code to C. As of right now (version 0.5.x), it provides extreme compatibility with the Python language and produces efficient code that results in moderate performance improvements over CPython.

Nuitka is quite different than Cython in the sense that it focuses on extreme compatibility with the Python language, and it doesn't extend the language with additional constructs.

Pyston is a new interpreter developed by Dropbox that powers JIT compilers. It differs substantially from PyPy as it doesn't employ a tracing JIT, but rather a method-at-a-time JIT (similar to what Numba does). Pyston, like Numba, is also built on top of the LLVM compiler infrastructure.

Pyston is still in early development (alpha stage) and only supports Python 2.7. Benchmarks show that it is faster than CPython but slower than PyPy; that said, it is still an interesting project to follow as new features are added and compatibility is increased.

Summary

Numba is a tool that compiles fast, specialized versions of Python functions at runtime. In this chapter, we learned how to compile, inspect, and analyze functions compiled by Numba. We also learned how to implement fast NumPy universal functions that are useful in a wide array of numerical applications. Finally, we implemented more complex data structures using the `nb.jitclass` decorator.

Tools such as PyPy allow us to run Python programs unchanged to obtain significant speed improvements. We demonstrated how to set up PyPy, and we assessed the performance improvements on our particle simulator application.

We also, briefly, described the current ecosystem of the Python compilers and compared them with each other.

In the next chapter, we will learn about concurrency and asynchronous programming. Using these techniques, we will be able to improve the responsiveness and design of applications that spend a lot of time waiting for network and disk resources.

6
Implementing Concurrency

So far, we have explored how to measure and improve the performance of programs by reducing the number of operations performed by the CPU through clever algorithms and more efficient machine code. In this chapter, we will shift our focus to programs where most of the time is spent waiting for resources that are much slower than the CPU, such as persistent storage and network resources.

Asynchronous programming is a programming paradigm that helps to deal with slow and unpredictable resources (such as users) and is widely used to build responsive services and user interfaces. In this chapter, we will show you how to program asynchronously in Python using techniques such as coroutines and reactive programming.

In this chapter, we will cover the following topics:

- The memory hierarchy
- Callbacks
- Futures
- Event loops
- Writing coroutines with `asyncio`
- Converting synchronous code to asynchronous code
- Reactive programming with RxPy
- Working with observables
- Building a memory monitor with RxPY

Asynchronous programming

Asynchronous programming is a way of dealing with slow and unpredictable resources. Rather than waiting idle for resources to become available, asynchronous programs are able to handle multiple resources concurrently and efficiently. Programming in an asynchronous way can be challenging because it is necessary to deal with external requests that can arrive in any order, may take a variable amount of time, or may fail unpredictably. In this section, we will introduce the topic by explaining the main concepts and terminology as well as by giving an idea of how asynchronous programs work.

Waiting for I/O

A modern computer employs different kinds of memory to store data and perform operations. In general, a computer possesses a combination of expensive memory that is capable of operating at fast speeds and cheaper, and more abundant memory that operates at lower speeds and is used to store a larger amount of data.

The memory hierarchy is shown in the following diagram:

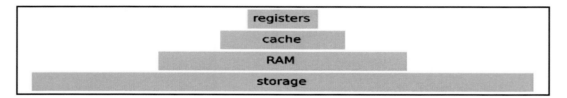

At the top of the memory hierarchy are the CPU registers. Those are integrated in the CPU and are used to store and execute machine instructions. Accessing data in a register generally takes one clock cycle. This means that if the CPU operates at 3 GHz, the time it takes to access one element in a CPU register is in the order of 0.3 nanoseconds.

At the layer just below the **registers**, you can find the CPU cache, which is comprised of multiple levels and is integrated in the processor. The **cache** operates at a slightly slower speed than the **registers** but within the same order of magnitude.

The next item in the hierarchy is the main memory (**RAM**), which holds much more data but is slower than the cache. Fetching an item from memory can take a few hundred clock cycles.

At the bottom layer, you can find persistent storage, such as a rotating disks (HDD) and **Solid State Drives (SSD)**. These devices hold the most data and are orders of magnitude slower than the main memory. An HDD may take a few milliseconds to seek and retrieve an item, while an SSD is substantially faster and takes only a fraction of a millisecond.

To put the relative speed of each memory type into perspective, if you were to have the CPU with a clock speed of about one second, a register access would be equivalent to picking up a pen from the table. A cache access will be equivalent to picking up a book from the shelf. Moving higher in the hierarchy, a RAM access will be equivalent to loading up the laundry (about twenty x slower than the cache). When we move to persistent storage, things are quite a bit different. Retrieving an element from an SSD will be equivalent to doing a four day trip, while retrieving an element from an HDD can take up to six months! The times can stretch even further if we move on to access resources over the network.

From the preceding example, it should be clear that accessing data from storage and other I/O devices is much slower compared to the CPU; therefore, it is very important to handle those resources so that the CPU is never stuck waiting aimlessly. This can be accomplished by carefully designing software capable of managing multiple, ongoing requests at the same time.

Concurrency

Concurrency is a way to implement a system that is able to deal with multiple requests at the same time. The idea is that we can move on and start handling other resources while we wait for a resource to become available. Concurrency works by splitting a task into smaller subtasks that can be executed out of order so that multiple tasks can be partially advanced without waiting for the previous tasks to finish.

As a first example, we will describe how to implement concurrent access to a slow network resource. Let's say we have a web service that takes the square of a number, and the time between our request and the response will be approximately one second. We can implement the `network_request` function that takes a number and returns a dictionary that contains information about the success of the operation and the result. We can simulate such services using the `time.sleep` function, as follows:

```
import time

def network_request(number):
    time.sleep(1.0)
    return {"success": True, "result": number ** 2}
```

We will also write some additional code that performs the request, verifies that the request was successful, and prints the result. In the following code, we define the `fetch_square` function and use it to calculate the square of the number two using a call to `network_request`:

```
def fetch_square(number):
    response = network_request(number)
    if response["success"]:
        print("Result is: {}".format(response["result"]))

fetch_square(2)
# Output:
# Result is: 4
```

Fetching a number from the network will take one second because of the slow network. What if we want to calculate the square of multiple numbers? We can call `fetch_square`, which will start a network request as soon as the previous one is done:

```
fetch_square(2)
fetch_square(3)
fetch_square(4)
# Output:
# Result is: 4
# Result is: 9
# Result is: 16
```

The previous code will take three seconds to run, but it's not the best we can do. Waiting for the previous result to finish is unnecessary as we can technically submit multiple requests at and wait for them parallely.

In the following diagram, the three tasks are represented as boxes. The time spent by the CPU processing and submitting the request is in orange while the waiting times are in blue. You can see how most of the time is spent waiting for the resources while our machine sits idle without doing anything else:

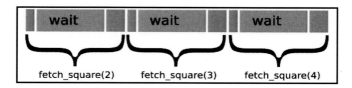

Ideally, we would like to start other new task while we are waiting for the already submitted tasks to finish. In the following figure, you can see that as soon as we submit our request in **fetch_square(2)**, we can start preparing for **fetch_square(3)** and so on. This allows us to reduce the CPU waiting time and to start processing the results as soon as they become available:

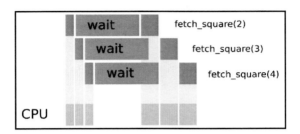

This strategy is made possible by the fact that the three requests are completely independent, and we don't need to wait for the completion of a previous task to start the next one. Also, note how a single CPU can comfortably handle this scenario. While distributing the work on multiple CPUs can further speedup the execution, if the waiting time is large compared to the processing times, the speedup will be minimal.

To implement concurrency, it is necessary to think and code differently; in the following sections, we'll demonstrate techniques and best practices to implement robust concurrent applications.

Callbacks

The code we have seen so far blocks the execution of the program until the resource is available. The call responsible for the waiting is `time.sleep`. To make the code start working on other tasks, we need to find a way to avoid blocking the program flow so that the rest of the program can go on with the other tasks.

One of the simplest ways to accomplish this behavior is through callbacks. The strategy is quite similar to what we do when we request a cab.

Imagine that you are at a restaurant and you've had a few drinks. It's raining outside, and you'd rather not take the bus; therefore, you request a taxi and ask them to call when they're outside so that you can come out, and you don't have to wait in the rain.

What you did in this case is request a taxi (that is, the slow resource) but instead of waiting outside until the taxi arrives, you provide your number and instructions (callback) so that you can come outside when they're ready and go home.

We will now show how this mechanism can work in code. We will compare the blocking code of `time.sleep` with the equivalent non-blocking code of `threading.Timer`.

For this example, we will write a function, `wait_and_print`, that will block the program execution for one second and then print a message:

```
def wait_and_print(msg):
    time.sleep(1.0)
    print(msg)
```

If we want to write the same function in a non-blocking way, we can use the `threading.Timer` class. We can initialize a `threading.Timer` instance by passing the amount of time we want to wait and a callback. A **callback** is simply a function that will be called when the timer expires. Note that we have to also call the `Timer.start` method to activate the timer:

```
import threading

def wait_and_print_async(msg):
    def callback():
        print(msg)

    timer = threading.Timer(1.0, callback)
    timer.start()
```

An important feature of the `wait_and_print_async` function is that none of the statements are blocking the execution flow of the program.

> How is `threading.Timer` capable of waiting without blocking? The strategy used by `threading.Timer` involves starting a new thread that is able to execute code in parallel. If this is confusing, don't worry, we will explore threading and parallel programming in detail in the following chapters.

This technique of registering callbacks for execution in response to certain events is commonly called the *Hollywood principle*. This is because, after an audition for a role at Hollywood, you may be told *"Don't call us, we'll call you"*, meaning that they won't tell you if they chose you for the role immediately, but they'll call you in case they do.

To highlight the difference between the blocking and non-blocking version of `wait_and_print`, we can test and compare the execution of the two versions. In the output comments, the waiting periods are indicated by `<wait...>`:

```
# Syncronous
wait_and_print("First call")
```

```
wait_and_print("Second call")
print("After call")
# Output:
# <wait...>
# First call
# <wait...>
# Second call
# After call
# Async
wait_and_print_async("First call async")
wait_and_print_async("Second call async")
print("After submission")
# Output:
# After submission
# <wait...>
# First call
# Second call
```

The synchronous version behaves in a very familiar way. The code waits for a second, prints First call, waits for another second, and then prints the Second call and After call messages.

In the asynchronous version, wait_and_print_async *submits* (rather than *execute*) those calls and moves on *immediately*. You can see this mechanism in action by acknowledging that the "After submission" message is printed immediately.

With this in mind, we can explore a slightly more complex situation by rewriting our network_request function using callbacks. In the following code, we define the network_request_async function. The biggest difference between network_request_async and its blocking counterpart is that network_request_async *doesn't return anything*. This is because we are merely submitting the request when network_request_async is called, but the value is available only when the request is completed.

If we can't return anything, how do we pass the result of the request? Rather than returning the value, we will pass the result as an argument to the on_done callback.

The rest of the function consists of submitting a callback (called timer_done) to the timer.Timer class that will call on_done when it's ready:

```
def network_request_async(number, on_done):

    def timer_done():
        on_done({"success": True,
                 "result": number ** 2})
```

```
timer = threading.Timer(1.0, timer_done)
timer.start()
```

The usage of `network_request_async` is quite similar to `timer.Timer`; all we have to do is pass the number we want to square and a callback that will receive the result *when it's ready*. This is demonstrated in the following snippet:

```
def on_done(result):
    print(result)

network_request_async(2, on_done)
```

Now, if we submit multiple network requests, we note that the calls get executed concurrently and do not block the code:

```
network_request_async(2, on_done)
network_request_async(3, on_done)
network_request_async(4, on_done)
print("After submission")
```

In order to use `network_request_async` in `fetch_square`, we need to adapt the code to use asynchronous constructs. In the following code, we modify `fetch_square` by defining and passing the `on_done` callback to `network_request_async`:

```
def fetch_square(number):
    def on_done(response):
        if response["success"]:
            print("Result is: {}".format(response["result"]))

    network_request_async(number, on_done)
```

You may have noted that the asynchronous code is significantly more convoluted than its synchronous counterpart. This is due to the fact that we are required to write and pass a callback every time we need to retrieve a certain result, causing the code to become nested and hard to follow.

Futures

Futures are a more convenient pattern that can be used to keep track of the results of asynchronous calls. In the preceding code, we saw that rather than returning values, we accept callbacks and pass the results when they are ready. It is interesting to note that, so far, there is no easy way to track the status of the resource.

A **future** is an abstraction that helps us keep track of the requested resources and that we are waiting to become available. In Python, you can find a future implementation in the `concurrent.futures.Future` class. A `Future` instance can be created by calling its constructor with no arguments:

```
fut = Future()
# Result:
# <Future at 0x7f03e41599e8 state=pending>
```

A future represents a value that is not yet available. You can see that its string representation reports the current status of the result which, in our case, is still pending. In order to make a result available, we can use the `Future.set_result` method:

```
fut.set_result("Hello")
# Result:
# <Future at 0x7f03e41599e8 state=finished returned str>

fut.result()
# Result:
# "Hello"
```

You can see that once we set the result, the `Future` will report that the task is finished and can be accessed using the `Future.result` method. It is also possible to subscribe a callback to a future so that, as soon as the result is available, the callback is executed. To attach a callback, it is sufficient to pass a function to the `Future.add_done_callback` method. When the task completes, the function will be called with the `Future` instance as its first argument and the result can be retrieved using the `Future.result()` method:

```
fut = Future()
fut.add_done_callback(lambda future: print(future.result(),
flush=True))
fut.set_result("Hello")
# Output:
# Hello
```

To get a grasp on how futures can be used in practice, we will adapt the `network_request_async` function to use futures. The idea is that, this time, instead of returning nothing, we return a `Future` that will keep track of the result for us. Note two things:

- We don't need to accept an `on_done` callback as callbacks can be connected later using the `Future.add_done_callback` method. Also, we pass the generic `Future.set_result` method as the callback for `threading.Timer`.

- This time we are able to return a value, thus making the code a bit more similar to the blocking version we saw in the preceding section:

```
from concurrent.futures import Future

def network_request_async(number):
    future = Future()
    result = {"success": True, "result": number ** 2}
    timer = threading.Timer(1.0, lambda: future.set_result(result))
    timer.start()
    return future

fut = network_request_async(2)
```

 Even though we instantiate and manage futures directly in these examples; in practical applications, the futures are handled by frameworks.

If you execute the preceding code, nothing will happen as the code only consists of preparing and returning a `Future` instance. To enable further operation of the future results, we need to use the `Future.add_done_callback` method. In the following code, we adapt the `fetch_square` function to use futures:

```
def fetch_square(number):
    fut = network_request_async(number)

    def on_done_future(future):
        response = future.result()
        if response["success"]:
            print("Result is: {}".format(response["result"]))

    fut.add_done_callback(on_done_future)
```

The code still looks quite similar to the callback version. Futures are a different and slightly more convenient way of working with callbacks. Futures are also advantageous, because they can keep track of the resource status, cancel (unschedule) scheduled tasks, and handle exceptions more naturally.

Event loops

So far, we have implemented parallelism using OS threads. However, in many asynchronous frameworks, the coordination of concurrent tasks is managed by an **event loop**.

The idea behind an event loop is to continuously monitor the status of the various resources (for example, network connections and database queries) and trigger the execution of callbacks when events take place (for example, when a resource is ready or when a timer expires).

Why not just stick to threading?

Events loops are sometimes preferred as every unit of execution never runs at the same time as another and this can simplify dealing with shared variables, data structures, and resources. Read the next chapter for more details about parallel execution and its shortcomings.

As a first example, we will implement a thread-free version of `threading.Timer`. We can define a `Timer` class that will take a timeout and implement the `Timer.done` method that returns `True` if the timer has expired:

```
class Timer:

    def __init__(self, timeout):
        self.timeout = timeout
        self.start = time.time()

    def done(self):
        return time.time() - self.start > self.timeout
```

To determine whether the timer has expired, we can write a loop that continuously checks the timer status by calling the `Timer.done` method. When the timer expires, we can print a message and exit the cycle:

```
timer = Timer(1.0)

while True:
    if timer.done():
        print("Timer is done!")
        break
```

By implementing the timer in this way, the flow of execution is never blocked and we can, in principle, do other work inside the while loop.

Waiting for events to happen by continuously polling using a loop is commonly termed as *busy-waiting*.

Ideally, we would like to attach a custom function that executes when the timer goes off, just like we did in `threading.Timer`. To do this, we can implement a method, `Timer.on_timer_done`, that will accept a callback to be executed when the timer goes off:

```
class Timer:
    # ... previous code
    def on_timer_done(self, callback):
        self.callback = callback
```

Note that `on_timer_done` merely stores a reference to the callback. The entity that monitors the event and executes the callback is the loop. This concept is demonstrated as follows. Rather than using the print function, the loop will call `timer.callback` when appropriate:

```
timer = Timer(1.0)
timer.on_timer_done(lambda: print("Timer is done!"))

while True:
    if timer.done():
        timer.callback()
        break
```

As you can see, an asynchronous framework is starting to take place. All we did outside the loop was define the timer and the callback, while the loop took care of monitoring the timer and executing the associated callback. We can further extend our code by implementing support for multiple timers.

A natural way to implement multiple timers is to add a few `Timer` instances to a list and modify our event loop to periodically check all the timers and dispatch the callbacks when required. In the following code, we define two timers and attach a callback to each of them. Those timers are added to a list, `timers`, that is continuously monitored by our event loop. As soon as a timer is done, we execute the callback and remove the event from the list:

```
timers = []

timer1 = Timer(1.0)
timer1.on_timer_done(lambda: print("First timer is done!"))

timer2 = Timer(2.0)
timer2.on_timer_done(lambda: print("Second timer is done!"))

timers.append(timer1)
timers.append(timer2)

while True:
    for timer in timers:
```

```
    if timer.done():
        timer.callback()
        timers.remove(timer)
# If no more timers are left, we exit the loop
if len(timers) == 0:
    break
```

The main restriction of an event loop is, since the flow of execution is managed by a continuously running loop, that it **never uses blocking calls**. If we use any blocking statement (such as `time.sleep`) inside the loop, you can imagine how the event monitoring and callback dispatching will stop until the blocking call is done.

To avoid this, rather than using a blocking call, such as `time.sleep`, we let the event loop detect and execute the callback when the resource is ready. By not blocking the execution flow, the event loop is free to monitor multiple resources in a concurrent way.

> The notification for events is usually implemented through operating system calls (such as the `select` Unix tool) that will resume the execution of the program whenever an event is ready (in contrast to busy-waiting).

The Python standard libraries include a very convenient event loop-based concurrency framework, `asyncio`, which will be the topic of the next section.

The asyncio framework

By now, you should have a solid foundation of how concurrency works, and how to use callbacks and futures. We can now move on and learn how to use the `asyncio` package present in the standard library since version 3.4. We will also explore the brand new `async/await` syntax to deal with asynchronous programming in a very natural way.

As a first example, we will see how to retrieve and execute a simple callback using `asyncio`. The `asyncio` loop can be retrieved by calling the `asyncio.get_event_loop()` function. We can schedule a callback for execution using `loop.call_later` that takes a delay in seconds and a callback. We can also use the `loop.stop` method to halt the loop and exit the program. To start processing the scheduled call, it is necessary to start the loop, which can be done using `loop.run_forever`. The following example demonstrates the usage of these basic methods by scheduling a callback that will print a message and halt the loop:

```
import asyncio
```

```
loop = asyncio.get_event_loop()

def callback():
    print("Hello, asyncio")
    loop.stop()

loop.call_later(1.0, callback)
loop.run_forever()
```

Coroutines

One of the main problems with callbacks is that they require you to break the program execution into small functions that will be invoked when a certain event takes place. As we saw in the earlier sections, callbacks can quickly become cumbersome.

Coroutines are another, perhaps a more natural, way to break up the program execution into chunks. They allow the programmer to write code that resembles synchronous code but will execute asynchronously. You may think of a coroutine as a function that can be stopped and resumed. A basic example of coroutines is generators.

Generators can be defined in Python using the `yield` statement inside a function. In the following example, we implement the `range_generator` function, which produces and returns values from 0 to n. We also add a print statement to log the internal state of the generator:

```
def range_generator(n):
    i = 0
    while i < n:
        print("Generating value {}".format(i))
        yield i
        i += 1
```

When we call the `range_generator` function, the code is not executed immediately. Note that nothing is printed to output when the following snippet is executed. Instead, a *generator object* is returned:

```
generator = range_generator(3)
generator
# Result:
# <generator object range_generator at 0x7f03e418ba40>
```

In order to start pulling values from a generator, it is necessary to use the `next` function:

```
next(generator)
# Output:
# Generating value 0

next(generator)
# Output:
# Generating value 1
```

Note that every time we invoke `next`, the code runs until it encounters the next `yield` statement and it is necessary to issue another `next` statement to resume the generator execution. You can think of a `yield` statement as a breakpoint where we can stop and resume execution (while also maintaining the internal state of the generator). This ability of stopping and resuming execution can be leveraged by the event loop to allow for concurrency.

It is also possible to *inject* (rather than *extract)* values in the generator through the `yield` statement. In the following example, we declare a function parrot that will repeat each message that we send. To allow a generator to receive a value, you can assign yield to a variable (in our case, it is `message = yield`). To insert values in the generator, we can use the `send` method. In the Python world, a generator that can also receive values is called a *generator-based coroutine*:

```
def parrot():
    while True:
        message = yield
        print("Parrot says: {}".format(message))

generator = parrot()
generator.send(None)
generator.send("Hello")
generator.send("World")
```

Note that we also need to issue a `generator.send(None)` before we can start sending messages; this is done to bootstrap the function execution and bring us to the first `yield` statement. Also, note that there is an infinite loop inside `parrot`; if we implement this without using generators, we will get stuck running the loop forever!

With this in mind, you can imagine how an event loop can partially progress several of these generators without blocking the execution of the whole program. You can also imagine how a generator can be advanced only when some resource is ready, therefore eliminating the need for a callback.

It is possible to implement coroutines in `asyncio` using the `yield` statement. However, Python supports the definition of powerful coroutines using a more intuitive syntax since version 3.5.

To define a coroutine with `asyncio`, you can use the `async def` statement:

```
async def hello():
    print("Hello, async!")

coro = hello()
coro
# Output:
# <coroutine object hello at 0x7f314846bd58>
```

As you can see, if we call the `hello` function, the function body is not executed immediately, but a *coroutine object* is returned. The `asyncio` coroutines do not support `next`, but they can be easily run in the `asyncio` event loop using the `run_until_complete` method:

```
loop = asyncio.get_event_loop()
loop.run_until_complete(coro)
```

 Coroutines defined with the `async def` statement are also called *native coroutines*.

The `asyncio` module provides resources (called *awaitables*) that can be requested inside coroutines through the `await` syntax. For example, if we want to wait for a certain time and then execute a statement, we can use the `asyncio.sleep` function:

```
async def wait_and_print(msg):
    await asyncio.sleep(1)
    print("Message: ", msg)

loop.run_until_complete(wait_and_print("Hello"))
```

The result is beautiful, clean code. We are writing perfectly functional asynchronous code without all the ugliness of callbacks!

 You may have noted how `await` provides a breakpoint for the event loop so that, as it wait for the resource, the event loop can move on and concurrently manage other coroutines.

Even better, coroutines are also `awaitable`, and we can use the `await` statement to chain coroutines asynchronously. In the following example, we rewrite the `network_request` function, which we defined earlier, by replacing the call to `time.sleep` with `asyncio.sleep`:

```
async def network_request(number):
    await asyncio.sleep(1.0)
    return {"success": True, "result": number ** 2}
```

We can follow up by reimplementing `fetch_square`. As you can see, we can await `network_request` directly without needing additional futures or callbacks.

```
async def fetch_square(number):
    response = await network_request(number)
    if response["success"]:
        print("Result is: {}".format(response["result"]))
```

The coroutines can be executed individually using `loop.run_until_complete`:

```
loop.run_until_complete(fetch_square(2))
loop.run_until_complete(fetch_square(3))
loop.run_until_complete(fetch_square(4))
```

Running tasks using `run_until_complete` is fine for testing and debugging. However, our program will be started with `loop.run_forever` most of the times, and we will need to submit our tasks while the loop is already running.

`asyncio` provides the `ensure_future` function, which schedules coroutines (as well as futures) for execution. `ensure_future` can be used by simply passing the coroutine we want to schedule. The following code will schedule multiple calls to `fetch_square` that will be executed concurrently:

```
asyncio.ensure_future(fetch_square(2))
asyncio.ensure_future(fetch_square(3))
asyncio.ensure_future(fetch_square(4))

loop.run_forever()
# Hit Ctrl-C to stop the loop
```

As a bonus, when passing a coroutine, the `asyncio.ensure_future` function will return a `Task` instance (which is a subclass of `Future`) so that we can take advantage of the await syntax without having to give up the resource tracking capabilities of regular futures.

Converting blocking code into non-blocking code

While `asyncio` supports connecting to resources in an asynchronous way, it is required to use blocking calls in certain cases. This happens, for example, when third-party APIs exclusively expose blocking calls (for example, many database libraries), but also when executing long-running computations. In this subsection, we will learn how to deal with blocking APIs and make them compatible with `asyncio`.

An effective strategy for dealing with blocking code is to run it in a separate thread. Threads are implemented at the **Operating System (OS)** level and allow parallel execution of blocking code. For this purpose, Python provides the `Executor` interface designed to run tasks in a separate thread and to monitor their progress using futures.

You can initialize a `ThreadPoolExecutor` by importing it from the `concurrent.futures` module. The executor will spawn a collection of threads (called `workers`) that will wait to execute whatever task we throw at them. Once a function is submitted, the executor will take care of dispatching its execution to an available worker thread and keep track of the result. The `max_workers` argument can be used to select the number of threads.

Note that the executor will not destroy a thread once a task is completed. By doing so, it reduces the cost associated with the creation and destruction of threads.

In the following example, we create a `ThreadPoolExecutor` with three workers, and we submit a `wait_and_return` function that will block the program execution for one second and return a message string. We then use the `submit` method to schedule its execution:

```
from concurrent.futures import ThreadPoolExecutor
executor = ThreadPoolExecutor(max_workers=3)

def wait_and_return(msg):
    time.sleep(1)
    return msg

executor.submit(wait_and_return, "Hello. executor")
# Result:
# <Future at 0x7ff616ff6748 state=running>
```

The `executor.submit` method immediately schedules the function and returns a future. It is possible to manage the execution of tasks in `asyncio` using the `loop.run_in_executor` method, which works quite similarly to `executor.submit`:

```
fut = loop.run_in_executor(executor, wait_and_return, "Hello, asyncio
executor")
# <Future pending ...more info...>
```

The `run_in_executor` method will also return an `asyncio.Future` instance that can be awaited from other code, the main difference being that the future will not be run until we start the loop. We can run and obtain the response using `loop.run_until_complete`:

```
loop.run_until_complete(fut)
# Result:
# 'Hello, executor'
```

As a practical example, we can use this technique to implement concurrent fetching of several web pages. To do this, we will import the popular (blocking) `requests` library and run the `requests.get` function in the executor:

```
import requests

async def fetch_urls(urls):
    responses = []
    for url in urls:
        responses.append(await loop.run_in_executor
                                (executor, requests.get, url))
    return responses

loop.run_until_complete(fetch_ruls(['http://www.google.com',
                                    'http://www.example.com',
                                    'http://www.facebook.com']))

# Result
# []
```

This version of `fetch_url` will not block the execution and allow other coroutines in `asyncio` to run; however, it is not optimal as the function will not fetch a URL in parallel. To do this, we can use `asyncio.ensure_future` or employ the `asyncio.gather` convenience function that will submit all the coroutines at once and gather the results as they come. The usage of `asyncio.gather` is demonstrated here:

```
def fetch_urls(urls):
    return asyncio.gather(*[loop.run_in_executor
                            (executor, requests.get, url)
                            for url in urls])
```

The number of URLs you can fetch in parallel with this method will be dependent on the number of worker threads you have. To avoid this limitation, you should use a natively non-blocking library, such as `aiohttp`.

Reactive programming

Reactive programming is a paradigm that aims at building better concurrent systems. Reactive applications are designed to comply with the requirements exemplified by the reactive manifesto:

- **Responsive**: The system responds immediately to the user.
- **Elastic**: The system is capable of handling different levels of load and is able to adapt to accommodate increasing demands.
- **Resilient**: The system deals with failure gracefully. This is achieved by modularity and avoiding having a single point of failure.
- **Message driven**: The system should not block and take advantage of events and messages. A message-driven application helps achieve all the previous requirements.

As you can see, the intent of reactive systems is quite noble, but how exactly does reactive programming work? In this section, we will learn about the principles of reactive programming using the RxPy library.

 The RxPy library is part of ReactiveX (`http://reactivex.io/`), which is a project that implements reactive programming tools for a large variety of languages.

Observables

As the name implies, the main idea of reactive programming is to *react* to events. In the preceding section, we saw some examples of this idea with callbacks; you subscribe to them and the callback is executed as soon as the event takes place.

In reactive programming, this idea is expanded by thinking of events as streams of data. This can be exemplified by showing examples of such streams in RxPy. A data stream can be created from an iterator using the `Observable.from_iterable` factory method, as follows:

```
from rx import Observable
obs = Observable.from_iterable(range(4))
```

In order to receive data from `obs`, we can use the `Observable.subscribe` method, which will execute the function we pass for each value that the data source emits:

```
obs.subscribe(print)
```

```
# Output:
# 0
# 1
# 2
# 3
```

You may have noted that observables are ordered collections of items just like lists or, more generally, iterators. This is not a coincidence.

 The term observable comes from the combination of observer and iterable. An *observer* is an object that reacts to changes of the variable it observes, while an *iterable* is an object that is capable of producing and keeping track of an iterator.

In Python, iterators are objects that define the __next__ method, and whose elements can be extracted by calling next. An iterator can generally be obtained by a collection using iter; then we can extract elements using next or a for loop. Once an element is consumed from the iterator, we can't go back. We can demonstrate its usage by creating an iterator from a list:

```
collection = list([1, 2, 3, 4, 5])
iterator = iter(collection)

print("Next")
print(next(iterator))
print(next(iterator))

print("For loop")
for i in iterator:
    print(i)

# Output:
# Next
# 1
# 2
# For loop
# 3
# 4
# 5
```

You can see how, every time we call next or we iterate, the iterator produces a value and advances. In a sense, we are *pulling* results from the iterator.

Iterators sound a lot like generators; however, they are more general. In Python, generators are returned by functions that use yield expressions. As we saw, generators support `next`, therefore, they are a special class of iterators.

Now you can appreciate the contrast between an iterator and an observable. An observable *pushes* a stream of data to us whenever it's ready, but that's not everything. An observable is also able to tell us when there is an error and where there is no more data. In fact, it is possible to register further callbacks to the `Observable.subscribe` method. In the following example, we create an observable and register callbacks to be called using `on_next` whenever the next item is available and using the `on_completed` argument when there is no more data:

```
obs = Observable.from_iter(range(4))
obs.subscribe(on_next=lambda x: print(on_next="Next item: {}"),
              on_completed=lambda: print("No more data"))
# Output:
# Next element: 0
# Next element: 1
# Next element: 2
# Next element: 3
# No more data
```

This analogy with the iterator is important because we can use the same techniques that can be used with iterators to handle streams of events.

RxPy provides operators that can be used to create, transform, filter, and group observables. The power of reactive programming lies in the fact that those operations return other observables that can be conveniently chained and composed together. For a quick taste, we will demonstrate the usage of the `take` operator.

Given an observable, `take` will return a new observable that will stop after n items. Its usage is straightforward:

```
obs = Observable.from_iterable(range(100000))
obs2 = obs.take(4)

obs2.subscribe(print)
# Output:
# 0
# 1
# 2
# 3
```

The collection of operations implemented in RxPy is varied and rich, and can be used to build complex applications using these operators as building blocks.

Useful operators

In this subsection, we will explore operators that transform the elements of a source observable in some way. The most prominent member of this family of operators is the familiar `map`, which emits the elements of the source observable after applying a function to them. For example, we may use `map` to calculate the square of a sequence of numbers:

```
(Observable.from_iterable(range(4))
            .map(lambda x:  x**2)
            .subscribe(print))
# Output:
# 0
# 1
# 4
# 9
```

Operators can be represented with marble diagrams that help us better understand how the operator works, especially when taking into account the fact that elements can be emitted over a region of time. In a marble diagram, a data stream (in our case, an observable) is represented by a solid line. A circle (or other shape) identifies a value emitted by the observable, an **X** symbol represents an error, and a vertical line represents the end of the stream.

In the following figure, we can see the marble diagram of **map**:

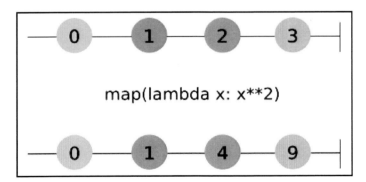

The source observable is placed at the top of the diagram, the transformation is placed in the middle, and the resulting observable is placed at the bottom.

Another example of a transformation is `group_by`, which sorts the items into groups based on a key. The `group_by` operator takes a function that extracts a key when given an element and produces an observable for each key with the elements associated to it.

The `group_by` operation can be expressed more clearly using a marble diagram. In the following figure, you can see how `group_by` emits two observables. Additionally, the items are dynamically sorted into groups *as soon as they are emitted*:

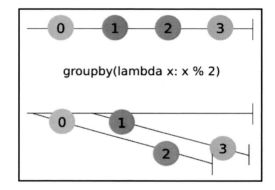

We can further understand how `group_by` works with a simple example. Let's say that we want to group the number according to the fact that they're even or odd. We can implement this using `group_by` by passing the `lambda x: x % 2` expression as a key function, which will return `0` if the number is even and `1` if the number is odd:

```
obs = (Observable.from_range(range(4))
            .group_by(lambda x: x % 2))
```

At this point, if we subscribe and print the content of `obs`, actually two observables are printed:

```
obs.subscribe(print)
# <rx.linq.groupedobservable.GroupedObservable object at
0x7f0fba51f9e8>
# <rx.linq.groupedobservable.GroupedObservable object at
0x7f0fba51fa58>
```

You can determine the group key using the `key` attribute. To extract all the even numbers, we can take the first observable (corresponding to a key equal to 0) and subscribe to it. In the following code, we show how this works:

```
obs.subscribe(lambda x: print("group key: ", x.key))
# Output:
# group key:   0
# group key:   1
obs.take(1).subscribe(lambda x: x.subscribe(print))
# Output:
# 0
# 2
```

With `group_by`, we introduced an observable that emits other observables. This turns out to be quite a common pattern in reactive programming, and there are functions that allow you to combine different observables.

Two useful tools for combining observables are `merge_all` and `concat_all`. Merge takes multiple observables and produces a single observable that contains the element of the two observables in the order they are emitted. This is better illustrated using a marble diagram:

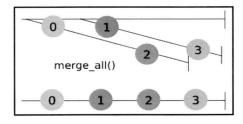

`merge_all` can be compared to a similar operator, `concat_all`, which returns a new observable that emits the elements of all the elements of the first observable, followed by the elements of the second observable and so on. The marble diagram for `concat_all` is presented here:

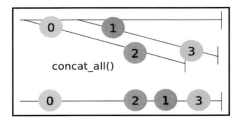

To demonstrate the usage of these two operators, we can apply those operations to the observable of observables returned by `group_by`. In the case of `merge_all`, the items are returned in the same order as they were initially (remember that `group_by` emits elements in the two groups as they come):

```
obs.merge_all().subscribe(print)
# Output
# 0
# 1
# 2
# 3
```

On the other hand, `concat_all` first returns the even elements and then the odd elements as it waits for the first observable to complete, and then starts emitting the elements of the second observable. This is demonstrated in the following snippet. In this specific example, we also applied a function, `make_replay`; this is needed because, by the time the "even" stream is consumed, the elements of the second stream have already been produced and will not be available to `concat_all`. This concept will become much clearer after reading the *Hot and cold observables* section:

```
def make_replay(a):
    result = a.replay(None)
    result.connect()
    return result

obs.map(make_replay).concat_all().subscribe(print)
# Output
# 0
# 2
# 1
# 3
```

This time around, the even numbers are printed first, followed by the odd numbers.

 RxPy also provides the `merge` and `concat` operations that can be used to combine individual observables

Hot and cold observables

In the preceding section, we learned how to create an observable using the `Observable.from_iterable` method. RxPy provides many other tools to create more interesting event sources.

`Observable.interval` takes a time interval in milliseconds, `period`, and will create an observable that emits a value every time the period has passed. The following line of code can be used to define an observable, `obs`, that will emit a number, starting from zero, every second. We use the `take` operator to limit the timer to four events:

```
obs = Observable.interval(1000)
obs.take(4).subscribe(print)
# Output:
# 0
# 1
# 2
# 3
```

A very important fact about `Observable.interval` is that the timer doesn't start until we subscribe. We can observe this by printing both the index and the delay from when the timer starts definition using `time.time()`, as follows:

```
import time

start = time.time()
obs = Observable.interval(1000).map(lambda a:
                                    (a, time.time() - start))

# Let's wait 2 seconds before starting the subscription
time.sleep(2)
obs.take(4).subscribe(print)
# Output:
# (0, 3.003735303878784)
# (1, 4.004871129989624)
# (2, 5.005947589874268)
# (3, 6.00749135017395)
```

As you can see, the first element (corresponding to a 0 index) is produced after three seconds, which means that the timer started when we issue the `subscribe(print)` method.

Observables, such as `Observable.interval`, are called *lazy* because they start producing values only when requested (think of them as vending machines, which won't dispense food unless we press the button). In Rx jargon, these kind of observables are called **cold**. A property of cold observables is that, if we attach two subscribers, the interval timer will be started multiple times. This is quite evident from the following example. Here, we add a new subscription 0.5 seconds after the first, and you can see how the output of the two subscriptions come at different times:

```
start = time.time()
obs = Observable.interval(1000).map(lambda a:
                                    (a, time.time() - start))

# Let's wait 2 seconds before starting the subscription
time.sleep(2)
obs.take(4).subscribe(lambda x: print("First subscriber:
                                      {}".format(x)))
time.sleep(0.5)
obs.take(4).subscribe(lambda x: print("Second subscriber:
                                      {}".format(x)))
# Output:
# First subscriber: (0, 3.0036110877990723)
# Second subscriber: (0, 3.5052847862243652)
# First subscriber: (1, 4.004414081573486)
# Second subscriber: (1, 4.506155252456665)
# First subscriber: (2, 5.005316972732544)
# Second subscriber: (2, 5.506817102432251)
# First subscriber: (3, 6.0062034130096436)
# Second subscriber: (3, 6.508296489715576)
```

Sometimes we may not want this behavior as we may want multiple subscribers to subscribe to the same data source. To make the observable produce the same data, we can delay the data production and ensure that all the subscribers will get the same data using the `publish` method.

Publish will transform our observable into a `ConnectableObservable`, which won't start pushing data immediately, but only when we call the `connect` method. The usage of `publish` and `connect` is demonstrated in the following snippet:

```
start = time.time()
obs = Observable.interval(1000).map(lambda a: (a, time.time() -
start)).publish()
obs.take(4).subscribe(lambda x: print("First subscriber:
                                      {}".format(x)))
obs.connect() # Data production starts here

time.sleep(2)
```

```
obs.take(4).subscribe(lambda x: print("Second subscriber:
                                {}".format(x)))
# Output:
# First subscriber: (0, 1.0016899108886719)
# First subscriber: (1, 2.0027990341186523)
# First subscriber: (2, 3.003532648086548)
# Second subscriber: (2, 3.003532648086548)
# First subscriber: (3, 4.004265308380127)
# Second subscriber: (3, 4.004265308380127)
# Second subscriber: (4, 5.005320310592651)
# Second subscriber: (5, 6.005795240402222)
```

In the preceding example, you can see how we first issue `publish`, then we subscribe the first subscriber and, finally, we issue `connect`. When `connect` is issued, the timer will start producing data. The second subscriber joins the party late and, in fact, won't receive the first two messages but will start receiving data from the third and so on. Note how, this time around, the subscribers share the exact same data. This kind of data source, where data is produced independently of the subscribers, is called **hot**.

Similar to `publish`, you can use the `replay` method that will produce the data *from the beginning* for each new subscriber. This is illustrated in the following example that, which is identical to the preceding one except that we replaced `publish` with `replay`:

```
import time

start = time.time()
obs = Observable.interval(1000).map(lambda a: (a, time.time() -
start)).replay(None)
obs.take(4).subscribe(lambda x: print("First subscriber:
                                {}".format(x)))

obs.connect()

time.sleep(2)
obs.take(4).subscribe(lambda x: print("Second subscriber:
                                {}".format(x)))

First subscriber: (0, 1.0008857250213623)
First subscriber: (1, 2.0019824504852295)
Second subscriber: (0, 1.0008857250213623)
Second subscriber: (1, 2.0019824504852295)
First subscriber: (2, 3.0030810832977295)
Second subscriber: (2, 3.0030810832977295)
First subscriber: (3, 4.004604816436768)
Second subscriber: (3, 4.004604816436768)
```

You can see how, this time around, even though the second subscriber arrives late to the party, it is still given all the items that have been given out so far.

Another way of creating hot observables is through the `Subject` class. `Subject` is interesting because it's capable of both receiving and pushing data, and thus it can be used to manually *push* items to an observable. Using `Subject` is very intuitive; in the following code, we create a `Subject` and subscribe to it. Later, we push values to it using the `on_next` method; as soon as we do that, the subscriber is called:

```
s = Subject()
s.subscribe(lambda a: print("Subject emitted value: {}".format(x))
s.on_next(1)
# Subject emitted value: 1
s.on_next(2)
# Subject emitted value: 2
```

Note that `Subject` is another example of hot observables.

Building a CPU monitor

Now that we have a grasp on the main reactive programming concepts, we can implement a sample application. In this subsection, we will implement a monitor that will give us real-time information about our CPU usage and is capable of detecting spikes.

 The complete code for the CPU monitor can be found in the `cpu_monitor.py` file.

As a first step, let's implement a data source. We will use the `psutil` module that provides a function, `psutil.cpu_percent`, that returns the latest available CPU usage as a percent (and doesn't block):

```
import psutil
psutil.cpu_percent()
# Result: 9.7
```

Since we are developing a monitor, we would like to sample this information over a few time intervals. To accomplish this we can use the familiar `Observable.interval`, followed by `map` just like we did in the previous section. Also, we would like to make this observable *hot* as, for this application, all subscribers should receive a single source of data; to make `Observable.interval` hot, we can use the `publish` and `connect` methods. The full code for the creation of the `cpu_data` observable is as follows

```
cpu_data = (Observable
            .interval(100) # Each 100 milliseconds
```

```
        .map(lambda x: psutil.cpu_percent())
        .publish())
cpu_data.connect() # Start producing data
```

We can test our monitor by printing a sample of 4 items

```
cpu_data.take(4).subscribe(print)
# Output:
# 12.5
# 5.6
# 4.5
# 9.6
```

Now that our main data source is in place, we can implement a monitor visualization using `matplotlib`. The idea is to create a plot that contains a fixed amount of measurements and, as new data arrives, we include the newest measurement and remove the oldest one. This is commonly referred to as a *moving window* and is better understood with an illustration. In the following figure, our `cpu_data` stream is represented as a list of numbers. The first plot is produced as soon as we have the first four numbers and, each time a new number arrives, we shift the window by one position and update the plot:

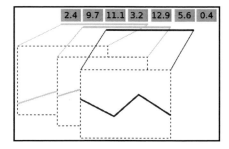

To implement this algorithm, we can write a function, called `monitor_cpu`, that will create and update our plotting window. The function will do the following things:

- Initialize an empty plot and set up the correct plot limits.
- Transform our `cpu_data` observable to return a moving window over the data. This can be accomplished using the `buffer_with_count` operator, which will take the number of points in our window, `npoints`, as parameters and the shift as 1.
- Subscribe to this new data stream and update the plot with the incoming data.

The complete code for the function is shown here and, as you can see, is extremely compact. Take some time to run the function and play with the parameters:

```python
import numpy as np
from matplotlib import pyplot as plt

def monitor_cpu(npoints):
    lines, = plt.plot([], [])
    plt.xlim(0, npoints)
    plt.ylim(0, 100) # 0 to 100 percent

    cpu_data_window = cpu_data.buffer_with_count(npoints, 1)

    def update_plot(cpu_readings):
        lines.set_xdata(np.arange(npoints))
        lines.set_ydata(np.array(cpu_readings))
        plt.draw()

    cpu_data_window.subscribe(update_plot)

    plt.show()
```

Another feature we may want to develop is, for example, an alert that triggers when the CPU has been high for a certain amount of time as this may indicate that some of the processes in our machine are working very hard. This can be accomplished by combining `buffer_with_count` and `map`. We can take the CPU stream and a window, and then we will test whether all items have a value higher than twenty percent usage (in a quad-core CPU that corresponds to about one processor working at hundred percent) in the map function. If all the points in the window have a higher than twenty percent usage, we display a warning in our plot window.

The implementation of the new observable can be written as follows and will produce an observable that emits `True` if the CPU has high usage, and `False` otherwise:

```python
alertpoints = 4
high_cpu = (cpu_data
            .buffer_with_count(alertpoints, 1)
            .map(lambda readings: all(r > 20 for r in readings)))
```

Now that the `high_cpu` observable is ready, we can create a `matplotlib` label and subscribe to it for updates:

```
label = plt.text(1, 1, "normal")
def update_warning(is_high):
    if is_high:
        label.set_text("high")
    else:
        label.set_text("normal")
high_cpu.subscribe(update_warning)
```

Summary

Asynchronous programming is useful when our code deals with slow and unpredictable resources, such as I/O devices and networks. In this chapter, we explored the fundamental concepts of concurrency and asynchronous programming and how to write concurrent code with the `asyncio` and RxPy libraries.

`asyncio` coroutines are an excellent choice when dealing with multiple, interconnected resources as they greatly simplify the code logic by cleverly avoiding callbacks. Reactive programming is also very good in these situations, but it truly shines when dealing with streams of data that are common in real-time applications and user interfaces.

In the next two chapters, we will learn about parallel programming and how to achieve impressive performance gain by taking advantage of multiple cores and multiple machines.

7
Parallel Processing

With parallel processing by using multiple cores, you can increase the amount of calculations your program can do in a given time frame without needing a faster processor. The main idea is to divide a problem into independent subunits and use multiple cores to solve those subunits in parallel.

Parallel processing is necessary to tackle large-scale problems. Companies produce massive quantities of data every day that need to be stored in multiple computers and analyzed. Scientists and engineers run parallel code on supercomputers to simulate massive systems.

Parallel processing allows you to take advantage of multicore CPUs as well as GPUs that work extremely well with highly parallel problems. In this chapter, we will cover the following topics:

- A brief introduction to the fundamentals of parallel processing
- Illustrating how to parallelize simple problems with the `multiprocessing` Python library
- Using the simple `ProcessPoolExecutor` interface
- Parallelizing our programs using multithreading with the help of Cython and OpenMP
- Achieving parallelism automatically with Theano and Tensorflow
- Executing code on a GPU with Theano, Tensorflow, and Numba

Introduction to parallel programming

In order to parallelize a program, it is necessary to divide the problem into subunits that can run independently (or almost independently) from each other.

A problem where the subunits are totally independent from each other is called **embarrassingly parallel**. An element-wise operation on an array is a typical example--the operation needs to only know the element it is handling at the moment. Another example is our particle simulator. Since there are no interactions, each particle can evolve independently from the others. Embarrassingly parallel problems are very easy to implement and perform very well on parallel architectures.

Other problems may be divided into subunits but have to share some data to perform their calculations. In those cases, the implementation is less straightforward and can lead to performance issues because of the communication costs.

We will illustrate the concept with an example. Imagine that you have a particle simulator, but this time the particles attract other particles within a certain distance (as shown in the following figure). To parallelize this problem, we divide the simulation box into regions and assign each region to a different processor. If we evolve the system one step at a time, some particles will interact with particles in a neighboring region. To perform the next iteration, communication with the new particle positions of the neighboring region is required.

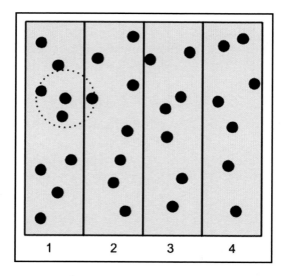

Communication between processes is costly and can seriously hinder the performance of parallel programs. There exist two main ways to handle data communication in parallel programs:

- **Shared memory**
- **Distributed memory**

In shared memory, the subunits have access to the same memory space. The advantage of this approach is that you don't have to explicitly handle the communication as it is sufficient to write or read from the shared memory. However, problems arise when multiple processes try to access and change the same memory location at the same time. Care should be taken to avoid such conflict using synchronization techniques.

In the distributed memory model, each process is completely separated from the others and possesses its own memory space. In this case, communication is handled explicitly between the processes. The communication overhead is typically costlier compared to shared memory as data can potentially travel through a network interface.

One common way to achieve parallelism with the shared memory model is **threads**. Threads are independent subtasks that originate from a process and share resources, such as memory. This concept is further illustrated in the following figure. Threads produce multiple execution context and share the same memory space, while processes provide multiple execution context that possess their own memory space and communication has to be handled explicitly.

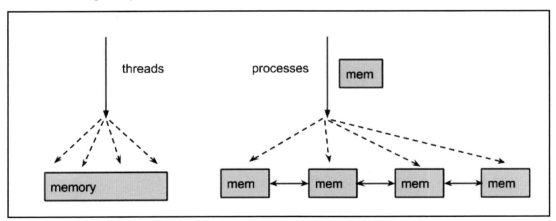

Python can spawn and handle threads, but they can't be used to increase performance; due to the Python interpreter design, only one Python instruction is allowed to run at a time-- this mechanism is called **Global Interpreter Lock (GIL)**. What happens is that each time a thread executes a Python statement, the thread acquires a lock and, when the execution is completed, the same lock is released. Since the lock can be acquired only by one thread at a time, other threads are prevented from executing Python statements while some other thread holds the lock.

Even though the GIL prevents parallel execution of Python instructions, threads can still be used to provide concurrency in situations where the lock can be released, such as in time-consuming I/O operations or in C extensions.

 Why not remove the GIL? In past years, many attempts have been made, including the most recent gilectomy experiment. First, removing the GIL is not an easy task and requires modification of most of the Python data structures. Additionally, such fine-grained locking can be costly and may introduce substantial performance loss in single-threaded programs. Despite this, some Python implementations (notable examples are Jython and IronPython) do not use the GIL.

The GIL can be completely sidestepped using processes instead of threads. Processes don't share the same memory area and are independent from each other--each process has its own interpreter. Processes have a few disadvantages: starting up a new process is generally slower than starting a new thread, they consume more memory, and inter-process communication can be slow. On the other hand, processes are still very flexible, and they scale better as they can be distributed on multiple machines.

Graphic processing units

Graphic processing units are special processors designed for computer graphics applications. Those applications usually require processing the geometry of a 3D scene and output an array of pixel to the screen. The operations performed by GPUs involve array and matrix operations on floating point numbers.

GPUs are designed to run this graphics-related operation very efficiently, and they achieve this by adopting a highly parallel architecture. Compared to a CPU, a GPU has many more (thousands) of small processing units. GPUs are intended to produce data at about 60 frames per second, which is much slower than the typical response time of a CPU, which possesses higher clock speeds.

GPUs possess a very different architecture from a standard CPU and are specialized for computing floating point operations. Therefore, to compile programs for GPUs, it is necessary to utilize special programming platforms, such as CUDA and OpenCL.

Compute Unified Device Architecture (**CUDA**) is a proprietary NVIDIA technology. It provides an API that can be accessed from other languages. CUDA provides the NVCC tool that can be used to compile GPU programs written in a language similar to C (CUDA C) as well as numerous libraries that implement highly optimized mathematical routines.

OpenCL is an open technology with the ability of writing parallel programs that can be compiled for a variety of target devices (CPUs and GPUs of several vendors) and is a good option for non-NVIDIA devices.

GPU programming sounds wonderful on paper. However, don't throw away your CPU yet. GPU programming is tricky and only specific use cases benefit from the GPU architecture. Programmers need to be aware of the costs incurred in memory transfers to and from the main memory and how to implement algorithms to take advantage of the GPU architecture.

Generally, GPUs are great at increasing the amount of operations you can perform per unit of time (also called **throughput**); however, they require more time to prepare the data for processing. In contrast, CPUs are much faster at producing an individual result from scratch (also called **latency**).

For the right problem, GPUs provide extreme (10 to 100 times) speedup. For this reason, they often constitute a very inexpensive (the same speedup will require hundreds of CPUs) solution to improve the performance of numerically intensive applications. We will illustrate how to execute some algorithms on a GPU in the *Automatic Parallelism* section.

Using multiple processes

The standard `multiprocessing` module can be used to quickly parallelize simple tasks by spawning several processes, while avoiding the GIL problem. Its interface is easy to use and includes several utilities to handle task submission and synchronization.

The Process and Pool classes

You can create a process that runs independently by subclassing `multiprocessing.Process`. You can extend the `__init__` method to initialize resources, and you can write the portion of the code that will be executed in a subprocess by implementing the `Process.run` method. In the following code, we define a `Process` class that will wait for one second and print its assigned `id`:

```
import multiprocessing
import time

class Process(multiprocessing.Process):
    def __init__(self, id):
        super(Process, self).__init__()
        self.id = id

    def run(self):
        time.sleep(1)
        print("I'm the process with id: {}".format(self.id))
```

To spawn the process, we have to instantiate the `Process` class and call the `Process.start` method. Note that you don't directly call `Process.run`; the call to `Process.start` will create a new process that, in turn, will call the `Process.run` method. We can add the following lines at the end of the preceding snippet to create and start the new process:

```
if __name__ == '__main__':
    p = Process(0)
    p.start()
```

The instructions after `Process.start` will be executed immediately without waiting for the p process to finish. To wait for the task completion, you can use the `Process.join` method, as follows:

```
if __name__ == '__main__':
    p = Process(0)
    p.start()
    p.join()
```

We can launch four different processes that will run parallely in the same way. In a serial program, the total required time will be four seconds. Since the execution is concurrent, the resulting wallclock time will be of one second. In the following code, we create four processes that will execute concurrently:

```
if __name__ == '__main__':
    processes = Process(1), Process(2), Process(3), Process(4)
    [p.start() for p in processes]
```

Note that the order of the execution for parallel processes is unpredictable and ultimately depends on how the OS schedules their execution. You can verify this behavior by executing the program multiple times; the order will likely be different between runs.

The multiprocessing module exposes a convenient interface that makes it easy to assign and distribute tasks to a set of processes that reside in the multiprocessing.Pool class.

The multiprocessing.Pool class spawns a set of processes--called **workers**--and lets us submit tasks through the apply/apply_async and map/map_async methods.

The Pool.map method applies a function to each element of a list and returns the list of results. Its usage is equivalent to the built-in (serial) map.

To use a parallel map, you should first initialize a multiprocessing.Pool object. It takes the number of workers as its first argument; if not provided, that number will be equal to the number of cores in the system. You can initialize a multiprocessing.Pool object in the following way:

```
pool = multiprocessing.Pool()
pool = multiprocessing.Pool(processes=4)
```

Let's see pool.map in action. If you have a function that computes the square of a number, you can map the function to the list by calling Pool.map and passing the function and the list of inputs as arguments, as follows:

```
def square(x):
    return x * x

inputs = [0, 1, 2, 3, 4]
outputs = pool.map(square, inputs)
```

The `Pool.map_async` function is just like `Pool.map` but returns an `AsyncResult` object instead of the actual result. When we call `Pool.map`, the execution of the main program is stopped until all the workers are finished processing the result. With `map_async`, the `AsyncResult` object is returned immediately without blocking the main program and the calculations are done in the background. We can then retrieve the result using the `AsyncResult.get` method at any time, as shown in the following lines:

```
outputs_async = pool.map_async(square, inputs)
outputs = outputs_async.get()
```

`Pool.apply_async` assigns a task consisting of a single function to one of the workers. It takes the function and its arguments and returns an `AsyncResult` object. We can obtain an effect similar to `map` using `apply_async`, as shown:

```
results_async = [pool.apply_async(square, i) for i in range(100))]
results = [r.get() for r in results_async]
```

The Executor interface

From version 3.2 onward, it is possible to execute Python code in parallel using the `Executor` interface provided in the `concurrent.futures` module. We already saw the `Executor` interface in action in the previous chapter, when we used `ThreadPoolExecutor` to perform multiple tasks concurrently. In this subsection, we'll demonstrate the usage of the `ProcessPoolExecutor` class.

`ProcessPoolExecutor` exposes a very lean interface, at least when compared to the more featureful `multiprocessing.Pool`. A `ProcessPoolExecutor` can be instantiated, similar to `ThreadPoolExecutor`, by passing a number of worker threads using the `max_workers` argument (by default, `max_workers` will be the number of CPU cores available). The main methods available to the `ProcessPoolExecutor` are `submit` and `map`.

The `submit` method will take a function and return a `Future` (see the last chapter) that will keep track of the execution of the submitted function. The method map works similarly to the `Pool.map` function, except that it returns an iterator rather than a list:

```
from concurrent.futures import ProcessPoolExecutor

executor = ProcessPoolExecutor(max_workers=4)
fut = executor.submit(square, 2)
# Result:
# <Future at 0x7f5b5c030940 state=running>

result = executor.map(square, [0, 1, 2, 3, 4])
```

```
list(result)
# Result:
# [0, 1, 4, 9, 16]
```

To extract the result from one or more `Future` instances, you can use the `concurrent.futures.wait` and `concurrent.futures.as_completed` functions. The `wait` function accepts a list of `future` and will block the execution of the programs until all the futures have completed their execution. The result can then be extracted using the `Future.result` method. The `as_completed` function also accepts a function but will, instead, return an iterator over the results:

```
from concurrent.futures import wait, as_completed

fut1 = executor.submit(square, 2)
fut2 = executor.submit(square, 3)
wait([fut1, fut2])
# Then you can extract the results using fut1.result() and
fut2.result()

results = as_completed([fut1, fut2])
list(results)
# Result:
# [4, 9]
```

Alternatively, you can generate futures using the `asyncio.run_in_executor` function and manipulate the results using all the tools and syntax provided by the `asyncio` libraries so that you can achieve concurrency and parallelism at the same time.

Monte Carlo approximation of pi

As an example, we will implement a canonical, embarrassingly parallel program--the **Monte Carlo approximation of pi**. Imagine that we have a square of size 2 units; its area will be 4 units. Now, we inscribe a circle of 1 unit radius in this square; the area of the circle will be $pi * r\verb|^|2$. By substituting the value of r in the previous equation, we get that the numerical value for the area of the circle is $pi * (1)\verb|^|2 = pi$. You can refer to the following figure for a graphical representation.

If we shoot a lot of random points on this figure, some points will fall into the circle, which we'll call **hits,** while the remaining points, **misses,** will be outside the circle. The area of the circle will be proportional to the number of hits, while the area of the square will be proportional to the total number of shots. To get the value of *pi*, it is sufficient to divide the area of the circle (equal to *pi*) by the area of the square (equal to 4):

```
hits/total = area_circle/area_square = pi/4
pi = 4 * hits/total
```

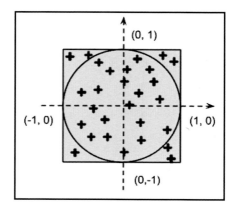

The strategy we will employ in our program will be as follows:

- Generate a lot of uniformly random (*x, y*) numbers in the range (**-1, 1**)
- Test whether those numbers lie inside the circle by checking whether $x^{**}2 + y^{**}2$ *<= 1*

The first step when writing a parallel program is to write a serial version and verify that it works. In a real-world scenario, you also want to leave the parallelization as the last step of your optimization process. First, we need to identify the slow parts, and second, parallelization is time-consuming and gives you *at most* a speedup equal to the number of processors. The implementation of the serial program is as follows:

```
import random

samples = 1000000
hits = 0

for i in range(samples):
    x = random.uniform(-1.0, 1.0)
    y = random.uniform(-1.0, 1.0)

    if x**2 + y**2 <= 1:
```

```
        hits += 1

    pi = 4.0 * hits/samples
```

The accuracy of our approximation will improve as we increase the number of samples. You can note that each loop iteration is independent from the other--this problem is embarrassingly parallel.

To parallelize this code, we can write a function, called `sample`, that corresponds to a single hit-miss check. If the sample hits the circle, the function will return 1; otherwise, it will return 0. By running `sample` multiple times and summing the results, we'll get the total number of hits. We can run `sample` over multiple processors with `apply_async` and get the results in the following way:

```python
def sample():
    x = random.uniform(-1.0, 1.0)
    y = random.uniform(-1.0, 1.0)

    if x**2 + y**2 <= 1:
        return 1
    else:
        return 0

pool = multiprocessing.Pool()
results_async = [pool.apply_async(sample) for i in range(samples)]
hits = sum(r.get() for r in results_async)
```

We can wrap the two versions in the `pi_serial` and `pi_apply_async` functions (you can find their implementation in the `pi.py` file) and benchmark the execution speed, as follows:

```
$ time python -c 'import pi; pi.pi_serial()'
real    0m0.734s
user    0m0.731s
sys     0m0.004s
$ time python -c 'import pi; pi.pi_apply_async()'
real    1m36.989s
user    1m55.984s
sys     0m50.386
```

As shown in the earlier benchmark, our first parallel version literally cripples our code. The reason is that the time spent doing the actual calculation is small compared to the overhead required to send and distribute the tasks to the workers.

To solve the issue, we have to make the overhead negligible compared to the calculation time. For example, we can ask each worker to handle more than one sample at a time, thus reducing the task communication overhead. We can write a `sample_multiple` function that processes more than one hit and modifies our parallel version by dividing our problem by 10; more intensive tasks are shown in the following code:

```
def sample_multiple(samples_partial):
    return sum(sample() for i in range(samples_partial))

n_tasks = 10
chunk_size = samples/n_tasks
pool = multiprocessing.Pool()
results_async = [pool.apply_async(sample_multiple, chunk_size)
                 for i in range(n_tasks)]
hits = sum(r.get() for r in results_async)
```

We can wrap this in a function called `pi_apply_async_chunked` and run it as follows:

```
$ time python -c 'import pi; pi.pi_apply_async_chunked()'
real    0m0.325s
user    0m0.816s
sys     0m0.008s
```

The results are much better; we more than doubled the speed of our program. You can also notice that the `user` metric is larger than `real`; the total CPU time is larger than the total time because more than one CPU worked at the same time. If you increase the number of samples, you will note that the ratio of communication to calculation decreases, giving even better speedups.

Everything is nice and simple when dealing with embarrassingly parallel problems. However, sometimes you have to share data between processes.

Synchronization and locks

Even if `multiprocessing` uses processes (with their own independent memory), it lets you define certain variables and arrays as shared memory. You can define a shared variable using `multiprocessing.Value`, passing its data type as a string (`i` integer, `d` double, `f` float, and so on). You can update the content of the variable through the `value` attribute, as shown in the following code snippet:

```
shared_variable = multiprocessing.Value('f')
shared_variable.value = 0
```

When using shared memory, you should be aware of concurrent accesses. Imagine that you have a shared integer variable and each process increments its value multiple times. You will define a process class as follows:

```
class Process(multiprocessing.Process):

    def __init__(self, counter):
        super(Process, self).__init__()
        self.counter = counter

    def run(self):
        for i in range(1000):
            self.counter.value += 1
```

You can initialize the shared variable in the main program and pass it to 4 processes, as shown in the following code:

```
def main():
    counter = multiprocessing.Value('i', lock=True)
    counter.value = 0

    processes = [Process(counter) for i in range(4)]
    [p.start() for p in processes]
    [p.join() for p in processes] # processes are done
    print(counter.value)
```

If you run this program (`shared.py` in the code directory), you will note that the final value of `counter` is not 4000, but it has random values (on my machine, they are between 2000 and 2500). If we assume that the arithmetic is correct, we can conclude that there's a problem with the parallelization.

What happens is that multiple processes are trying to access the same shared variable at the same time. The situation is best explained by looking at the following figure. In a serial execution, the first process reads (the number 0), increments it, and writes the new value (1); the second process reads the new value (1), increments it, and writes it again (2).

In the parallel execution, the two processes read (0), increment it, and write the value (1) at the same time, leading to a wrong answer:

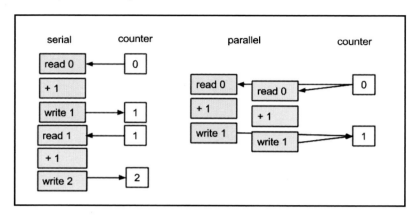

To solve this problem, we need to synchronize the access to this variable so that only one process at a time can access, increment, and write the value on the shared variable. This feature is provided by the multiprocessing.Lock class. A lock can be acquired and released through the acquire method and release, or using the lock as a context manager. Since the lock can be acquired by only one process at a time, this method prevents multiple processes from executing the protected section of code at the same time.

We can define a global lock and use it as a context manager to restrict the access to the counter, as shown in the following code snippet:

```python
lock = multiprocessing.Lock()

class Process(multiprocessing.Process):

    def __init__(self, counter):
        super(Process, self).__init__()
        self.counter = counter

    def run(self):
        for i in range(1000):
            with lock: # acquire the lock
                self.counter.value += 1
            # release the lock
```

Synchronization primitives, such as locks, are essential to solve many problems, but they should be kept to a minimum to improve the performance of your program.

 The `multiprocessing` module includes other communication and synchronization tools; you can refer to the official documentation at http ://docs.python.org/3/library/multiprocessing.html for a complete reference.

Parallel Cython with OpenMP

Cython provides a convenient interface to perform shared-memory parallel processing through **OpenMP**. This lets you write extremely efficient parallel code directly in Cython without having to create a C wrapper.

OpenMP is a specification and an API designed to write multithreaded, parallel programs. The OpenMP specification includes a series of C preprocessor directives to manage threads and provides communication patterns, load balancing, and other synchronization features. Several C/C++ and Fortran compilers (including GCC) implement the OpenMP API.

We can introduce the Cython parallel features with a small example. Cython provides a simple API based on OpenMP in the `cython.parallel` module. The simplest way to achieve parallelism is through `prange`, which is a construct that automatically distributes loop operations in multiple threads.

First of all, we can write the serial version of a program that computes the square of each element of a NumPy array in the `hello_parallel.pyx` file. We define a function, `square_serial`, that takes a buffer as input and populates an output array with the squares of the input array elements; `square_serial` is shown in the following code snippet:

```
import numpy as np

def square_serial(double[:] inp):
    cdef int i, size
    cdef double[:] out
    size = inp.shape[0]
    out_np = np.empty(size, 'double')
    out = out_np

    for i in range(size):
        out[i] = inp[i]*inp[i]

    return out_np
```

Implementing a parallel version of the loop over the array elements involves substituting the range call with prange. There's a caveat--to use prange, it is necessary that the body of the loop is interpreter-free. As already explained, we need to release the GIL and, since interpreter calls generally acquire the GIL, they need to be avoided to make use of threads.

In Cython, you can release the GIL using the nogil context, as follows:

```
with nogil:
    for i in prange(size):
        out[i] = inp[i]*inp[i]
```

Alternatively, you can use the option nogil=True of prange that will automatically wrap the loop body in a nogil block:

```
for i in prange(size, nogil=True):
    out[i] = inp[i]*inp[i]
```

Attempts to call Python code in a prange block will produce an error. Prohibited operations include function calls, objects initialization, and so on. To enable such operations in a prange block (you may want to do so for debugging purposes), you have to re-enable the GIL using the with gil statement:

```
for i in prange(size, nogil=True):
    out[i] = inp[i]*inp[i]
    with gil:
        x = 0 # Python assignment
```

We can now test our code by compiling it as a Python extension module. To enable OpenMP support, it is necessary to change the setup.py file so that it includes the compilation option -fopenmp . This can be achieved by using the distutils.extension.Extension class in distutils and passing it to cythonize. The complete setup.py file is as follows:

```
from distutils.core import setup
from distutils.extension import Extension
from Cython.Build import cythonize

hello_parallel = Extension('hello_parallel',
                           ['hello_parallel.pyx'],
                           extra_compile_args=['-fopenmp'],
                           extra_link_args=['-fopenmp'])

setup(
    name='Hello',
    ext_modules = cythonize(['cevolve.pyx', hello_parallel]),
)
```

Using `prange`, we can easily parallelize the Cython version of our `ParticleSimulator`. The following code contains the `c_evolve` function of the `cevolve.pyx` Cython module that was written in `Chapter 4`, *C Performance with Cython*:

```
def c_evolve(double[:, :] r_i,double[:] ang_speed_i,
             double timestep,int nsteps):

    # cdef declarations

    for i in range(nsteps):
        for j in range(nparticles):
            # loop body
```

First, we will invert the order of the loops so that the outermost loop will be executed in parallel (each iteration is independent from the other). Since the particles don't interact with each other, we can change the order of iteration safely, as shown in the following snippet:

```
    for j in range(nparticles):
        for i in range(nsteps):

            # loop body
```

Next, we will replace the `range` call of the outer loop with `prange` and remove calls that acquire the GIL. Since our code was already enhanced with static types, the `nogil` option can be applied safely as follows:

```
    for j in prange(nparticles, nogil=True)
```

We can now compare the functions by wrapping them in the benchmark function to assess any performance improvement:

```
In [3]: %timeit benchmark(10000, 'openmp') # Running on 4 processors
1 loops, best of 3: 599 ms per loop
In [4]: %timeit benchmark(10000, 'cython')
1 loops, best of 3: 1.35 s per loop
```

Interestingly, we achieved a 2x speedup by writing a parallel version using `prange`.

Automatic parallelism

As we mentioned earlier, normal Python programs have trouble achieving thread parallelism because of the GIL. So far, we worked around this problem using separate processes; starting a process, however, takes significantly more time and memory than starting a thread.

We also saw that sidestepping the Python environment allowed us to achieve a 2x speedup on an already fast Cython code. This strategy allowed us to achieve lightweight parallelism but required a separate compilation step. In this section, we will further explore this strategy using special libraries that are capable of automatically translating our code into a parallel version for efficient execution.

Examples of packages that implement automatic parallelism are the (by now) familiar JIT compilers `numexpr` and Numba. Other packages have been developed to automatically optimize and parallelize array and matrix-intensive expressions, which are crucial in specific numerical and machine learning applications.

Theano is a project that allows you to define a mathematical expression on arrays (more generally, *tensors*), and compile them to a fast language, such as C or C++. Many of the operations that Theano implements are parallelizable and can run on both CPU and GPU.

Tensorflow is another library that, similar to Theano, is targeted towards expression of array-intensive mathematical expression but, rather than translating the expressions to specialized C code, executes the operations on an efficient C++ engine.

Both Theano and Tensorflow are ideal when the problem at hand can be expressed in a chain of matrix and element-wise operations (such as *neural networks*).

Getting started with Theano

Theano is somewhat similar to a compiler but with the added bonuses of being able to express, manipulate, and optimize mathematical expressions as well as run code on CPU and GPU. Since 2010, Theano has improved release after release and has been adopted by several other Python projects as a way to automatically generate efficient computational models on the fly.

In Theano, you first *define* the function you want to run by specifying variables and transformation using a pure Python API. This specification will then be compiled to machine code for execution.

As a first example, let's examine how to implement a function that computes the square of a number. The input will be represented by a scalar variable, a, and then we will transform it to obtain its square, indicated by a_sq. In the following code, we will use the T.scalar function to define the variable and use the normal ** operator to obtain a new variable:

```
import theano.tensor as T
import theano as th
a = T.scalar('a')
a_sq = a ** 2
```

```
print(a_sq)
# Output:
# Elemwise{pow,no_inplace}.0
```

As you can see, no specific value is computed and the transformation we apply is purely symbolic. In order to use this transformation, we need to generate a function. To compile a function, you can use the `th.function` utility that takes a list of the input variables as its first argument, and the output transformation (in our case `a_sq`) as its second argument:

```
compute_square = th.function([a], a_sq)
```

Theano will take some time and translate the expression to efficient C code and compile it, all in the background! The return value of `th.function` will be a ready-to-use Python function and its usage is demonstrated in the next line of code:

```
compute_square(2)
4.0
```

Unsurprisingly, `compute_square` correctly returns the input value squared. Note, however, that the return type is not an integer (like the input type) but a floating point number. This is because the Theano default variable type is `float64`. you can verify that by inspecting the `dtype` attribute of the `a` variable:

```
a.dtype
# Result:
# float64
```

The Theano behavior is very different compared to what we saw with Numba. Theano doesn't compile generic Python code and, also, doesn't do any type inference; defining Theano functions requires a more precise specification of the types involved.

The real power of Theano comes from its support for array expressions. Defining a one-dimensional vector can be done with the `T.vector` function; the returned variable supports broadcasting operations with the same semantics of NumPy arrays. For instance, we can take two vectors and compute the element-wise sum of their squares, as follows:

```
a = T.vector('a')
b = T.vector('b')
ab_sq = a**2 + b**2
compute_square = th.function([a, b], ab_sq)

compute_square([0, 1, 2], [3, 4, 5])
# Result:
# array([  9.,   17.,   29.])
```

The idea is, again, to use the Theano API as a mini-language to combine various Numpy array expressions will be compiled to efficient machine code.

 One of the selling points of Theano is its ability to perform arithmetic simplifications and automatic gradient calculations. For more information, refer to the official documentation (http://deeplearning.net/software/theano/introduction.html).

To demonstrate Theano functionality on a familiar use case, we can implement our parallel calculation of pi again. Our function will take a collection of two random coordinates as input and return the `pi` estimate. The input random numbers will be defined as vectors named `x` and `y`, and we can test their position inside the circle using standard element-wise operation that we will store in the `hit_test` variable:

```
x = T.vector('x')
y = T.vector('y')

hit_test = x ** 2 + y ** 2 < 1
```

At this point, we need to count the number of `True` elements in `hit_test`, which can be done taking its sum (it will be implicitly cast to integer). To obtain the pi estimate, we finally need to calculate the ratio of hits versus the total number of trials. The calculation is illustrated in the following code block:

```
hits = hit_test.sum()
total = x.shape[0]
pi_est = 4 * hits/total
```

We can benchmark the execution of the Theano implementation using `th.function` and the `timeit` module. In our test, we will pass two arrays of size 30,000 and use the `timeit.timeit` utility to execute the `calculate_pi` function multiple times:

```
calculate_pi = th.function([x, y], pi_est)

x_val = np.random.uniform(-1, 1, 30000)
y_val = np.random.uniform(-1, 1, 30000)

import timeit
res = timeit.timeit("calculate_pi(x_val, y_val)",
"from __main__ import x_val, y_val, calculate_pi", number=100000)
print(res)
# Output:
# 10.905971487998613
```

The serial execution of this function takes about 10 seconds. Theano is capable of automatically parallelizing the code by implementing element-wise and matrix operations using specialized packages, such as OpenMP and the **Basic Linear Algebra Subprograms (BLAS)** linear algebra routines. Parallel execution can be enabled using configuration options.

In Theano, you can set up configuration options by modifying variables in the `theano.config` object at import time. For example, you can issue the following commands to enable OpenMP support:

```
import theano
theano.config.openmp = True
theano.config.openmp_elemwise_minsize = 10
```

The parameters relevant to OpenMP are as follows:

- `openmp_elemwise_minsize`: This is an integer number that represents the minimum size of the arrays where element-wise parallelization should be enabled (the overhead of the parallelization can harm performance for small arrays)
- `openmp`: This is a Boolean flag that controls the activation of OpenMP compilation (it should be activated by default)

Controlling the number of threads assigned for OpenMP execution can be done by setting the `OMP_NUM_THREADS` environmental variable before executing the code.

We can now write a simple benchmark to demonstrate the OpenMP usage in practice. In a file `test_theano.py`, we will put the complete code for the pi estimation example:

```
# File: test_theano.py
import numpy as np
import theano.tensor as T
import theano as th
th.config.openmp_elemwise_minsize = 1000
th.config.openmp = True

x = T.vector('x')
y = T.vector('y')

hit_test = x ** 2 + y ** 2 <= 1
hits = hit_test.sum()
misses = x.shape[0]
pi_est = 4 * hits/misses

calculate_pi = th.function([x, y], pi_est)
```

```
x_val = np.random.uniform(-1, 1, 30000)
y_val = np.random.uniform(-1, 1, 30000)

import timeit
res = timeit.timeit("calculate_pi(x_val, y_val)",
                    "from __main__ import x_val, y_val,
                    calculate_pi", number=100000)
print(res)
```

At this point, we can run the code from the command line and assess the scaling with an increasing number of threads by setting the OMP_NUM_THREADS environment variable:

```
$ OMP_NUM_THREADS=1 python test_theano.py
10.905971487998613
$ OMP_NUM_THREADS=2 python test_theano.py
7.538279129999864
$ OMP_NUM_THREADS=3 python test_theano.py
9.405846934998408
$ OMP_NUM_THREADS=4 python test_theano.py
14.634153957000308
```

Interestingly, there is a small speedup when using two threads, but the performance degrades quickly as we increase their number. This means that for this input size, it is not advantageous to use more than two threads as the price you pay to start new threads and synchronize their shared data is higher than the speedup that you can obtain from the parallel execution.

Achieving good parallel performance can be tricky as it will depend on the specific operations and how they access the underlying data. As a general rule, measuring the performance of a parallel program is crucial and obtaining substantial speedups is a work of trial and error.

As an example, we can see that the parallel performance quickly degrades using a slightly different code. In our hit test, we used the sum method directly and relied on the explicit casting of the hit_tests Boolean array. If we make the cast explicit, Theano will generate a slightly different code that benefits less from multiple threads. We can modify the test_theano.py file to verify this effect:

```
# Older version
# hits = hit_test.sum()
hits = hit_test.astype('int32').sum()
```

If we rerun our benchmark, we see that the number of threads does not affect the running time significantly. Despite that, the timings improved considerably as compared to the original version:

```
$ OMP_NUM_THREADS=1 python test_theano.py
5.822126664999814
$ OMP_NUM_THREADS=2 python test_theano.py
5.697357518001809
$ OMP_NUM_THREADS=3 python test_theano.py
5.636914656002773
$ OMP_NUM_THREADS=4 python test_theano.py
5.764030176000233
```

Profiling Theano

Given the importance of measuring and analyzing performance, Theano provides powerful and informative profiling tools. To generate profiling data, the only modification needed is the addition of the `profile=True` option to `th.function`:

```
calculate_pi = th.function([x, y], pi_est, profile=True)
```

The profiler will collect data as the function is being run (for example, through `timeit` or direct invocation). The profiling summary can be printed to output by issuing the `summary` command, as follows:

```
calculate_pi.profile.summary()
```

To generate profiling data, we can rerun our script after adding the `profile=True` option (for this experiment, we will set the `OMP_NUM_THREADS` environmental variable to 1). Also, we will revert our script to the version that performed the casting of `hit_tests` implicitly.

You can also set up profiling globally using the `config.profile` option.

The output printed by `calculate_pi.profile.summary()` is quite long and informative. A part of it is reported in the next block of text. The output is comprised of three sections that refer to timings sorted by `Class`, `Ops`, and `Apply`. In our example, we are concerned with `Ops`, which roughly maps to the functions used in the Theano compiled code. As you can see, roughly 80% of the time is spent in taking the element-wise square and sum of the two numbers, while the rest of the time is spent calculating the sum:

```
Function profiling
==================
  Message: test_theano.py:15

... other output
Time in 100000 calls to Function.__call__: 1.015549e+01s
... other output

Class
---
<% time> <sum %> <apply time> <time per call> <type> <#call> <#apply>
<Class name>
.... timing info by class

Ops
---
<% time> <sum %> <apply time> <time per call> <type> <#call> <#apply> <Op
name>
   80.0%    80.0%         6.722s          6.72e-05s    C    100000          1
Elemwise{Composite{LT((sqr(i0) + sqr(i1)), i2)}}
   19.4%    99.4%         1.634s          1.63e-05s    C    100000          1
Sum{acc_dtype=int64}
    0.3%    99.8%         0.027s          2.66e-07s    C    100000          1
Elemwise{Composite{((i0 * i1) / i2)}}
    0.2%   100.0%         0.020s          2.03e-07s    C    100000          1
Shape_i{0}
   ... (remaining 0 Ops account for   0.00%(0.00s) of the runtime)

Apply
------
<% time> <sum %> <apply time> <time per call> <#call> <id> <Apply name>
... timing info by apply
```

This information is consistent with what was found in our first benchmark. The code went from about 11 seconds to roughly 8 seconds when two threads were used. From these numbers, we can analyze how the time was spent.

Out of these 11 seconds, 80% of the time (about 8.8 seconds) was spent doing element-wise operations. This means that, in perfectly parallel conditions, the increase in speed by adding two threads will be 4.4 seconds. In this scenario, the theoretical execution time will be 6.6 seconds. Considering that we obtained a timing of about 8 seconds, it looks like there is some extra overhead (1.4 seconds) for the thread usage.

Tensorflow

Tensorflow is another library designed for fast numerical calculations and automatic parallelism. It was released as an open source project by Google in 2015. Tensorflow works by building mathematical expressions similar to Theano, except that the computation is not compiled to machine code but is executed on an external engine written in C++. Tensorflow supports execution and deployment of parallel codes on one or more CPUs and GPUs.

The usage of Tensorflow is quite similar to that of Theano. To create a variable in Tensorflow, you can use the `tf.placeholder` function that takes a data type as input:

```
import tensorflow as tf

a = tf.placeholder('float64')
```

Tensorflow mathematical expressions can be expressed quite similarly to Theano, except for a few different naming conventions as well as a more restricted support for the NumPy semantics.

Tensorflow doesn't compile functions to C and then machine code like Theano, but serializes the defined mathematical functions (the data structure containing variables and transformations is called **computation graph**) and executes them on specific devices. The configuration of devices and context can be done using the `tf.Session` object.

Once the desired expression is defined, a `tf.Session` needs to be initialized and can be used to execute computation graphs using the `Session.run` method. In the following example, we demonstrate the usage of the Tensorflow API to implement a simple element-wise sum of squares:

```
a = tf.placeholder('float64')
b = tf.placeholder('float64')
ab_sq = a**2 + b**2

with tf.Session() as session:
    result = session.run(ab_sq, feed_dict={a: [0, 1, 2],
                                            b: [3, 4, 5]})
```

```
        print(result)
# Output:
# array([  9.,  17.,  29.])
```

Parallelism in Tensorflow is achieved automatically by its smart execution engine, and it generally works well without much fiddling. However, note that it is mostly suited for deep learning workloads that involve the definition of complex functions that use a lot of matrix multiplications and calculate their gradient.

We can now replicate the estimation of the pi example using Tensorflow capabilities and benchmark its execution speed and parallelism against the Theano implementation. What we will do is this:

- Define our x and y variables and perform a hit test using broadcasted operations.
- Calculate the sum of `hit_tests` using the `tf.reduce_sum` function.
- Initialize a `Session` object with the `inter_op_parallelism_threads` and `intra_op_parallelism_threads` configuration options. These options control the number of threads used for different classes of parallel operations. Note that the first `Session` created with such options sets the number of threads for the whole script (even future `Session` instances).

We can now write a script name, `test_tensorflow.py`, containing the following code. Note that the number of threads is passed as the first argument of the script (`sys.argv[1]`):

```
import tensorflow as tf
import numpy as np
import time
import sys

NUM_THREADS = int(sys.argv[1])
samples = 30000

print('Num threads', NUM_THREADS)
x_data = np.random.uniform(-1, 1, samples)
y_data = np.random.uniform(-1, 1, samples)

x = tf.placeholder('float64', name='x')
y = tf.placeholder('float64', name='y')

hit_tests = x ** 2 + y ** 2 <= 1.0
hits = tf.reduce_sum(tf.cast(hit_tests, 'int32'))

with tf.Session
    (config=tf.ConfigProto
```

```
        (inter_op_parallelism_threads=NUM_THREADS,
         intra_op_parallelism_threads=NUM_THREADS)) as sess:
    start = time.time()
    for i in range(10000):
        sess.run(hits, {x: x_data, y: y_data})
    print(time.time() - start)
```

If we run the script multiple times with different values of NUM_THREADS, we see that the performance is quite similar to Theano and that the speedup increased by parallelization is quite modest:

```
$ python test_tensorflow.py 1
13.059704780578613
$ python test_tensorflow.py 2
11.938535928726196
$ python test_tensorflow.py 3
12.783955574035645
$ python test_tensorflow.py 4
12.158143043518066
```

The main advantage of using software packages such as Tensorflow and Theano is the support for parallel matrix operations that are commonly used in machine learning algorithms. This is very effective because those operations can achieve impressive performance gains on GPU hardware that is designed to perform these operations with high throughput.

Running code on a GPU

In this subsection, we will demonstrate the usage of a GPU with Theano and Tensorflow. As an example, we will benchmark the execution of a very simple matrix multiplication on the GPU and compare it to its running time on a CPU.

 The code in this subsection requires the possession of a GPU. For learning purposes, it is possible to use the Amazon EC2 service (https://aws.amaz on.com/ec2) to request a GPU-enabled instance.

The following code performs a simple matrix multiplication using Theano. We use the T.matrix function to initialize a two-dimensional array, and then we use the T.dot method to perform the matrix multiplication:

```
from theano import function, config
import theano.tensor as T
import numpy as np
```

```
import time

N = 5000

A_data = np.random.rand(N, N).astype('float32')
B_data = np.random.rand(N, N).astype('float32')

A = T.matrix('A')
B = T.matrix('B')

f = function([A, B], T.dot(A, B))

start = time.time()
f(A_data, B_data)

print("Matrix multiply ({}) took {} seconds".format(N, time.time() -
start))
    print('Device used:', config.device)
```

It is possible to ask Theano to execute this code on a GPU by setting the
`config.device=gpu` option. For added convenience, we can set up the configuration value
from the command line using the `THEANO_FLAGS` environmental variable, shown as
follows. After copying the previous code in the `test_theano_matmul.py` file, we can
benchmark the execution time by issuing the following command:

```
$ THEANO_FLAGS=device=gpu python test_theano_gpu.py
Matrix multiply (5000) took 0.4182612895965576 seconds
Device used: gpu
```

We can analogously run the same code on the CPU using the `device=cpu` configuration
option:

```
$ THEANO_FLAGS=device=cpu python test_theano.py
Matrix multiply (5000) took 2.9623231887817383 seconds
Device used: cpu
```

As you can see, the GPU is 7.2 times faster than the CPU version for this example!

For comparison, we may benchmark equivalent code using Tensorflow. The
implementation of a Tensorflow version is reported in the next code snippet. The main
differences with the Theano version are as follows:

- The usage of the `tf.device` config manager that serves to specify the target
  device (`/cpu:0` or `/gpu:0`)

- The matrix multiplication is performed using the `tf.matmul` operator:

```
import tensorflow as tf
import time
import numpy as np
N = 5000

A_data = np.random.rand(N, N)
B_data = np.random.rand(N, N)

# Creates a graph.

with tf.device('/gpu:0'):
    A = tf.placeholder('float32')
    B = tf.placeholder('float32')

    C = tf.matmul(A, B)

with tf.Session() as sess:
    start = time.time()
    sess.run(C, {A: A_data, B: B_data})
    print('Matrix multiply ({}) took: {}'.format(N, time.time() -
start))
```

If we run the `test_tensorflow_matmul.py` script with the appropriate `tf.device` option, we obtain the following timings:

```
# Ran with tf.device('/gpu:0')
Matrix multiply (5000) took: 1.417285680770874

# Ran with tf.device('/cpu:0')
Matrix multiply (5000) took: 2.9646761417388916
```

As you can see, the performance gain is substantial (but not as good as the Theano version) in this simple case.

Another way to achieve automatic GPU computation is the now familiar Numba. With Numba, it is possible to compile Python code to programs that can be run on a GPU. This flexibility allows for advanced GPU programming as well as more simplified interfaces. In particular, Numba makes extremely easy-to-write, GPU-ready, generalized universal functions.

In the next example, we will demonstrate how to write a universal function that applies an exponential function on two numbers and sums the results. As we already saw in Chapter 5, *Exploring Compilers* this can be accomplished using the nb.vectorize function (we'll also specify the cpu target explicitly):

```python
import numba as nb
import math
@nb.vectorize(target='cpu')
def expon_cpu(x, y):
    return math.exp(x) + math.exp(y)
```

The expon_cpu universal function can be compiled for the GPU device using the target='cuda' option. Also, note that it is necessary to specify the input types for CUDA universal functions. The implementation of expon_gpu is as follows:

```python
@nb.vectorize(['float32(float32, float32)'], target='cuda')
def expon_gpu(x, y):
    return math.exp(x) + math.exp(y)
```

We can now benchmark the execution of the two functions by applying the functions on two arrays of size 1,000,000. Also, note that we execute the function before measuring the timings to trigger the Numba just-in-time compilation:

```python
import numpy as np
import time

N = 1000000
niter = 100

a = np.random.rand(N).astype('float32')
b = np.random.rand(N).astype('float32')

# Trigger compilation
expon_cpu(a, b)
expon_gpu(a, b)

# Timing
start = time.time()
for i in range(niter):
    expon_cpu(a, b)
print("CPU:", time.time() - start)

start = time.time()
for i in range(niter):
    expon_gpu(a, b)
print("GPU:", time.time() - start)
# Output:
```

```
# CPU: 2.4762887954711914
# GPU: 0.8668839931488037
```

Thanks to the GPU execution, we were able to achieve a 3x speedup over the CPU version. Note that transferring data on the GPU is quite expensive; therefore, GPU execution becomes advantageous only for very large arrays.

Summary

Parallel processing is an effective way to improve performance on large datasets. Embarrassingly parallel problems are excellent candidates for parallel execution that can be easily implemented to achieve good performance scaling.

In this chapter, we illustrated the basics of parallel programming in Python. We learned how to circumvent Python threading limitation by spawning processes using the tools available in the Python standard library. We also explored how to implement a multithreaded program using Cython and OpenMP.

For more complex problems, we learned how to use the Theano, Tensorflow, and Numba packages to automatically compile array-intensive expressions for parallel execution on CPU and GPU devices.

In the next chapter, we will learn how to write and execute parallel programs on multiple processors and machines using libraries such as dask and PySpark.

8

Distributed Processing

In the last chapter, we introduced the concept of parallel processing and learned how to leverage multicore processors and GPUs. Now, we can step up our game a bit and turn our attention on distributed processing, which involves executing tasks across multiple machines to solve a certain problem.

In this chapter, we will illustrate the challenges, use cases, and examples of how to run code on a cluster of computers. Python offers easy-to-use and reliable packages for distribute processing, which will allow us to implement scalable and fault-tolerant code with relative ease.

The list of topics for this chapter is as follows:

- Distributed computing and the MapReduce model
- Directed Acyclic Graphs with Dask
- Writing parallel code with Dask's `array`, `Bag`, and `DataFrame` data structures
- Distributing parallel algorithms with Dask Distributed
- An introduction to PySpark
- Spark's Resilient Distributed Datasets and DataFrame
- Scientific computing with `mpi4py`

Introduction to distributed computing

In today's world, computers, smartphones, and other devices have become an integral part of our lives. Every day, massive quantities of data is produced. Billions of people access services on the Internet, and companies are constantly collecting data to learn about their users to better target products and improve user experience.

Handling this ever increasing amount of data presents substantial challenges. Large companies and organizations often build clusters of machines designed to store, process, and analyze large and complex datasets. Similar datasets are also produced in data-intensive fields such as environmental sciences and health care. These large-scale datasets have been recently called **big data**. The analysis techniques applied to big data usually involve a combination of machine learning, information retrieval, and visualization.

Computing clusters have been used for decades in scientific computing, where the study of complex problems requires the use of parallel algorithms executed on high-performance distributed systems. For such applications, universities and other organizations provide and manage supercomputers for research and engineering purposes. Applications that run on supercomputers are generally focused on highly numerical workloads, such as protein and molecular simulations, quantum mechanical calculations, climate models, and much more.

The challenges of programming for distributed systems are apparent if we think back on how the cost of communication increases as we distribute data and computational tasks across a local network. Network transfers are extremely slow compared to the processor speed, and when using distributed processing, it is even more important to keep network communications as limited as possible. This can be achieved using a few different strategies that favor local data processing and resort to data transfers only when strictly necessary.

Other challenges of distributed processing involve the general unreliability of computer networks. When you think that in a computing cluster there may be thousands of machines, it becomes clear that (probabilistically speaking) faulty nodes become very common. For this reason, distributed systems need to be able to handle node failures gracefully and without disrupting the ongoing work. Luckily, companies have invested a great deal of resources in developing fault-tolerant distributed engines that take care of these aspects automatically.

An introduction to MapReduce

MapReduce is a programming model that allows you to express algorithms for efficient execution on a distributed system. The MapReduce model was first introduced by Google in 2004 (`https://research.google.com/archive/mapreduce.html`), as a way to automatically partition datasets over different machines and for automatic local processing and the communication between *cluster nodes*.

The MapReduce framework was used in cooperation with a distributed filesystem, the **Google File System** (GFS or GoogleFS), which was designed to partition and replicate data across the computing cluster. Partitioning was useful for storing and processing datasets that wouldn't fit on a single node while replication ensured that the system was able to handle failures gracefully. MapReduce was used by Google, in conjunction with GFS, for indexing of their web pages. Later on, the MapReduce and GFS concepts were implemented by Doug Cutting (at the time, an employee at Yahoo!), resulting in the first versions of the **Hadoop Distributed File System (HDFS)** and Hadoop MapReduce.

The programming model exposed by MapReduce is actually quite simple. The idea is to express the computation as a combination of two, fairly generic, steps: *Map* and *Reduce*. Some readers will probably be familiar with Python's `map` and `reduce` functions; however, in the context of MapReduce, the Map and Reduce steps are capable of representing a broader class of operations.

Map takes a collection of data as input and produces a *transformation* on this data. What is generally emitted by Map is a series of key value pairs that can be passed to a Reduce step. The Reduce step will aggregate items with the same key and apply a function to the collection to form a usually smaller collection of values.

The estimation of *pi*, which was shown in the last chapter, can be trivially converted using a series of Map and Reduce steps. In that case, the input was a collection of pairs of random numbers. The transformation (Map step) was the hit test, and the Reduce step was counting the number of times the hit test was True.

The prototypical example of the MapReduce model is the implementation of a word count; the program takes a series of documents as input, and returns, for each word, the total number of occurrences in the document collection. The following figure illustrates the Map and Reduce steps of the word count program. On the left, we have the input documents. The Map operation will produce a (key, value) entry where the first element is the word and the second element is **1** (that's because every word contributes **1** to the final count).

We then perform the reduce operation to aggregate all the elements of the same key and produce the global count for each of the words. In the figure, we can see how all values of the items with key **the** are summed to produce the final entry (**the, 4**):

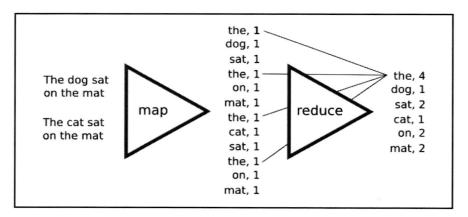

If we implement our algorithm using the Map and Reduce operation, the framework implementation will ensure that data production and aggregation is done efficiently, by limiting the communication between nodes through clever algorithms.

However, how does MapReduce manage to keep communication to a minimum? Let's go through the journey of a MapReduce task. Imagine that you have a cluster with two nodes, and a partition of the data (this is usually found locally in each node) is loaded in each node from disk and is ready for processing. A mapper process is created in each node and processes the data to produce the intermediate results.

Next, it is necessary to send the data to the reducer for further processing. In order to do this, however, it is necessary that all the items that possess the same key are shipped to the same reducer. This operation is called **shuffling** and is the principal communication task in the MapReduce model:

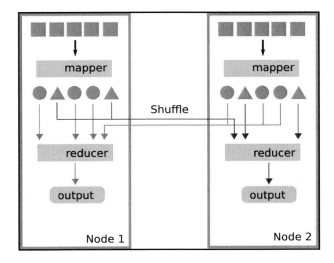

Note that, before the data exchange happens, it is necessary to assign a subset of keys to each reducer; this step is called **partitioning**. Once a reducer receives its own partition of keys, it is free to process data and write the resulting output on disk.

The MapReduce framework (through the Apache Hadoop project) has been extensively used in its original form by many companies and organizations. More recently, new frameworks that extend the ideas introduced by MapReduce have been developed to create systems able to express more complex workflows, to use memory more efficiently and to support a lean and efficient execution of distributed tasks.

In the following sections, we will describe two of the most used libraries in the Python distributed landscape: Dask and PySpark.

Dask

Dask is a project of Continuum Analytics (the same company that's responsible for Numba and the `conda` package manager) and a pure Python library for parallel and distributed computation. It excels at performing data analysis tasks and is very well integrated in the Python ecosystem.

Dask was initially conceived as a package for bigger-than-memory calculations on a single machine. Recently, with the Dask Distributed project, its code has been adapted to execute tasks on a cluster with excellent performance and fault-tolerance capabilities. It supports MapReduce-style tasks as well as complex numerical algorithms.

Directed Acyclic Graphs

The idea behind Dask is quite similar to what we already saw in the last chapter with Theano and Tensorflow. We can use a familiar Pythonic API to build an execution plan, and the framework will automatically split the workflow into tasks that will be shipped and executed on multiple processes or computers.

Dask expresses its variables and operations as a **Directed Acyclic Graph (DAG)** that can be represented through a simple Python dictionary. To briefly illustrate how this works, we will implement the sum of two numbers with Dask. We will define our computational graph by storing the values of our input variables in the dictionary. The a and b input variables will be given a value of 2:

```
dsk = {
  "a" : 2,
  "b" : 2,
}
```

Each variable represents a node in the DAG. The next step necessary to build our DAG is the execution of operations on the nodes we just defined. In Dask, a task can be defined by placing a tuple containing a Python function and its positional arguments in the dsk dictionary. To implement a sum, we can add a new node, named result, (the actual name is completely arbitrary) with a tuple containing the function we intend to execute, followed by its arguments. This is illustrated in the following code:

```
dsk = {
  "a" : 2,
  "b" : 2,
  "result": (lambda x, y: x + y, "a", "b")
}
```

For better style and clarity, we can calculate the sum by replacing the lambda statement with the standard operator.add library function:

```
from operator import add
dsk = {
  "a" : 2,
  "b" : 2,
  "result": (add, "a", "b")
}
```

It's important to note that the arguments we intend to pass to the function are the `"a"` and `"b"` strings, which refer to the a and b nodes in the graph. Note that we didn't use any Dask-specific functions to define the DAG; this is the first indication of how the framework is flexible and lean since all manipulations are performed on simple and familiar Python dictionaries.

The execution of tasks is performed by a scheduler, which is a function that takes a DAG and the task or tasks we'd like to perform and returns the computed value. The default Dask scheduler is the `dask.get` function, which can be used as follows:

```
import dask

res = dask.get(dsk, "result")
print(res)
# Output:
# 4
```

All the complexity is hidden behind the scheduler, which will take care of distributing the tasks across threads, processes, or even different machines. The `dask.get` scheduler is a synchronous and serial implementation that is useful for testing and debugging purposes.

Defining graphs using a simple dictionary is useful to understand how Dask does its magic and for debugging purposes. Raw dictionaries can also be used to implement more complex algorithms not covered by the Dask API. Now, we will learn how Dask is capable of generating tasks automatically through a familiar NumPy- and Pandas-like interface.

Dask arrays

One of the main use-cases of Dask is the automatic generation of parallel array operations, which greatly simplifies the handling of arrays that don't fit into memory. The strategy employed by Dask is to split the array into a number of subunits that, in Dask array terminology, are called **chunks**.

Dask implement a NumPy-like interface for arrays in the `dask.array` module (which we will abbreviate as da). An array can be created from a NumPy-like array using the `da.from_array` function, which requires the specification of a chunk size. The `da.from_array` function will return a `da.array` object that will handle the splitting of the original array into subunits of the specified chunk size. In the following example, we create an array of 30 elements, and we split it into chunks with 10 elements each:

```
import numpy as np
import dask.array as da
```

```
a = np.random.rand(30)

a_da = da.from_array(a, chunks=10)
# Result:
# dask.array<array-4..., shape=(30,), dtype=float64, chunksize=(10,)>
```

The a_da variable maintains a Dask graph that can be accessed using the dask attribute. To understand what Dask does under the hood, we can inspect its content. In the following example, we can see that the Dask graph contains four nodes. One of them is the source array, denoted by the 'array-original-4c76' key, the other three keys in the a_da.dask dictionary are tasks that are used to access a chunk of the original array using the dask.array.core.getarray function and, as you can see, each task extracts a slice of 10 elements:

```
dict(a_da.dask)
# Result
{('array-4c76', 0): (<function dask.array.core.getarray>,
                     'array-original-4c76',
                     (slice(0, 10, None),)),
 ('array-4c76', 2): (<function dask.array.core.getarray>,
                     'array-original-4c76',
                     (slice(20, 30, None),)),
 ('array-4c76', 1): (<function dask.array.core.getarray>,
                     'array-original-4c76',
                     (slice(10, 20, None),)),
 'array-original-4c76': array([ ... ])
}
```

If we perform an operation on the a_da array, Dask will generate more subtasks that operate on the smaller chunks, opening the possibility of achieving parallelism. The interface exposed by da.array is compatible with common NumPy semantics and broadcasting rules. The complete code, shown as follows, demonstrates the good compatibility of Dask with NumPy broadcasting rules, element-wise operations, and other methods:

```
N = 10000
chunksize = 1000

x_data = np.random.uniform(-1, 1, N)
y_data = np.random.uniform(-1, 1, N)

x = da.from_array(x_data, chunks=chunksize)
y = da.from_array(y_data, chunks=chunksize)

hit_test = x ** 2 + y ** 2 < 1
```

```
hits = hit_test.sum()
pi = 4 * hits / N
```

The value of pi can be calculated using the `compute` method, which can also be called with the `get` optional argument to specify a different scheduler (by default, `da.array` uses a multithreaded scheduler):

```
pi.compute() # Alternative: pi.compute(get=dask.get)
# Result:
# 3.1804000000000001
```

Even deceptively simple algorithms, such as the estimation of pi, may require a lot of tasks to be executed. Dask provides utilities to visualize the computational graph. The following figure shows part of the Dask graph for the estimation of pi, which can be obtained by executing the method `pi.visualize()`. In the graph, circles refer to transformations that get applied on the nodes, which are represented as rectangles. This example helps us to get a feel of the complexity of the Dask graph and to appreciate the scheduler's job of creating an efficient execution plan that includes proper ordering of tasks and the selection of tasks that will be executed in parallel:

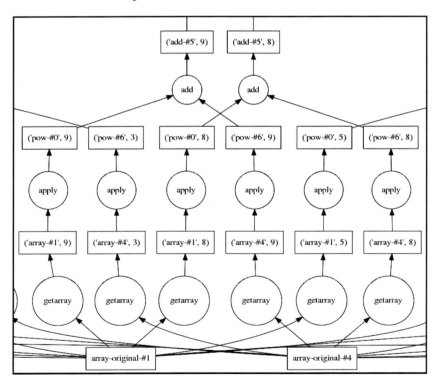

Dask Bag and DataFrame

Dask provides other data structures for automatic generation of computation graphs. In this subsection, we'll take a look at `dask.bag.Bag`, a generic collection of elements that can be used to code MapReduce-style algorithms, and `dask.dataframe.DataFrame`, a distributed version of `pandas.DataFrame`.

A `Bag` can be easily created from a Python collection. For example, you can create a `Bag` from a list using the `from_sequence` factory function. The level of parallelism can be specified using the `npartitions` argument (this will distribute the `Bag` content into a number of partitions). In the following example, we create a `Bag` containing numbers from `0` to `99`, partitioned into four chunks:

```
import dask.bag as dab
dab.from_sequence(range(100), npartitions=4)
# Result:
# dask.bag<from_se..., npartitions=4>
```

In the next example, we will demonstrate how to perform a word count of a set of strings using an algorithm that's similar to MapReduce. Given our collection of sequences, we apply `str.split`, followed by `concat` to obtain a linear list of words in the documents. Then, for each word, we produce a dictionary that contains a word and the value 1 (refer to the *An introduction to MapReduce* section for an illustration). We then write a *Reduce* step using the `foldby` operator to calculate the word count.

The `foldby` transformation is useful to implement a Reduce step that combines the word counts without having to shuffle all the elements over the network. Imagine that our word dataset is divided into two partitions. A good strategy to calculate the total count is to first sum the word occurrences in each partition and then combine those partial sums to get the final result. The following figure illustrates the concept. On the left, we have our input partitions. The partial sum is calculated for each individual partition (this is done using a binary operation, **binop**), and then the final sums are computed by combining the partial sums using a **combine** function.

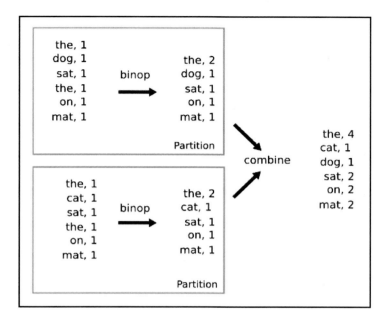

The following code illustrates how to use `Bag` and the `foldby` operator to compute the word count. For the `foldby` operator, we need to define two functions that take five arguments:

- `key`: This is a function that returns the key for the reduce operation.
- `binop`: This is a function that takes two arguments: `total` and `x`. Given a `total` value (the values accumulated so far), `binop` incorporates the next item into the total.
- `initial`: This is the initial value for the `binop` accumulation.
- `combine`: This is a function that combines the totals for each partition (in this case it is a simple sum).
- `initial_combine`: This is the initial value for the `combine` accumulation.

Now, let's look at the code:

```
collection = dab.from_sequence(["the cat sat on the mat",
                               "the dog sat on the mat"],
  npartitions=2)

binop = lambda total, x: total + x["count"]
combine = lambda a, b: a + b
(collection
 .map(str.split)
```

```
    .concat()
    .map(lambda x: {"word": x, "count": 1})
    .foldby(lambda x: x["word"], binop, 0, combine, 0)
    .compute())
# Output:
# [('dog', 1), ('cat', 1), ('sat', 2), ('on', 2), ('mat', 2), ('the',
4)]
```

As we just saw, expressing complex operations in an efficient way using `Bag` can become cumbersome. For this reason, Dask provides another data structure designed for analytical workloads--`dask.dataframe.DataFrame`. A `DataFrame` can be initialized in Dask using a variety of methods, such as from `CSV` files on distributed filesystems, or directly from a `Bag`. Just like `da.array` provides an API that closely mirrors NumPy features, Dask `DataFrame` can be used as a distributed version of `pandas.DataFrame`.

As a demonstration, we will re-implement the word count using a `DataFrame`. We first load the data to obtain a `Bag` of words, and then we convert the `Bag` to a `DataFrame` using the `to_dataframe` method. By passing a column name to the `to_dataframe` method, we can initialize a `DataFrame`, which contains a single column, named `words`:

```
collection = dab.from_sequence(["the cat sat on the mat",
                               "the dog sat on the mat"],
npartitions=2)
words = collection.map(str.split).concat()
df = words.to_dataframe(['words'])
df.head()
# Result:
#    words
# 0    the
# 1    cat
# 2    sat
# 3     on
# 4    the
```

Dask `DataFrame` closely replicates the `pandas.DataFrame` API. To compute the word count, we only need to call the `value_counts` method on the words column, and Dask will automatically devise a parallel computation strategy. To trigger the calculation, it is sufficient to call the `compute` method:

```
df.words.value_counts().compute()
# Result:
# the    4
# sat    2
# on     2
# mat    2
# dog    1
```

```
#  cat       1
#  Name:  words,  dtype:  int64
```

An interesting question one may ask is *"what kind of algorithm does DataFrame use under the hood?"*. The answer can be found by looking at the upper part of the generated Dask graph, which is displayed in the following figure. The first two rectangles at the bottom represent two partitions of the dataset, which are stored as two pd.Series instances. To calculate the overall count, Dask will first execute value_counts on each of the pd.Series and then combine the counts along with the value_counts_aggregate step:

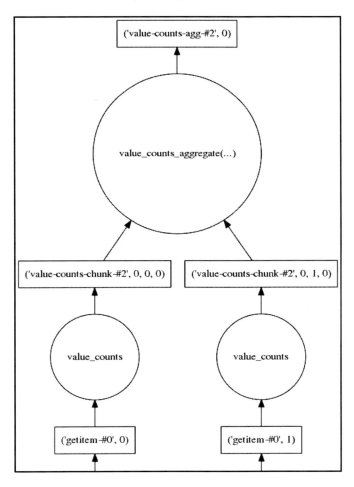

As you can see, both Dask `array` and `DataFrame` take advantage of the fast vectorized implementations of NumPy and Pandas to achieve excellent performance and stability.

Dask distributed

The first iterations of the Dask project were designed to run on a single computer using a thread-based or a process-based scheduler. Recently, the implementation of a new distributed backend can be used to set up and run Dask graphs on a network of computers.

 Dask distributed is not installed automatically with Dask. The library is available through the `conda` package manager (use the `$ conda install distributed` command) as well as `pip` (with the `$ pip install distributed` command).

Getting started with Dask distributed is really easy. The most basic setup is obtained by instantiating a `Client` object:

```
from dask.distributed import Client

client = Client()
# Result:
# <Client: scheduler='tcp://127.0.0.1:46472' processes=4 cores=4>
```

By default, Dask will start a few key processes (on the local machine) necessary for scheduling and executing distributed tasks through the `Client` instance. The main components of a Dask cluster are a single *scheduler* and a collection of *workers*.

The **scheduler** is the process responsible for distributing the work across the workers and to monitor and manage the results. Generally, when a task is submitted to the user, the scheduler will find a free worker and submit a task for execution. Once the worker is done, the scheduler is informed that the result is available.

A worker is a process that accepts incoming tasks and produces results. Workers can reside on different machines over the network. Workers execute tasks using `ThreadPoolExecutor`. This can be used to achieve parallelism when using functions that do not acquire the GIL (such as Numpy, Pandas, and Cython functions in `nogil` blocks). When executing pure Python code, it is advantageous to start many single-threaded worker processes as this will enable parallelism for code that acquires the GIL.

The `Client` class can be used to submit tasks manually to the scheduler using familiar asynchronous methods. For example, to submit a function for execution on the cluster, one can use the `Client.map` and `Client.submit` methods. In the following code, we demonstrate the use of `Client.map` and `Client.submit` to calculate the square of a few numbers. The `Client` will submit a series of tasks to the scheduler and we will receive a `Future` instance for each task:

```
def square(x):
    return x ** 2

fut = client.submit(square, 2)
# Result:
# <Future: status: pending, key:
square-05236e00d545104559e0cd20f94cd8ab>

client.map(square)
futs = client.map(square, [0, 1, 2, 3, 4])
# Result:
# [<Future: status: pending, key: square-
d043f00c1427622a694f518348870a2f>,
#  <Future: status: pending, key:
square-9352eac1fb1f6659e8442ca4838b6f8d>,
#    <Future: status: finished, type: int, key:
#    square-05236e00d545104559e0cd20f94cd8ab>,
#    <Future: status: pending, key:
#    square-c89f4c21ae6004ce0fe5206f1a8d619d>,
#    <Future: status: pending, key:
#    square-a66f1c13e2a46762b092a4f2922e9db9>]
```

So far, this is quite similar to what we saw in the earlier chapters with `TheadPoolExecutor` and `ProcessPoolExecutor`. Note however, that Dask Distributed not only submits the tasks, but also caches the computation results on the worker memory. You can see caching in action by looking at the preceding code example. When we first invoke `client.submit`, the `square(2)` task is created and its status is set to *pending*. When we subsequently invoke `client.map`, the `square(2)` task is resubmitted to the scheduler, but this time, rather than recalculating its value, the scheduler directly retrieves the result for the worker. As a result, the third `Future` returned by map already has a finished status.

Results from a collection of `Future` instances can be retrieved using the `Client.gather` method:

```
client.gather(futs)
# Result:
# [0, 1, 4, 9, 16]
```

`Client` can also be used to run arbitrary Dask graphs. For example, we can trivially run our approximation of pi by passing the `client.get` function as an optional argument to `pi.compute`:

```
pi.compute(get=client.get)
```

This feature makes Dask extremely scalable as it is possible to develop and run algorithms on the local machine using one of the simpler schedulers and, in case the performance is not satisfactory, to reuse the same algorithms on a cluster of hundreds of machines.

Manual cluster setup

To instantiate scheduler and workers manually, one can use the `dask-scheduler` and `dask-worker` command-line utilities. First, we can initialize a scheduler using the `dask-scheduler` command:

```
$ dask-scheduler
distributed.scheduler - INFO - ------------------------------------------------
---
distributed.scheduler - INFO - Scheduler at: tcp://192.168.0.102:8786
distributed.scheduler - INFO - bokeh at: 0.0.0.0:8788
distributed.scheduler - INFO - http at: 0.0.0.0:9786
distributed.bokeh.application - INFO - Web UI:
http://127.0.0.1:8787/status/
distributed.scheduler - INFO - ------------------------------------------------
---
```

This will provide an address for the scheduler and a Web UI address that can be accessed to monitor the state of the cluster. Now, we can assign some workers to the scheduler; this can be accomplished using the `dask-worker` command and by passing the address of the scheduler to the worker. This will automatically start a worker with four threads:

```
$ dask-worker 192.168.0.102:8786
distributed.nanny - INFO - Start Nanny at: 'tcp://192.168.0.102:45711'
distributed.worker - INFO - Start worker at: tcp://192.168.0.102:45928
distributed.worker - INFO - bokeh at: 192.168.0.102:8789
distributed.worker - INFO - http at: 192.168.0.102:46154
distributed.worker - INFO - nanny at: 192.168.0.102:45711
```

```
distributed.worker - INFO - Waiting to connect to: tcp://192.168.0.102:8786
distributed.worker - INFO - -----------------------------------------------
--
distributed.worker - INFO - Threads: 4
distributed.worker - INFO - Memory: 4.97 GB
distributed.worker - INFO - Local Directory: /tmp/nanny-jh1esoo7
distributed.worker - INFO - -----------------------------------------------
--
distributed.worker - INFO - Registered to: tcp://192.168.0.102:8786
distributed.worker - INFO - -----------------------------------------------
--
distributed.nanny - INFO - Nanny 'tcp://192.168.0.102:45711' starts worker
process 'tcp://192.168.0.102:45928'
```

The Dask scheduler is fairly resilient in the sense that if we add and remove a worker, it is able to track which results are unavailable and recompute them on-demand. Finally, in order to use the initialized scheduler from a Python session, it is sufficient to initialize a Client instance and provide the address for the scheduler:

```
client = Client(address='192.168.0.102:8786')
# Result:
# <Client: scheduler='tcp://192.168.0.102:8786' processes=1 cores=4>
```

Dask also provides a convenient diagnostic Web UI that can be used to monitor the status and time spent for each of the tasks performed on the cluster. In the next figure, the **Task Stream** shows the time taken for executing the pi estimation. In the plot, each horizontal gray line corresponds to a thread used by the workers (in our case, we have one worker with four threads, also called **Worker Core**), and each rectangular box corresponds to a task, colored so that the same task types have the same color (for example, addition, power, or exponent). From this plot, you can observe how all the boxes are very small and far from each other. This means that the tasks are quite small compared to the overhead of communication.

In this case, an increase in chunk size, which implies to an increase in the time required to run each task compared to the time of communication, will be beneficial.

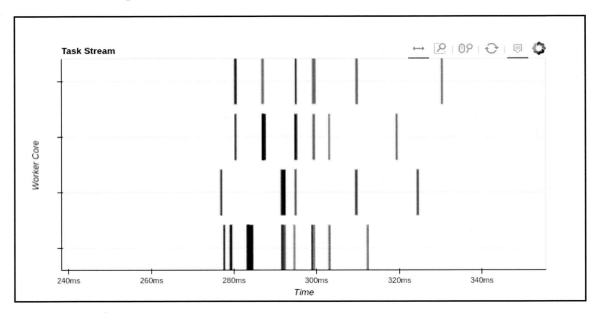

Using PySpark

Nowadays, Apache Spark is one of the most popular projects for distributed computing. Developed in Scala, Spark was released in 2014, and integrates with HDFS and provides several advantages and improvements over the Hadoop MapReduce framework.

Contrary to Hadoop MapReduce, Spark is designed to process data interactively and supports APIs for the Java, Scala, and Python programming languages. Given its different architecture, especially by the fact that Spark keep results in memory, Spark is generally much faster than Hadoop MapReduce.

Setting up Spark and PySpark

Setting up PySpark from scratch requires the installation of the Java and Scala runtimes, the compilation of the project from source, and the configuration of Python and Jupyter notebook so that they can be used alongside the Spark installation. An easier and less error-prone way to set up PySpark is to use an already configured Spark cluster made available through a **Docker** container.

Docker can be downloaded at `https://www.docker.com/`. If you're new to containers, you can read the next chapter for an introduction.

To set up a Spark cluster, it is sufficient to go in this chapter's code files (where a file named `Dockerfile` is located) and issue the following command:

```
$ docker build -t pyspark
```

This command will automatically download, install, and configure Spark, Python, and Jupyter notebook in an isolated environment. To start Spark and a Jupyter notebook session, you can execute the following command:

```
$ docker run -d -p 8888:8888 -p 4040:4040 pyspark
22b9dbc2767c260e525dcbc562b84a399a7f338fe1c06418cbe6b351c998e239
```

The command will print a unique ID (called *container id*) that you can use to reference the application container and will start Spark and Jupyter notebook in the background. The `-p` option ensures that we can access the SparkUI and Jupyter network ports from the local machine. After issuing the command, you can open a browser to `http://127.0.0.1:8888` to access the Jupyter notebook session. You can test the correct initialization of Spark by creating a new notebook and executing the following content inside a cell:

```python
import pyspark
sc = pyspark.SparkContext('local[*]')

rdd = sc.parallelize(range(1000))
rdd.first()
# Result:
# 0
```

This will initialize a `SparkContext` and take the first element in a collection (those new terms will be explained in detail later). Once the `SparkContext` is initialized, we can also head over to `http://127.0.0.1:4040` to open the Spark Web UI.

Now that the setup is complete, we will understand how Spark works and how to implement simple parallel algorithms using its powerful API.

Spark architecture

A Spark cluster is a set of processes distributed over different machines. The **Driver Program** is a process, such as a Scala or Python interpreter, used by the user to submit the tasks to be executed.

The user can build task graphs, similar to Dask, using a special API and submit those tasks to the **Cluster Manager** that is responsible for assigning these tasks to **Executors**, processes responsible for executing the tasks. In a multi-user system, the Cluster Manager is also responsible for allocating resources on a per-user basis.

The user interacts with the Cluster Manager through the Driver Program. The class responsible for communication between the user and the Spark cluster is called `SparkContext`. This class is able to connect and configure the Executors on the cluster based on the resources available to the user.

For its most common use-cases, Spark manages its data through a data structure called **Resilient Distributed Datasets** (**RDD**), which represents a collection of items. RDDs are capable of handling massive datasets by separating their elements into partitions and operating on the partitions in parallel (note that this mechanism is mainly hidden from the user). RDDs can also be stored in memory (optionally, and when appropriate) for fast access and to cache expensive intermediate results.

Using RDDs, it is possible to define tasks and transformations (similarly to how we were automatically generating computation graphs in Dask) and, when requested, the Cluster Manager will automatically dispatch and execute tasks on the available Executors.

The Executors will receive the tasks from the Cluster Manager, execute them, and keep the results around if needed. Note that an Executor can have multiple cores and each node in the cluster may have multiple Executors. Generally speaking, Spark is fault tolerant on Executor's failures.

In the following diagram, we show how the aforementioned components interact in a Spark cluster. The **Driver Program** interacts with the **Cluster Manager** that manages the **Executor** instances on different nodes (each Executor instance can also have multiple threads). Note that, even if the **Driver Program** doesn't directly control the Executors, the results, which are stored in the **Executor** instances, are transferred directly between the Executors and the Driver Program. For this reason, it's important that the **Driver Program** is network-reachable from the **Executor** processes:

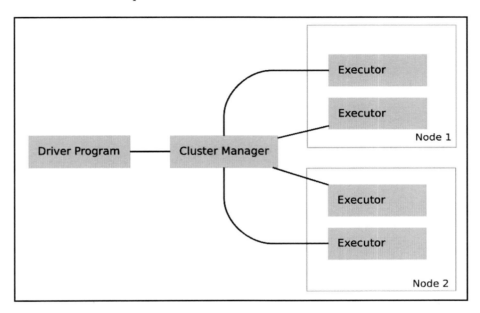

A natural question to ask is: How is Spark, a software written in Scala, able to execute Python code? The integration is done through the Py4J library, which maintains a Python process under-the-hood and communicates with it through sockets (a form of interprocess communication). In order to run the tasks, Executors maintain a series of Python processes so that they are able to process Python code in parallel.

RDDs and variables defined in a Python process in the Driver Program are serialized, and the communication between the Cluster Manager and the Executors (including shuffling) is dealt with by Spark's Scala code. The extra serialization steps necessary for the Python and Scala interchange, all contribute to the overhead of communication; therefore, when using PySpark, extra care must be taken to ensure that the data structures used are serialized efficiently and that the data partitions are big enough so that the cost of communication is negligible compared to the cost of execution.

The following diagram illustrates the additional Python processes needed for PySpark execution. These additional Python processes come with associated memory costs and an extra layer of indirection that complicate error reporting:

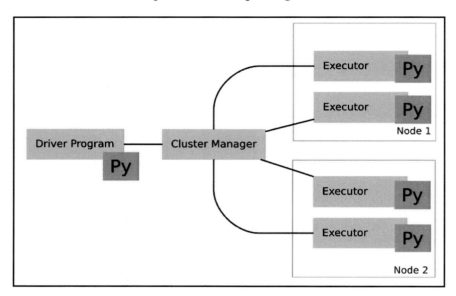

Despite these drawbacks, PySpark is still a widely used tool because it bridges the vivid Python ecosystem with the industrial strength of the Hadoop infrastructure.

Resilient Distributed Datasets

The easiest way to create an RDD in Python is with the `SparkContext.parallelize` method. This method was also used earlier where we parallelized a collection of integers between 0 and 1000:

```
rdd = sc.parallelize(range(1000))
# Result:
# PythonRDD[3] at RDD at PythonRDD.scala:48
```

The `rdd` collection will be divided into a number of partitions which, in this case, correspond to a default value of four (the default value can be changed using configuration options). To explicitly specify the number of partitions, one can pass an extra argument to `parallelize`:

```
rdd = sc.parallelize(range(1000), 2)
rdd.getNumPartitions() # This function will return the number of
```

```
partitions
    # Result:
    # 2
```

RDDs support a lot of functional programming operators, similar to what we used back in Chapter 6, *Implementing Concurrency*, with reactive programming and data streams (even though, in that case, the operators were designed to work on events over time rather than normal collections). For example, we may illustrate the basic map function which, by now, should be quite familiar. In the following code, we use map to calculate the square of a series of numbers:

```
square_rdd = rdd.map(lambda x: x**2)
# Result:
# PythonRDD[5] at RDD at PythonRDD.scala:48
```

The map function will return a new RDD but won't compute anything just yet. In order to trigger the execution, you can use the collect method, which will retrieve all the elements in the collection, or take, which will return only the first ten elements:

```
square_rdd.collect()
# Result:
# [0, 1, ... ]

square_rdd.take(10)
# Result:
# [0, 1, 4, 9, 16, 25, 36, 49, 64, 81]
```

For a comparison between PySpark, Dask, and the other parallel programming libraries we explored in the earlier chapters, we will reimplement the approximation of pi. In the PySpark implementation, we will first create two RDDs of random numbers using parallelize, then we combine the datasets using the zip function (this is equivalent to Python's zip), and we finally test whether the random points are inside the circle:

```
import numpy as np

N = 10000
x = np.random.uniform(-1, 1, N)
y = np.random.uniform(-1, 1, N)

rdd_x = sc.parallelize(x)
rdd_y = sc.parallelize(y)

hit_test = rdd_x.zip(rdd_y).map(lambda xy: xy[0] ** 2 + xy[1] ** 2 < 1)
pi = 4 * hit_test.sum()/N
```

It's important to note that both the `zip` and `map` operations produce new RDDs and do not actually execute the instruction on the underlying data. In the preceding example, code execution is triggered when we call the `hit_test.sum` function, which returns an integer. This behavior is different from the Dask API where the whole computation (including the final result, `pi`) did not trigger the execution.

We can now move on to a more interesting application to demonstrate more RDD methods. We will learn how to count the number of visits each user of a website performs in a day. In a real-world scenario, the data would have been collected in a database and/or stored in a distributed filesystem, such as HDFS. However, in our example, we will generate some data that we will then analyze.

In the following code, we generate a list of dictionaries, each containing a `user` (selected among twenty users) and a `timestamp`. The steps to produce the dataset are as follows:

1. Create a pool of 20 users (the `users` variable).
2. Define a function that returns a random time between two dates.
3. For 10,000 times, we choose a random user from our `users` pool and a random timestamp between the dates January 1, 2017 and January 7, 2017.

```python
import datetime

from uuid import uuid4
from random import randrange, choice

# We generate 20 users
n_users = 20
users = [uuid4() for i in range(n_users)]

def random_time(start, end):
    '''Return a random timestamp between start date and end
    date'''
    # We select a number of seconds
    total_seconds = (end - start).total_seconds()
    return start + \
    datetime.timedelta(seconds=randrange(total_seconds))

start = datetime.datetime(2017, 1, 1)
end = datetime.datetime(2017, 1, 7)

entries = []
N = 10000
for i in range(N):
    entries.append({
      'user': choice(users),
```

```
                   'timestamp': random_time(start, end)
              })
```

With the dataset at hand, we can start asking questions and use PySpark to find the answers. One common question is *"How many times has a given user visited the website?."* A naive way to compute this result can be achieved by grouping the entries RDD by user (using the `groupBy` operator) and counting how many items are present for each user. In PySpark, `groupBy` takes a function as argument to extract the grouping key for each element and returns a new RDD that contain tuples of the (key, group) form. In the following example, we use the user ID as the key for our `groupBy`, and we inspect the first element using `first`:

```
entries_rdd = sc.parallelize(entries)
entries_rdd.groupBy(lambda x: x['user']).first()
# Result:
# (UUID('0604aab5-c7ba-4d5b-b1e0-16091052fb11'),
#  <pyspark.resultiterable.ResultIterable at 0x7faced4cd0b8>)
```

The return value of `groupBy` contains a `ResultIterable` (which is basically a list) for each user ID. To count the number of visits per user, it's sufficient to calculate the length of each `ResultIterable`:

```
(entries_rdd
 .groupBy(lambda x: x['user'])
 .map(lambda kv: (kv[0], len(kv[1])))
 .take(5))
# Result:
# [(UUID('0604aab5-c7ba-4d5b-b1e0-16091052fb11'), 536),
#  (UUID('d72c81c1-83f9-4b3c-a21a-788736c9b2ea'), 504),
#  (UUID('e2e125fa-8984-4a9a-9ca1-b0620b113cdb'), 498),
#  (UUID('b90acaf9-f279-430d-854f-5df74432dd52'), 561),
#  (UUID('00d7be53-22c3-43cf-ace7-974689e9d54b'), 466)]
```

Even though this algorithm may work well in small datasets, `groupBy` requires us to collect and store the whole set of entries for each user in memory, and this can exceed the memory capacity of an individual node. Since we don't need the list but only the count, there's a better way to calculate this number without having to hold the list of visits for each user in memory.

When dealing with an RDD of (key, value) pairs, it is possible to use `mapValues` to apply a function only to the values. In the preceding code, we can replace the `map(lambda kv: (kv[0], len(kv[1])))` call with `mapValues(len)` for better readability.

For a more efficient calculation, we can leverage the `reduceByKey` function, which will perform a step similar to the Reduce step that we saw in the *An introduction to MapReduce* section. The `reduceByKey` function can be called from an RDD of tuples that contain a key as their first element and a value as their second element, and accepts a function as its first argument that will calculate the reduction. A simple example of the `reduceByKey` function is illustrated in the following snippet. We have a few string keys associated with integer numbers, and we want to get the sum of the values for each key; the reduction, expressed as a lambda, corresponds to the sum of the elements:

```
rdd = sc.parallelize([("a", 1), ("b", 2), ("a", 3), ("b", 4), ("c",
5)])
rdd.reduceByKey(lambda a, b: a + b).collect()
# Result:
# [('c', 5), ('b', 6), ('a', 4)]
```

The `reduceByKey` function is much more efficient than `groupBy` because the reduction is parallelizable and doesn't require the in-memory storage of the groups; also, it limits the data shuffled between Executors (it performs similar operations to Dask's `foldby`, which was explained earlier). At this point, we can rewrite our visit count calculation using `reduceByKey`:

```
(entries_rdd
 .map(lambda x: (x['user'], 1))
 .reduceByKey(lambda a, b: a + b)
 .take(3))
# Result:
# [(UUID('0604aab5-c7ba-4d5b-b1e0-16091052fb11'), 536),
#  (UUID('d72c81c1-83f9-4b3c-a21a-788736c9b2ea'), 504),
#  (UUID('e2e125fa-8984-4a9a-9ca1-b0620b113cdb'), 498)]
```

With Spark's RDD API, it is also easy to answer questions such as "*How many visits did the website receive each day?*." This can be computed using `reduceByKey` with the appropriate key (which is the date extracted from the timestamp). In the following example, we demonstrate the calculation. Also, note the usage of the `sortByKey` operator to return the counts sorted by date:

```
(entries_rdd
 .map(lambda x: (x['timestamp'].date(), 1))
 .reduceByKey(lambda a, b: a + b)
 .sortByKey()
 .collect())
# Result:
# [(datetime.date(2017, 1, 1), 1685),
#  (datetime.date(2017, 1, 2), 1625),
#  (datetime.date(2017, 1, 3), 1663),
```

```
#    (datetime.date(2017, 1, 4), 1643),
#    (datetime.date(2017, 1, 5), 1731),
#    (datetime.date(2017, 1, 6), 1653)]
```

Spark DataFrame

For numerical and analytical tasks, Spark provides a convenient interface available through the `pyspark.sql` module (also called SparkSQL). The module includes a `spark.sql.DataFrame` class that can be used for efficient SQL-style queries similar to those of Pandas. Access to the SQL interface is provided through the `SparkSession` class:

```
from pyspark.sql import SparkSession
spark = SparkSession.builder.getOrCreate()
```

`SparkSession` can then be used to create a `DataFrame` through the function `createDataFrame`. The function `createDataFrame` accepts either a RDD, a list, or a `pandas.DataFrame`.

In the following example, we will create a `spark.sql.DataFrame` by converting an RDD, `rows`, which contains a collection of `Row` instances. The `Row` instances represent an association between a set of column names and a set of values, just like a row in a `pd.DataFrame`. In this example, we have two columns--x and y--to which we will associate random numbers:

```
# We will use the x_rdd and y_rdd defined previously.
rows = rdd_x.zip(rdd_y).map(lambda xy: Row(x=float(xy[0]),
y=float(xy[1])))

rows.first() # Inspect the first element
# Result:
# Row(x=0.18432163061239137, y=0.632310101419016)
```

After obtaining our collection of `Row` instances, we can combine them in a `DataFrame`, as follows. We can also inspect the `DataFrame` content using the `show` method:

```
df = spark.createDataFrame(rows)
df.show(5)
# Output:
# +-------------------+--------------------+
# |                  x|                   y|
# +-------------------+--------------------+
# |0.18432163061239137|   0.632310101419016|
# | 0.8159145525577987|  -0.9578448778029829|
# |-0.6565050226033042|   0.4644773453129496|
# |-0.1566191476553318|-0.11542211978216432|
# | 0.7536730082381564|  0.26953055476074717|
# +-------------------+--------------------+
# only showing top 5 rows
```

`spark.sql.DataFrame` supports performing transformations on the distributed dataset using a convenient SQL syntax. For example, you can use the `selectExpr` method to calculate a value using a SQL expression. In the following code, we compute the hit test using the `x` and `y` columns and the `pow` SQL function:

```
hits_df = df.selectExpr("pow(x, 2) + pow(y, 2) < 1 as hits")
hits_df.show(5)
# Output:
# +-----+
# | hits|
# +-----+
# | true|
# |false|
# | true|
# | true|
# | true|
# +-----+
# only showing top 5 rows
```

To demonstrate the expressivity of SQL, we can also calculate the estimation of pi using a single expression. The expression involves using SQL functions such as `sum`, `pow`, `cast`, and `count`:

```
result = df.selectExpr('4 * sum(cast(pow(x, 2) +
                       pow(y, 2) < 1 as int))/count(x) as pi')
result.first()
# Result:
# Row(pi=3.13976)
```

Spark SQL follows the same syntax as Hive, a SQL engine for distributed datasets built on Hadoop. Refer to `https://cwiki.apache.org/confluence/display/Hive/LanguageManua l` for a complete syntax reference.

DataFrames are a great way to leverage the power and optimization of Scala while using the Python interface. The main reason is that queries are interpreted symbolically by SparkSQL and the execution happens directly in Scala without having to pass intermediate results through Python. This greatly reduces the serialization overhead and takes advantage of the query optimizations performed by SparkSQL. Optimizations and query planning allows the use of SQL operators, such as `GROUP BY`, without incurring in performance penalties, such as the one we experienced using `groupBy` directly on an RDD.

Scientific computing with mpi4py

Even though Dask and Spark are great technologies widely used in the IT industry, they have not been widely adopted in academic research. High-performance supercomputers with thousands of processors have been used in academia for decades to run intense numerical applications. For this reason, supercomputers are generally configured using a very different software stack that focuses on a computationally-intensive algorithm implemented in a low-level language, such as C, Fortran, or even assembly.

The principal library used for parallel execution on these kinds of systems is **Message Passing Interface** (**MPI**), which, while less convenient or sophisticated than Dask or Spark, is perfectly capable of expressing parallel algorithms and achieving excellent performance. Note that, contrary to Dask and Spark, MPI does not follow the MapReduce model and is best used for running thousands of processes with very little data sent between them.

MPI works quite differently compared to what we've seen so far. Parallelism in MPI is achieved by running *the same script* in multiple processes (which possibly exist on different nodes); communication and synchronization between processes is handled by a designated process, which is commonly called **root** and is usually identified by a 0 ID.

In this section, we will briefly demonstrate the main concepts of MPI using its `mpi4py` Python interface. In the following example, we demonstrate the simplest possible parallel code with MPI. The code imports the MPI module and retrieves COMM_WORLD, which is an interface that can be used to interact with other MPI processes. The Get_rank function will return an integer identifier for the current process:

```
from mpi4py import MPI

comm = MPI.COMM_WORLD
rank = comm.Get_rank()
print("This is process", rank)
```

We can place the preceding code in a file, `mpi_example.py`, and execute it. Running this script normally won't do anything special as it involves the execution of a single process:

```
$ python mpi_example.py
This is process 0
```

MPI jobs are meant to be executed using the `mpiexec` command, which takes a -n option to indicate the number of parallel processes. Running the script using the following command will generate four independent executions of the same script, each with a different ID:

```
$ mpiexec -n 4 python mpi_example.py
This is process 0
This is process 2
This is process 1
This is process 3
```

Distributing processes among the network is performed automatically through a resource manager (such as TORQUE). Generally, supercomputers are configured by the system administrator, which will also provide instructions on how to run MPI software.

To get a feel as to what an MPI program looks like, we will reimplement the approximation of *pi*. The complete code is shown here. The program will do the following:

- Create a random array of N / n_procs size for each process so that each process will test the same amount of samples (n_procs is obtained through the Get_size function)
- In each separate process, calculate the sum of the hit tests and store it in hits_counts, which will represent the partial counts for each process
- Use the reduce function to calculate the total sum of the partial counts. When using reduce, we need to specify the root argument to specify which process will receive the result

- Print the final result only on the process corresponding to the root process:

```
from mpi4py import MPI

comm = MPI.COMM_WORLD
rank = comm.Get_rank()

import numpy as np

N = 10000

n_procs = comm.Get_size()

print("This is process", rank)

# Create an array
x_part = np.random.uniform(-1, 1, int(N/n_procs))
y_part = np.random.uniform(-1, 1, int(N/n_procs))

hits_part = x_part**2 + y_part**2 < 1
hits_count = hits_part.sum()

print("partial counts", hits_count)

total_counts = comm.reduce(hits_count, root=0)

if rank == 0:
    print("Total hits:", total_counts)
    print("Final result:", 4 * total_counts/N)
```

We can now place the preceding code in a file named `mpi_pi.py` and execute it using `mpiexec`. The output shows how the four process executions are intertwined until we get to the `reduce` call:

```
$ mpiexec -n 4 python mpi_pi.py
This is process 3
partial counts 1966
This is process 1
partial counts 1944
This is process 2
partial counts 1998
This is process 0
partial counts 1950
Total hits: 7858
Final result: 3.1432
```

Summary

Distributed processing can be used to implement algorithms capable of handling massive datasets by distributing smaller tasks across a cluster of computers. Over the years, many software packages, such as Apache Hadoop, have been developed to implement performant and reliable execution of distributed software.

In this chapter, we learned about the architecture and usage of Python packages, such as Dask and PySpark, which provide powerful APIs to design and execute programs capable of scaling to hundreds of machines. We also briefly looked at MPI, a library that has been used for decades to distribute work on supercomputers designed for academic research.

Throughout this book, we explored several techniques to improve the performance of our program, and to increase the speed of our programs and the size of the datasets we are able to process. In the next chapter, we will describe the strategies and best practices to write and maintain high-performance code.

9
Designing for High Performance

In the earlier chapters, we learned how to use the vast array of tools available in Python's standard library and third-party packages to assess and improve the performance of Python applications. In this chapter, we will provide some general guidelines on how to approach different kinds of applications as well as illustrate some good practices that are commonly adopted by several Python projects.

In this chapter, we will learn the following:

- Picking the right performance technique for generic, number crunching, and big data applications
- Structuring a Python project
- Isolating Python installations with virtual environments and containerization
- Setting up continuous integration with Travis CI

Choosing a suitable strategy

Many packages are available for improving the performance of programs, but how do we determine the best optimization strategy for our program? A variety of factors dictate the decision on which method to use. In this section, we will try to answer this question as comprehensively as possible, based on broad application categories.

The first aspect to take into consideration is the type of application. Python is a language that serves multiple and very diverse communities that span web services, system scripting, games, machine learning, and much more. Those different applications will require optimization efforts for different parts of the program.

For example, a web service can be optimized to have a very short response time. Also, it has to be able to answer as many requests as possible using as little resources as possible (that is, it will try to achieve lower latency), while numerical code may require weeks to run. It's important to improve the amount of data the system may process, even if there's a significant start up overhead (in this case, we are interested in throughput).

Another aspect is the platform and architecture we are developing for. While Python has support for a lot of platforms and architectures, many of the third-party libraries may have limited support for certain platforms, especially when dealing with packages that bind into C extensions. For this reason, it's necessary to check the availability of libraries for the target platforms and architectures.

Also, some architectures, such as embedded systems and small devices, may have severe CPU and memory restrictions. This is an important factor to take into consideration as, for instance, some techniques (such as multiprocessing) may consume too much memory or require the execution of additional software.

Finally, the business requirements are equally important. Many times, software products require fast iterations and the ability to change the code quickly. Generally speaking, you want to keep your software stack as minimal as possible so that modification, testing, deployment, and introducing additional platform support becomes easy and feasible in a short period of time. This also applies to the team--installing the software stack and starting the development should be as smooth as possible. For this reason, one should generally prefer pure Python libraries over extensions, with the possible exception of solid, battle-tested libraries, such as NumPy. Additionally, various business aspects will help determine which operations need to be optimized first (always remember that *premature optimization is the root of all evil*).

Generic applications

Generic applications, such as web apps or mobile app backends, usually involve calls to remote services and databases. For such cases, it can be useful to take advantage of asynchronous frameworks, such as the ones presented in `Chapter 6`, *Implementing Concurrency*; this will improve application logic, system design, responsiveness and, also, it will simplify the handling of network failures.

Use of asynchronous programming also makes it easier to implement and use microservices. A **microservice**, although there is no standard definition, can be thought of as a remote service that focuses on a specific aspect of the application (for example, authentication).

The idea behind microservices is that you can build an application by composing different microservices that communicate through a simple protocol (such as gRPC, REST calls, or through a dedicated message queue). This architecture is in contrast with a monolithic application where all the services are handled by the same Python process.

Advantages of microservices include strong decoupling of different parts of the application. Small, simple services can be implemented and maintained by different teams as well as be updated and deployed at different times. This also allows microservices to be easily replicated so that they can handle more users. Additionally, since the communication is done through a simple protocol, microservices can be implemented in a different language that can be more appropriate than Python for the specific application.

If the performance of a service is not satisfactory, the application can often be executed on a different Python interpreter, such as PyPy (provided that all the third-party extensions are compatible) to achieve sufficient speed gains. Otherwise, algorithmic strategies as well as porting bottlenecks to Cython is generally sufficient to achieve satisfactory performance.

Numerical code

If your goal is to write numerical code, an excellent strategy is to start directly with a NumPy implementation. Using NumPy is a safe bet because it is available and tested on many platforms and, as we have seen in the earlier chapters, many other packages treat NumPy arrays as first-class citizens.

When properly written (such as by taking advantage of broadcasting and other techniques we learned in `Chapter 2`, *Pure Python Optimizations*), NumPy performance is already quite close to the native performance achievable by C code, and won't require further optimization. That said, certain algorithms are hard to express efficiently using NumPy's data structures and methods. When this happens, two very good options can be, for example, Numba or Cython.

Cython is a very mature tool used intensely by many important projects, such as `scipy` and `scikit-learn`. Cython code, with its explicit, static type declarations, makes it very understandable, and most Python programmers will have no problem picking up its familiar syntax. Additionally, the absence of "magic" and good inspection tools make it easy for the programmer to predict its performance and have educated guesses as to what to change to achieve maximum performance.

Cython, however, has some drawbacks. Cython code needs to be compiled before it can be executed, thus breaking the convenience of the Python edit-run cycle. This also requires the availability of a compatible C compiler for the target platform. This also complicates distribution and deployment, as multiple platforms, architectures, configurations, and compilers need to be tested for every target.

On the other hand, Numba API requires only the definition of pure-Python functions, which get compiled on the fly, maintaining the fast Python edit-run cycle. In general, Numba requires a LLVM toolchain installation to be available on the target platform. Note that, as of version 0.30, there is some limited support for **Ahead-Of-Time (AOT)** compilation of Numba functions so that Numba-compiled functions can be packaged and deployed without requiring a Numba and LLVM installation.

Note that both Numba and Cython are usually available pre-packaged with all of their dependencies (including compilers) on the default channels of the conda package manager. Therefore, deployment of Cython can be greatly simplified on the platforms where the conda package manager is available.

 What if Cython and Numba are still not enough? While this is generally not required, an additional strategy would be to implement a pure C module (which can be further optimized using compiler flags or hand-tuning) and use it from a Python module using either the `cffi` package (h ttps://cffi.readthedocs.io/en/latest/) or Cython.

Using NumPy, Numba, and Cython is a very effective strategy to obtain near-optimal performance on serial codes. For many applications, serial codes are certainly enough and, even if the ultimate plan is to have a parallel algorithm, it's still very worthy working on a serial reference implementation for debugging purposes and because a serial implementation is likely to be faster on small datasets.

Parallel implementations vary considerably in complexity depending on the particular application. In many cases, the program can be easily expressed as a series of independent calculations followed by some sort of *aggregation* and is parallelizable using simple process-based interfaces, such as `multiprocessing.Pool` or `ProcessPoolExecutor`, which have the advantage of being able to execute generic Python code in parallel without much trouble.

To avoid the time and memory overhead of starting multiple processes, one can use threads. NumPy functions typically release the GIL and are good candidates for thread-base parallelization. Additionally, Cython and Numba provide special `nogil` statements as well as automatic parallelization, which makes them suitable for simple, lightweight parallelization.

For more complex use cases, you may have to change the algorithm significantly. In those cases, Dask arrays are a decent option, which provide an almost-drop-in replacement for standard NumPy. Dask has the further advantage of operating very transparently and is easy to tweak.

Specialized applications that make intensive use of linear algebra routines (such as deep learning and computer graphics) may benefit from packages such as Theano and Tensorflow, which are capable of highly performant and automatic parallelization with built-in GPU support.

Finally, `mpi4py` usage can be used for deploying parallel python scripts on a MPI-based supercomputer (commonly available for researchers in universities).

Big data

Large datasets (typically larger than 1 TB) are becoming increasingly common and a lot of resources have been invested in developing technologies capable of collecting, storing, and analyzing them. Typically, the choice of which framework to use is bound to how the data is stored in the first place.

Many times, even if the complete dataset doesn't fit in a single machine, it is still possible to devise strategies to extract the answers without having to probe the whole dataset. For example, it is quite often possible to answer questions by extracting a small, interesting subset of data that can be easily loaded in memory and analyzed with highly convenient and performant libraries, such as Pandas. By filtering or randomly sampling data points, one can often find a good enough answer to a business question without having to resort to big data tools.

If the bulk of the company's software is written in Python, and you have the freedom to decide your software stack, it would make sense to use Dask distributed. The software package has a very simple setup and is tightly integrated with the Python ecosystem. Using something such as Dask `array` and `DataFrame`, it's very easy to scale your already-existing Python algorithms by adapting NumPy and Pandas code.

Quite often, some companies may have already set up a Spark cluster. In this case, PySpark is the optimal choice, and the use of SparkSQL is encouraged for higher performance. One of the Spark advantages is that it allows the use of other languages, such as Scala and Java.

Organizing your source code

The repository structure of a typical Python project consists, at a minimum, of a directory containing a README.md file, a Python module or package containing the source code for the application or library, and a setup.py file. Projects may also adopt different conventions to comply with company policies or specific frameworks in use. In this section, we will illustrate some common practices that are commonly found in community-driven Python projects which can include some of the tools we illustrated in the earlier chapters.

A typical directory structure for a Python project named myapp can look like this. Now, we will elucidate the role of each file and directory:

```
myapp/
  README.md
  LICENSE
  setup.py
  myapp/
    __init__.py
    module1.py
    cmodule1.pyx
    module2/
      __init__.py
  src/
    module.c
    module.h
  tests/
    __init__.py
    test_module1.py
    test_module2.py
  benchmarks/
    __init__.py
    test_module1.py
    test_module2.py
  docs/
  tools/
```

README.md is a text file that contains general information about the software, such as project scope, installation, a quick start, and useful links. If the software is released to the public, a LICENSE file is used to specify terms and conditions for its usage.

Python software is commonly packaged using the setuptools library in a setup.py file. As we have seen in the earlier chapters, setup.py is also an effective way to compile and distribute Cython code.

The myapp package contains the source code for the application, including Cython modules. Sometimes, it's convenient to maintain pure-Python implementations besides their Cython-optimized counterparts. Commonly, the Cython version of a module is named with a c prefix (such as cmodule1.pyx in the preceding example).

If the external .c and .h files are needed, those are usually stored under an additional src/ directory placed in the top-level (myapp) project directory.

The tests/ directory contains testing code for application (usually in the form of unit tests), which can be run using a test runner, such as unittest or pytest. However, some projects prefer to place the tests/ directory inside the myapp package. Since high-performance code is tweaked and rewritten continuously, having a solid test suite is crucial to spot bugs as early as possible and to improve the developer experience by shortening the test-edit-run cycle.

Benchmarks can be placed in the benchmarks directory; the advantage of having benchmarks separated from tests is that benchmarks can potentially take more time to execute. Benchmarks can also be run on a build server (see the *Continuous integration* section) as a simple mean to compare the performance of versions. While benchmarks usually take longer to run than unit tests, it's best to keep their execution as short as possible to avoid waste of resources.

Finally, the docs/ directory contains user and developer documentation and API references. This usually also includes configuration files for documentation tools, such as sphinx. Other tools and scripts can be placed in the tools/ directory.

Isolation, virtual environments, and containers

The importance of having isolated environments for code testing and execution becomes quite apparent by noticing what happens when you ask a friend to run one of your Python scripts. What happens is that you provide instructions to install Python version X and dependent packages Y, X, and ask them to copy and execute the script on their machine.

In many cases, your friend will proceed and download Python for its platform as well as the dependent libraries and try to execute the script. However, it can happen (more often than not) that the script will fail because either their computer has a different operating system than yours, or the installed libraries are not the same version as the one you installed on your machine. At other times, there can be previous installations that are improperly removed and will cause hard-to-debug conflicts and a lot of frustration.

A very easy way to avoid this scenario is to use virtual environments. Virtual environments are used to create and manage several Python installations by isolating Python, related executables, and third-party packages. Since Python's 3.3 version, the standard library includes the `venv` module (previously known as **virtualenv**), which is a tool designed to create and manage simple isolated environments. Python packages in `venv`-based virtual environments can be installed using `setup.py` files or through `pip`.

Providing exact and specific library versions is crucial when dealing with high-performance code. Libraries evolve all the time between releases and changes in the algorithms may dramatically affect the performance. For instance, popular libraries, such as `scipy` and `scikit-learn`, often port some of their codes and data structures to Cython, so it's really important that the user installs the correct version for optimal performance.

Using conda environments

Most of the time, using `venv` is a fine choice. However, when writing high-performance code, it often happens that some high-performance libraries also require non-Python software to be installed. This typically involves additional setting up of compilers and high-performance native libraries (in C, C++, or Fortran) to which Python packages link. As `venv` and `pip` are designed to deal with Python packages only, this scenario is poorly supported by these tools.

The `conda` package manager was created specifically to handle such cases. Creating a virtual environment with conda can be done using the `conda create` command. The command takes a `-n` argument (`-n` stands for `--name`) that specifies an identifier for the newly created environment and the packages we intend to install. If we wish to create an environment that uses python version `3.5` and the latest version of NumPy, we use the following command:

```
$ conda create -n myenv Python=3.5 numpy
```

Conda will take care of fetching the relative packages from their repositories and placing them in an isolated Python installation. To enable the virtual environment, you can use the `source activate` command:

```
$ source activate myenv
```

After executing this command, the default Python interpreter will be switched to the version we specified earlier. You can easily verify the location of your Python executable using the `which` command, which returns the full path of the executable:

```
(myenv) $ which python
/home/gabriele/anaconda/envs/myenv/bin/python
```

At this point, you are free to add, remove, and modify packages in the virtual environment without affecting the global Python installation. Further packages can be installed using the `conda install <package name>` command or through `pip`.

The beauty of virtual environments is that you can install or compile any software you want in a well-isolated fashion. This means that if, for some reason, your environment gets corrupted, you can scratch it and start from zero.

To remove the `myenv` environment, you first need to deactivate it, and then use the `conda env remove` command, as follows:

```
(myenv) $ source deactivate
$ conda env remove -n myenv
```

What if a package is not available on the standard `conda` repositories? One option is to look whether it is available in the `conda-forge` community channel. To search for a package in `conda-forge`, you can add the `-c` option (which stands for `--channel`) to the `conda search` command:

```
$ conda search -c conda-forge scipy
```

The command will list a series of packages and versions available that match the `scipy` query string. Another option is to search for the package in the public channels hosted on **Anaconda Cloud**. The command-line client for Anaconda Cloud can be downloaded by installing the `anaconda-client` package:

```
$ conda install anaconda-client
```

Once the client is installed, you can use the `anaconda` command-line client to search for packages. In the following example, we demonstrate how to look for the `chemview` package:

```
$ anaconda search chemview
Using Anaconda API: https://api.anaconda.org
Run 'anaconda show <USER/PACKAGE>' to get more details:
Packages:
  Name                          | Version | Package Types   | Platforms
  ----------------------------- | ------- | --------------- | ---------------
  cjs14/chemview                | 0.3     | conda           | linux-64, win-64,
osx-64
                                           : WebGL Molecular Viewer for IPython
notebook.
  gabrielelanaro/chemview       | 0.7     | conda           | linux-64, osx-64
                                           : WebGL Molecular Viewer for IPython
notebook.
```

Installation can then be easily performed by specifying the appropriate channel with the `-c` option:

```
$ conda install -c gabrielelanaro chemlab
```

Virtualization and Containers

Virtualization has been around for a long time as a way to run multiple operating systems on the same machine in order to better utilize physical resources.

One way to achieve virtualization is to employ a *virtual machine*. Virtual machines work by creating virtual hardware resources, such as CPU, memory, and devices, and use those to install and run multiple operating systems on the same machine. Virtualization can be accomplished by installing a hypervisor application on top of an operating system (called *host*). The hypervisor is capable of creating, managing, and monitoring virtual machines and their respective operating systems (called *guests*).

It's important to note that virtual environments, despite their name, have nothing to do with virtual machines. A virtual environment is Python-specific and works by setting up different Python interpreters through shell scripts.

Containers are a way to isolate an application by creating an environment separated from the host operating system and contain only the necessary dependencies. Containers are an operating system feature that allows you to share the hardware resources (provided by the operating system kernel) for multiple instances. A container is different from a virtual machine because it does not abstract hardware resources, but merely shares the operating system's kernel.

Containers are very efficient at utilizing hardware resources as those are accessed natively through the kernel. For this reason, they are an excellent solution for high-performance applications. They are also fast to create and destroy and can be used to quickly test an application in isolation. Containers are also used to simplify deployments (especially microservices) and to develop build servers, such as the ones we mentioned in the preceding section.

In `Chapter 8`, *Distributed Processing*, we used **docker** to easily set up a PySpark installation. Docker is one of the most popular containerization solutions available today. The best way to install docker is by following the instructions on the official website (`https://www.docker.com/`). After installation, it is possible to easily create and manage containers using the docker command-line interface.

You can start a new container by using the `docker run` command. In the following example, we will demonstrate how to use `docker run` to execute a shell session in an Ubuntu 16.04 container. To do this, we will need to specify the following arguments:

- `-i` specifies that we are trying to start an interactive session. It is also possible to execute individual docker commands without interactivity (for example, when starting a web server).
- `-t <image name>` specifies which system image to use. In the following example, we use the `ubuntu:16.04` image.
- `/bin/bash`, which is the command to run inside the container, demonstrated as follows:

```
$ docker run -i -t ubuntu:16.04 /bin/bash
root@585f53e77ce9:/#
```

This command will immediately take us into a separate, isolated shell where we can play around with the system and install software without touching the host operating system. Using a container is a very good way to test installations and deployments on different Linux flavors. After we are done with the interactive shell, we can type the `exit` command to return to the host system.

In the last chapter, we also made use of the port and detach options, `-p` and `-d`, to run the executable `pyspark`. The `-d` option simply asks Docker to run the command in the background. The `-p <host_port>:<guest_port>` option was, instead, necessary to map a network port of the host operating system to the guest system; without this option, the Jupyter Notebook would not have been reachable from a browser running in the host system.

We can monitor the status of the containers with `docker ps`, as shown in the following snippet. The `-a` option (which stands for *all*) serves to output information about all the containers, whether they are currently running or not:

```
$ docker ps -a
CONTAINER ID IMAGE          COMMAND     CREATED       STATUS       PORTS NAMES
585f53e77ce9 ubuntu:16.04 "/bin/bash" 2 minutes ago Exited (0)         2
minutes ago pensive_hamilton
```

The information provided by `docker ps` includes a hexadecimal identifier, `585f53e77ce9`, as well as a human readable name, `pensive_hamilton`, both of which can be used to specify the container in other docker commands. It also includes additional information about the command executed, creation time, and the execution's current status.

You can resume the execution of an exited container using the `docker start` command. To gain shell access to the container, you can use `docker attach`. Both these commands can be followed by either the container ID or its human readable name:

```
$ docker start pensive_hamilton
pensive_hamilton
$ docker attach pensive_hamilton
root@585f53e77ce9:/#
```

A container can be easily removed using the `docker run` command followed by a container identifier:

```
$ docker rm pensive_hamilton
```

As you can see, you are free to execute commands, run, stop, and resume containers as needed, in less than a second. Using docker containers interactively is a great way to test things out and play with new packages without disturbing the host operating system. Since you can run many containers at the same time, docker can also be used to simulate a distributed system (for testing and learning purposes) without having to own an expensive computing cluster.

Docker also allows you to create your own system images, which is useful for distribution, testing, deployment, and documentation purposes. This will be the topic of the next subsection.

Creating docker images

Docker images are ready-to-use, pre-configured systems. The `docker run` command can be used to access and install the docker images available on the **DockerHub** (`https://hub.docker.com/`), a web service where package maintainers upload ready-to-use images to test and deploy various applications.

One way to create a docker image is by using the `docker commit` command on an existing container. The docker commit command takes a container reference and the output image names as arguments:

```
$ docker commit <container_id> <new_image_name>
```

Using this method is useful to save snapshots of a certain container but, if the image is removed from the system, the steps to recreate the image are lost as well.

A better way to create an image is to build it using a **Dockerfile**. A Dockerfile is a text file that provides instructions on how to build an image starting from another image. As an example, we will illustrate the contents of the Dockerfile we used in the last chapter to set up PySpark with Jupyter notebook support. The complete file is reported here.

Each Dockerfile needs a starting image, which can be declared with the `FROM` command. In our case, the starting image is `jupyter/scipy-notebook`, which is available through DockerHub (`https://hub.docker.com/r/jupyter/scipy-notebook/`).

Once we have defined our starting image, we can start issuing shell commands to install packages and perform other configurations using a series of RUN and ENV commands. In the following example, you can recognize installation of Java Runtime Environment (openjdk-7-jre-headless) as well as downloading Spark and setting up relevant environment variables. The USER instructions can be used to specify which user executes the subsequent commands:

```
FROM jupyter/scipy-notebook
MAINTAINER Jupyter Project <jupyter@googlegroups.com>
USER root

# Spark dependencies
ENV APACHE_SPARK_VERSION 2.0.2
RUN apt-get -y update &&
    apt-get install -y --no-install-recommends
    openjdk-7-jre-headless &&
    apt-get clean &&
    rm -rf /var/lib/apt/lists/*
RUN cd /tmp &&
    wget -q http://d3kbcqa49mib13.cloudfront.net/spark-
    ${APACHE_SPARK_VERSION}-bin-hadoop2.6.tgz       &&
    echo "ca39ac3edd216a4d568b316c3af00199
          b77a52d05ecf4f9698da2bae37be998a
          *spark-${APACHE_SPARK_VERSION}-bin-hadoop2.6.tgz" |
    sha256sum -c - &&
    tar xzf spark-${APACHE_SPARK_VERSION}
    -bin-hadoop2.6.tgz -C /usr/local &&
    rm spark-${APACHE_SPARK_VERSION}-bin-hadoop2.6.tgz
RUN cd /usr/local && ln -s spark-${APACHE_SPARK_VERSION}
    -bin-hadoop2.6 spark

# Spark and Mesos config
ENV SPARK_HOME /usr/local/spark
ENV PYTHONPATH $SPARK_HOME/python:$SPARK_HOME/python/lib/
    py4j-0.10.3-src.zip
ENV SPARK_OPTS --driver-java-options=-Xms1024M
    --driver-java-options=-
    Xmx4096M --driver-java-options=-Dlog4j.logLevel=info

USER $NB_USER
```

Dockerfiles can be used to create images using the following command from the directory where the Dockerfile is located. The -t option can be used to specify the tag that will be used to store the image. With the following line, we can create the image named pyspark from the preceding Dockerfile:

```
$ docker build -t pyspark .
```

The command will automatically retrieve the starting image, `jupyter/scipy-notebook`, and produce a new image, named `pyspark`.

Continuous integration

Continuous integration is a great way to ensure that the application stays bug-free at every development iteration. The main idea behind continuous integration is to run the test suite for the project very frequently, usually on a separate build server that pulls the code directly from the main project repository.

Setting up a build server can be accomplished by manually setting up software such as Jenkins (`https://jenkins.io/`), Buildbot (`http://buildbot.net/`), and Drone (`https://github.com/drone/drone`) on a machine. This a convenient and cheap solution, especially for small teams and private projects.

Most open source projects take advantage of Travis CI (`https://travis-ci.org/`), a service capable of building and testing your code automatically from your repository because it's tightly integrated with GitHub. As of today, Travis CI provides a free plan for open source projects. Many open source Python projects take advantage of Travis CI to ensure that the programs run correctly on multiple Python versions and platforms.

Travis CI can be set up easily from a GitHub repository by including a `.travis.yml` file containing the build instruction for the project and activating the builds on the Travis CI website (`https://travis-ci.org/`) after registering an account.

An example `.travis.yml` for a high performance application is illustrated here. The file contains instructions to build and run the software that are specified using a few sections written in YAML syntax.

The `python` section specifies which Python versions to use. The `install` section will download and set up conda for testing, installing dependencies, and setting up the project. While this step is not necessary (one can use `pip` instead), conda is a great package manager for high-performance applications as it contains useful native packages.

The `script` section contains the code needed to test the code. In this example, we limit ourselves to run our tests and benchmarks:

```
language: python
python:
  - "2.7"
  - "3.5"
install:
```

```
# Setup miniconda
- sudo apt-get update
- if [[ "$TRAVIS_PYTHON_VERSION" == "2.7" ]]; then
    wget https://repo.continuum.io/miniconda/
    Miniconda2-latest-Linux-x86_64.sh -O miniconda.sh;
  else
    wget https://repo.continuum.io/miniconda/
    Miniconda3-latest-Linux-x86_64.sh -O miniconda.sh;
  fi
- bash miniconda.sh -b -p $HOME/miniconda
- export PATH="$HOME/miniconda/bin:$PATH"
- hash -r
- conda config --set always_yes yes --set changeps1 no
- conda update -q conda
# Installing conda dependencies
- conda create -q -n test-environment python=
  $TRAVIS_PYTHON_VERSION numpy pandas cython pytest
- source activate test-environment
# Installing pip dependencies
- pip install pytest-benchmark
- python setup.py install

script:
  pytest tests/
  pytest benchmarks/
```

Every time new code is pushed (as well as other configurable events) to the GitHub repository, Travis CI will spin up a container, install dependencies, and run the test suite. Using Travis CI in open source projects is a great practice as it is a form of constant feedback about the status of the project and also provides up-to-date installation instructions through a continuously tested .travis.yml file.

Summary

Deciding on a strategy to optimize your software is a complex and delicate task that depends on the application type, target platforms, and business requirements. In this chapter, we provided some guidelines to help you think and choose an appropriate software stack for your own applications.

High-performance numerical applications sometimes require managing installation and deployment of third-party packages that may require handling of external tools and native extensions. In this chapter, we saw how to structure your Python project, including tests, benchmarks, documentation, Cython modules, and C extensions. Also, we introduced the continuous integration service Travis CI, which can be used to enable continuous testing for your projects hosted on GitHub.

Finally, we also learned about virtual environments and docker containers that can be used to test applications in isolation and to greatly simplify deployments and ensure that multiple developers have access to the same platform.

Index

O

object mode 120, 122
observable 156, 158
OpenCL 175
optimal performance
  reaching, with numexpr 73, 74

P

pairing function 123
Pandas
  about 75
  database-style operations 80
  fundamentals 75, 76, 77
Parallel Cython
  with OpenMP 185, 186, 187
particle simulator test application
  designing 8, 9, 10, 11, 12, 13
particle simulator, Cython 102, 104, 105, 106
particle simulator
  rewriting, in NumPy 69, 72
  running, in PyPy 133
partitioning 207
pd.Panel
  reference 77
performance improvement strategy
  big data 239, 240
  generic applications 236, 237
  numerical code 237, 238, 239
Pool classes 176
process
  creating 176
  launching 177
  spawning 176
profile module 22
profiler 7
profiling 7
psutil module
  reference 32
PyPy project 131, 132
PyPy
  particle simulator, running in 133
  setting up 132
PySpark
  setting up 221

using 220
Pyston 134
pytest documentation
  reference 19
pytest-benchmark
  reference 21
  using, for better tests and benchmarks 19, 21

Q

QCacheGrind
  reference 24

R

reactive programming
  about 156
  cold observable 163
  CPU monitor, building 166, 168
  hot observable 163
  observables 156, 158
  operators 159, 160, 162
ReactiveX
  reference 156
Resilient Distributed Datasets (RDD)
  about 222
  creating 224, 226, 228
root 231

S

scheduler 216
scientific computing
  with mpi4py 231, 232
sets 46
shared memory 173
shuffling 206
simulator 8
slicing 62
Solid State Drives (SSD) 139
source code
  organizing 240, 241
Spark architecture 222, 223
Spark DataFrame 229
Spark
  setting up 221
static types
  adding 90